Redskins

Insult and Brand   C. Richard King

UNIVERSITY OF NEBRASKA PRESS | LINCOLN AND LONDON

Library of Congress Control Number: 2015954951

Set in Lyon by L. Auten.
Designed by N. Putens.

For the haters, the warriors, and the future

CONTENTS

ILLUSTRATIONS

ACKNOWLEDGMENTS

This project took shape over many years and owes much to many people. While it took shape in the wake of the resurgent controversy surrounding the Washington professional football team, it builds on many established collaborations and ongoing conversations. I have benefited over the years leading up to this book from the guidance, council, and inspiration of many leaders and scholars, including Amanda Blackhorse, Laurel Davis, Stephanie Fryberg, Michael Giardina, Jennifer Guiliano, Jennifer Harvey and Carol Gunderson, Suzan Shown Harjo, Tara Houska, Jacqueline Keeler, Adrienne Keene, Cornell Pewewardy, David Prochaska, Rob Schmidt, Carol Spindel, Ellen Staurowsky, Pauline Turner Strong, Charlene Teeters, Linda Waggoner, and especially Chuck Springwood. Of equal importance, this work derives from the blood, sweat, and tears that countless advocates, activists, artists, and educators within and beyond Indian Country have invested in the pursuit of justice, civil rights, and dignity. To them I owe my deepest debt of gratitude, both for what they have taught me and for how they endeavored to make the world a better place.

Throughout the publication process, I have had the good fortune of working with the staff of the University of Nebraska Press. Their support and expertise have proven invaluable to me. Of particular note have been the efforts of Heather Stauffer and my editor, Matthew Bokovoy.

I am grateful as well to the artists and photographers who have provided illustrations for this book and routinely deepened my thinking about indigenous issues, social justice, and the human condition. I appreciate Marty Two Bulls, Doug Nemanic, and Fibonacci Blue agreeing to include their work. A special thanks to Gregg Deal for his many creative interventions, especially the art featured on the cover.

Over the years, the Colleges of Arts and Sciences at Washington State University have provided regular and meaningful support of my research, for which I am particularly grateful. Of special note, my colleagues in Critical Culture, Gender, and Race Studies at Washington State University deserve much credit for creating an intellectual community that nurtures good work. I appreciate especially the contributions of David J. Leonard, Carmen Lugo-Lugo, Mary Bloodsworth-Lugo, and Lisa Guerrero. I have benefited, moreover, from the hard work of Debbie Brudie, Cerissa Harper, and Rose Smetana. My students have routinely allowed me to engage with aspects of this project, often pushing to refine my thinking and argumentation.

I presented portions of this work previously at the National Museum of the American Indian, as part of its symposium "Racist Stereotypes and Cultural Appropriation in American Sports," and at lectures at the University of Graz, University of Maribor, University of Passau, and University of Regensburg. I am especially grateful to Karsten Fitz and Nassim Balestrini for their support during these visits. A presentation at the White Privilege Conference, at the invitation of Abby Ferber, and interest from Chuck Modiano, who maintains popsspots.com, also proved instrumental to my early thinking on this project.

Last, but certainly not least, I must again acknowledge the love and support of my family. My daughters, Abbey and Ellory, continue to inspire with how they think about the world and amaze me with how they try make it a better place. And I really cannot say enough to thank my life partner and best friend, Marcie, for all she has done for me. She has given me more than she knows and made me capable of more than I ever imagined over the years. She is a rare jewel I cherish more each day.

AUTHOR'S NOTE ON LANGUAGE

Names and naming, as this book details, always carry a charge in the study of indigenous people, precisely because they articulate power, identity, and representation so succinctly, forcefully, and often invisibly. Thus, one must take great care in the interpretation and application of language. Colonial histories, national narratives, and cultural practices do not make this easy. In what follows, I make two conscious language choices. First, I will use *American Indians*, *Native Americans*, *indigenous peoples*, and *native nations* interchangeably in this text. Second, I endeavor to avoid the r-word. I understand it to be a racial slur, on par with the n-word. While the former enjoys wider acceptance and use than the latter, this is not a defensible rationale for relying on it. In fact, persistent reiteration makes it appear reasonable and even appropriate, a pattern that I think important to disrupt and undermine. To this end, I will substitute phrases like *the Washington professional football team* and *the DC NFL franchise*, as well as *the team* and *the franchise*. When unavoidable, I employ an altered version of the word, *R*dskin(s)*, to underscore its unspeakable, problematic nature. I have not edited the usage of others in direct quotations, in part to remain faithful to my sources and in part to draw attention to the slur.

~~Redskins~~

Introduction

1

Redskin is a problem. It is an outdated reference to an American Indian. It is best regarded as a racial slur on par with other denigrating terms. In fact, while similar terms have been crossed out of our collective vocabulary as inappropriate and offensive, much like on the cover of this book, it still finds use. Most visibly, it remains the moniker of the Washington professional football team, long anchoring its brand and traditions. This should unsettle us. The word has deep connections to the history of anti-Indian violence, marked by ethnic cleansing, dispossession, and displacement. It is a term of contempt and derision that targets indigenous people. As much a weapon as a word, then, it injures and excludes, denying history and humanity. Its lingering presence undermines the pursuit of equality, inclusion, and empowerment by American Indians. Indeed, this continued use of a racial slur as the name of a professional sports team, the ongoing defense of it, and the willingness of the franchise, the National Football League (NFL), and their media partners to profit from it pose an even more troubling set of problems.

Sportscaster Bob Costas seemed to recognize as much when in October 2013, during halftime of the Sunday Night Football game between Dallas and Washington, he offered a sharply worded critique of the latter's team name, describing it as a "slur" and an "insult."[1] In denouncing the continued use of the moniker, he followed a growing number of high-profile journalists, from Peter King and Bill Simmons to Christine Brennan and Dave Zirin. At the same time, he joined media figures, including Howard Stern, Matthew Berry, and John Oliver, and athletes, like Billy Mills, Mike Tyson, and Martina Navratilova, who have all publicly spoken out against the name.[2] And in the subsequent NFL season, use of the team name declined by 27 percent, as sportscasters "deferred to 'Washington' more often."[3] Costas's comments, moreover, echoed the long-standing position of the National Congress of American Indians (NCAI) and nearly a dozen tribes. And they found support in positions taken by a number of professional organizations, including the American Studies Association, the American Sociological Association, and the Organization of American Historians; religious groups; and news outlets, like *Mother Jones*, the *Seattle Times*, and the *Washington City Paper*.[4] Even Larry Dolan, owner of the Cleveland Indians, infamous for its continued use of the caricature Chief Wahoo, has remarked, "If we were the Redskins, the day after I owned the team, the name would have been changed."[5]

These changing attitudes coincide with a recent ruling in *Blackhorse et al. v. Pro Football, Inc.*, which stripped the team of several of its trademarks (and was upheld by a federal court in the first round of appeals). They unfold alongside, if not in direct response to, Change the Mascot, a well-orchestrated campaign spearheaded by the National Congress of American Indians and the Oneida Nation, and a growing grassroots movement, armed with social media. The shifts in public opinion, moreover, find resonance in recent calls for action from members of the U.S. Congress, including fifty U.S. senators who demanded change in a letter to the organization, in President Obama's statement that he would think about changing the team name, and in efforts by the Obama administration to block the building of new stadium in the District of Columbia so long as the franchise has its current moniker. Some seventy years after its inception, the name makes many people uncomfortable. Some, in fact, are so uneasy, they have resolved not to use it. These individual epiphanies, actions, and condemnations together direct attention to a shift around popular understandings of racial images, ideas, and identities. While all of these actions were undoubtedly fomented by a broader movement within Indian Country intent on reclaiming dignity, sovereignty, and humanity, in part by bringing stereotypes like mascots to an end, Costas did not highlight these unsettling politics. Instead, he anchored his critique in the seemingly settled truths found in dictionaries, where the word is defined as an offensive, antiquated, and insulting reference to an American Indian.

As a scholar who has written about the history and significance of Native American mascots for more than two decades, I have long known the franchise to exemplify the practices associated with playing Indian in athletics, offering some of the most vivid and troubling examples of popular uses and understandings of American Indians.[6] Among the most prominent and profitable in sport, the organization since its inception has offered insights into the privileges and pleasures associated with taking and remaking Indianness. This alone would merit study and reflection, but in recent years, something even more significant has begun to unfold. Recent events suggest to me that we have reached something of a critical juncture, which makes this an especially opportune moment to reflect on the past, present, and possible futures of the Washington professional football team.

Perhaps most obviously, a dynamic, multifaceted opposition has converged around the moniker and logo. While far from united, this critical mass has its roots in Indian Country and has important connections to broader struggles for self-determination and decolonization. Unprecedented in size, scope, and diversity, it has made the once-unremarkable, and often-celebrated, team and its traditions the subject of debate, rendering them increasingly indefensible. In doing so, it has actively challenged anti-Indian racism, while pushing to restore dignity and humanity to indigenous people.

The ongoing debate, moreover, has fostered a shifting defense of the organization and its use of American Indians, which has appealed to and exposed the complex contours of racial politics and cultural identity today. Much of the defense casts the franchise and fans in a positive light, stressing that they have good intentions and mean to convey honor with the moniker, logo, and associated practices. And more, it has stressed indigenous support, highlighting the importance of public opinion polls as well as endorsements of the team by prominent individuals and reservation communities. Importantly, the defense is about more than Indianness. In particular, it turns in spoken and unspoken ways on whiteness. On the one hand, it invokes the attachments and sentimentality of white fans to legitimate the team and its traditions. On the other hand, it derives from and defends a series of entitlements or prerogatives anchoring a long history of owning Indians and Indianness in U.S. settler society.

Current events also focus our understanding of the past. They provide much-needed critical distance to assess the creation of the brand and its broader significance. That the team would have settled on its name unselfconsciously underscores how deep the entitlement and attachment to things "Indian" were at the time and how deeply embedded anti-Indian racism was in American public culture. It was, not to overstate things, a paradoxical love of imagined Indians and a loathing of actual, embodied Indians that continues to this day. Not surprisingly, the franchise, in common with other sports teams, Hollywood films, and commercial culture generally, traded in stereotypical renderings of Native Americans that, like the moniker, distorted and dehumanized them. To fans, journalists, and owners alike, the logo, fight song, and marching band all were in good fun. And while they meant no harm, a point many make today, these traditions create hostile environments that do in fact harm. Then, as now, such images and attitudes encouraged a kind of thoughtlessness. Such thoughtlessness allowed people to take the team and its traditions for granted without the burdens of history or introspection.

Finally, the critical juncture produced by recent events may be the beginning of the end. It is certainly a moment of change, a moment when countless people call for the team to change, when individuals create new team names and logos, and when many others imagine a time after the current moniker and mascot have been changed. Of course, this moment of change and what it has brought into being are about much more than the brand, its use of a slur, or even the intransigence of the current owner. The issue is about dignity and respect, combating anti-Indian racism while furthering self-determination and decolonization. As such, when the name changes, for that action to be of lasting and meaningful importance, it must be paired with deeper transformations, including education, coming to terms with the past, and expressing honor for indigenous people by honoring treaties made with native nations.

The critical juncture explored in this book has been marked by public condemnations of the team and calls for change, which have heighten public awareness of the word and its origins. Recent events likely played a key role in the increase in online searches. In 2014 Dictionary.com dubbed the team name, along with *caliphate*, *Ebola*, and *sociopath*, one of its eleven trending words.[7] Growing interest and increased attention, moreover, may explain why Americans generally remain supportive of the franchise but have growing unease about the word. A recent survey, for instance, found that 83 percent of Americans indicated they would not use the word in a conversation with a Native American.[8] One pizza restaurant in Washington DC learned how profoundly attitudes have shifted around the term. In fall 2014, when it ran a promotion, "Redskins score, You score," the reaction from its customers was so negative that it felt compelled to issue an apology less than six hours later. It read in part, "We are listening to all of your feedback. . . . We agree that the use of the name is wrong, offensive, and hurtful to all. In our future promotions and emails, we will make sure not to make the same mistake."[9]

Whatever the precise cause, the conservative columnist Charles Krauthammer rightly concludes that words and public usage of and attitudes toward them change:

> Fifty years ago the preferred, most respectful term for African Americans was Negro. The word appears 15 times in Martin Luther King's "I have a dream" speech. . . . The preferred term is now black or African American. With a rare few legacy exceptions, Negro carries an unmistakably patronizing and demeaning tone.
>
> If you were detailing the racial composition of Congress, you wouldn't say: "Well, to start with, there are 44 Negroes." . . . Similarly, regarding the further racial breakdown of Congress, you wouldn't say: "And by my count, there are two redskins." It's inconceivable, because no matter how the word was used 80 years ago, it carries invidious connotations today.[10]

For Krauthammer, like Costas and growing numbers of people, these changing sensibilities do not simply argue against use of the slur to describe a American Indian, they also argue against the continued its continued use as name for a professional football team.

Even as the past few years have witnessed an unparalleled push toward and increasing momentum for change, it would be wrong to conclude that concern with the team and its traditions is of recent origin or driven by forces outside of Indian Country. For more than four decades, American Indians and their allies have voiced their opposition. They have appealed to the ownership, held rallies and demonstrations at NFL games, and filed lawsuits to strip the team of its trademarks. They have created art, produced public service announcements, and formed organizations devoted to change. They have funded studies, launched protests on social media, and lodged complaints with governmental bodies, like the Federal Communications Commission. Through it all, they have worked to developed a diverse coalition within and beyond Indian Country and across cultural and racial lines in the nation's capital. These efforts have had noticeable impacts on public opinion. They have also prompted the franchise and the league to repeatedly respond to questions and criticism, secure support among indigenous people—often through questionable, if not fraudulent, means—and wage a series of public relations campaigns.

Even as Costas, Congress, and myriad others have called the team and its name into question, it has remained one of the most valuable franchises in professional sports. It has an easily recognizable and familiar brand, which is at once hugely popular and highly profitable. It is, according to *Forbes*, the third most valuable NFL franchise.[11] By way of comparison, in 2014 the Bureau of Indian Affairs had a total operating budget of $2.6 billion, while the team had a total value of $2.4 billion and total revenues of $395 million.[12] The franchise's ownership has bristled at the ongoing critique, suggesting that the team name is in fact quite positive, enjoying support from the majority of Americans and American Indians. Far from being an ethnic slur, the team has long asserted, its moniker conveys respect and honor. The franchise, moreover, has sought to reframe the controversy through a sophisticated promotional campaign rooted in focus groups, polls, and philanthropic initiatives. The National Football League, for its part, has actively defended the team, endorsed its interpretation of the name and its origins, and supported it in court. And even as more journalists and news outlets have spoken out against the team name, according to the *Washington Business Journal*, in an editorial ending its use of the moniker, "The vast majority of media outlets continue to use it. Our sister paper, the *Sports Business Journal*, reported last week that 44 of 48 major newspapers—those in cities with NFL teams along with the *Wall Street Journal*, *L.A. Times* and *USA Today*—still use the name."[13] Finally, fans largely have continued to support the team. Disappointing play has not diminished pride or attendance appreciably. And many are quite vocal in defense of the team and its traditions of social media. Nevertheless, merchandise sales, in a possible sign of things to come, were down 35 percent in 2014.[14] Despite this and in keeping with the general support of the organization, according to *Forbes*, the valuation and revenues for the team rose during the same period.[15]

The ongoing struggle lends itself to binary thinking, moral declarations, and public denunciations. To many, either the moniker is respectful or it is racist. It is a stereotype or not. Such arguments, whatever their merits, simplify the conflict and its cultural import. They discourage full understanding of the significance of the debate, competing claims, and key words. Indeed, the struggle over the team name, what it means, and why it matters raises important questions about popular perceptions of American Indians, the cultural life of brands, and existing obstacles to inclusion and equality. It also encourages deeper reflection on race and racism, the shifting contours of American attitudes and identities, and the possibilities and limitations of change in consumer society.

Some of these complexities find expression in the city that has long celebrated the franchise. Washington DC exemplifies racial politics in the United States. Built in part by slave labor, on land taken from native nations, the seat of American democracy was long marked by pronounced segregation and black-white racial tensions. For much of its first three decades in DC, the team played off these tensions, endeavoring to cast itself as the team of the South. Even as the city has changed, the centrality of race has not, and a rising Latino population has introduced a new dynamic that has complicated established assumptions. Economic and demographic shifts, moreover, have fostered a whitening of the urban core, increasingly pushing the poor and people of color to the margins. For all of this, on any given Sunday, residents of the metropolitan area form an imagined community united in shared identification with a team and becoming cultural citizens by exalting imaginary Indians. Even as they dress in feathers and sing the praises of their braves on the warpath, fans erase indigenous people. They make claims on and through images of them but disclaim their histories or continued relevance. In the process, they forget the past and its legacies. They forget about dispossession, displacement, and death. Few will remember that the team currently plays on the ancestral territory of the Piscataway Tribe or that the capital is built on the homelands of the Patawomeck Tribe. And even as they don its colors or sing its fight song, fewer still will acknowledge the ways in which a professional football team continues to profit from anti-Indian stereotypes and stories.

The creation, consumption, and contestation of the brand, then, have emerged and evolved in a context marked by the interplay of racisms. What the team means and how individuals and institutions make sense of it can be understood only in light of overlapping identities, ideologies, and exclusions. Perhaps most obviously, the moniker and logo reflect the force of anti-Indian racism to dehumanize and deny. As such, they underscore the importance and invisibility of U.S. settler society, particularly the ingrained prerogatives of taking and remaking land, culture, and identity, which actively contribute to the erasure and exclusion of indigenous people. At the same time, arguments around the team and its traditions also reveal the centrality of a model of black-white race relations for assessing the shape and significance of racism generally.

Of course, one cannot speak of settler colonialism, prevailing understandings of race and racism, or the team and its traditions without talking about the construction of whiteness. The assumptions, aspirations, and anxieties of Euro-Americans not only introduce Indianness into athletics in the form of mascots and monikers but anchor the ongoing defense of them as well. At root, this cultural complex, as embodied by the Washington professional football team, turns on owning Indians. The franchise has long regarded Indianness as a resource or raw material to exploit for pleasure and profit. The establishment of its brand depended on embellishments of pseudo-Indian motifs. In fact, over its first three decades, the organization elaborated on popular stereotypes and romantic images of American Indians to create a logo, rituals, marching band, cheer squad, and identity. Fans and the franchise alike have felt entitled to use Indians and Indianness as they have seen fit. Even as the franchise ownership has become uneasy with outside criticism of its name, the organization has fought to prop up the brand through philanthropy that some interpret as little more than bribery and fake instances of indigenous support for its racist image. Anxiety, along with entitlement, has shaped the origin, elaboration, and defense of the brand. Jennifer Guiliano has identified the historic anxieties that prompted the emergence of American Indian mascots. She has argued in particular that the changing shape and significance of white masculinities in the wake of modernity, urbanization, and industrialization gave rise to American Indian mascots and monikers like those associated with the Washington professional football team.[16] Today a new set of anxieties paces the defense of the team and its traditions; specifically, it reflects the shape and significance of white masculinities in the wake of multiculturalism, feminism, and postindustrialization. Arguments for the team and its traditions, then, often hinge on other issues, circle around whites and whiteness, and display deep-seated resentments about a changing world as much as they purport to pay homage and convey respect. Thus, while it may be easy to see the team name as a slur, it is difficult, even for many critics, to recognize and respond to the ways that attachment, entitlement, identity, and anxiety shape the debate and stymie change.

Ultimately, the name, the team, and the brand matter not just because they reference an offensive racial slur or profit on hurtful stereotypes. They have pressing significance because of how they encourage anti-Indian racism, reinforce white privilege, and perpetuate distorted understandings of people and the past. As Amanda Blackhorse, lead plaintiff in a current legal challenge, notes, "Native American people have been targeted for their race, their land, and their resources. So when the dominant culture believes they are superior to the indigenous population they will dehumanize and dominate us for their own good. This includes the dehumanization of our entire being, especially our identity."[17] Clearly part of a deeper history and larger struggle, the prerogative to imagine and exploit popular ideas about American Indians for pleasure and profit, as the franchise has long done, negatively affects indigenous people, belittling, disempowering, and marginalizing them on any given Sunday. For Blackhorse, this pattern raises two questions seldom asked: "Why have we not achieved true self-determination as indigenous people?" and "Why is it that in this day and age are we still fighting for common decency to be respected by our non-native counterparts?"[18] Tracing the history of the team and studying the defense of its use of racial slur may be a first and necessarily partial step toward addressing these big questions. Such efforts offer an important opportunity to better comprehend the problem posed by R*dskin today, creating an important means of combating the ongoing dehumanization of indigenous people in the United States. Echoing Blackhorse, for the franchise and its fans, for the league and its media partners, for politicians and the public, the key challenge posed by the critique of the team and its traditions might be phrased as two overlapping questions: How do we stop the dehumanization of indigenous peoples? And how do we create new stories and spaces, reimagine self and society, and otherwise transform traditions to rehumanize them?

Origins

2

Samuel Henry would "love to see a boycott of all things Redskins." He reached this conclusion while serving on the Oregon Board of Education, which he currently chairs. Hearing testimony from Native Americans about the impact of American Indian mascots led the board to institute a ban on such symbols in public high schools in the state. While controversial, even in a state like Oregon, Henry's decision would strike many as odd. After all, he grew up a fan of the Washington professional football team. Like many young people in DC, he and his friends "had the jerseys and knew the lore." One such story he vividly recalls is their understanding of how and why the team's headquarters had its peculiar reddish-brown tint: they thought it "came from the blood of Native Americans.... We really thought that they had captured and killed Native Americans and pasted them all over the building.... We were just kids, we didn't know any better. But we really, honestly believed that."[1]

While one might be tempted to dismiss this tale as an urban legend, the work of childhood imaginations, or just a story, the stories people tell, especially when those stories endeavor to account for social arrangements, explain cultural practices, or recall historical events, offer deepen insights into power, identity, and community. They give us a better sense of how people interpret the world, understand their place in it, and comprehend events within it. Stories prove particularly useful when people relate the origins of beliefs and behaviors, detailing where things came from and how things came to be as they are. And at no time is this more true than when origins are in question, intentions in doubts, and outcomes unsettled. Origin stories play an especially important role in the controversy surrounding the Washington professional football team, providing constituencies a means to make sense of the past and empower the present. The franchise and its supporters, in particular, have increasingly turned to narratives to identify origins, explain away problems and perceptions, and settle the uneasy contentions associated with the word *R*dskin*, its use as a moniker, and its role as a fount of tradition.

In this chapter I examine, in turn, five origin stories that might be best phrased as questions:

Where did the word *r*dskin* originate?
When did it become a slur?
How did it become the name of a professional football team?
Who produced the team logo?
When did opposition to the team begin?

In unpacking the answers to these questions, I will be as interested in the uses to which individuals and organizations put these stories as their veracity, for their ultimate significance lies in their telling and retelling and what such reiterations reveal about cultural politics, racial meanings, and interpretive frames.

Word

As with many words, determining the precise origin of the word *r*dskin* frustrates the efforts of scholars. Few records from the period survive; fewer people still, indigenous and settler, were literate or recorded the minutia of daily life.[2] This lack of clarity has not stopped the circulation of stories purporting to ascertain the history of the word, usually to advance a position on its significance today. Two competing theories dominate public discourse: (1) the term originated among Native Americans and (2) the term emerged in association with a thriving trade in American Indian scalps, part of larger campaign to eradicate indigenous people. Not surprisingly, the former frequently finds use in efforts to defend the team and its traditions, while the latter routinely ground critiques of them.

Shifting Stories

Although one would doubt that George Preston Marshall gave etymology much thought when selecting the name of the team or elaborating its traditions, the franchise and its fans regularly make reference to the history of the word. Significantly, the stories have shifted over time. In 2005 Mike Wise noted that in "the team's media guide, readers are even given a Reader's Digest version of where the term came from. 'The term redskin . . . was inspired not by their natural complexion but by their fondness for vermillion makeup.'"[3] In other words, whatever else might be said, it is not a racist term. More recently, the organization has suggested that it is an expression that American Indians used to describe themselves and/or that it has benign origins, concluding that hence it cannot be racist, should not be problematic, is not really about us. Bruce Allen, president of the franchise, offered such an account in a letter defending the organization in May 2014: "The term redskin originated as a Native American expression of solidarity. . . . Our use of 'Redskins' as the name of our football team for more than 81 years has always been respectful of and shown reverence for the proud legacy and traditions of Native Americans."[4] Of course, there is not a single American Indian language, but hundreds of them. Even if one concludes that the word originated among Native American speakers in the past, that does not mean that the meanings of the word have not changed, that we can disregard context, or that any or all uses would be deemed congruent, appropriate, or defensible. Both of these versions work to explain away the term and disentangle the franchise from it, absolving it of racism while recuperating its embattled reputation.

Native Roots

The Washington professional football team began to alter its account of the origin of the term in the wake of a study by the Smithsonian Institution linguist Ives Goddard. In fact, it cites his study online to buttress its most recent origin story.[5]

Goddard argues in his history of the term that r*dskin has an "entirely benign" origin among indigenous peoples in French colonial territory, which was referred to as "Illinois Country" at the time. He dates the initial usage to 1769 in a private conversation recorded in the French plural form as *peaux rouges*. He identifies the first public usages four decades later in diplomatic speeches delivered to mixed audiences of Native Americans and Euro-Americans. For instance, on July 20, 1815, the Meskawki chief Black Thunder said to such an assembly, "I turn to all, red skins and white skins, and challenge an accusation against me." Translators adopted the term as a convention and journalists soon followed suit. Goddard credits James Fennimore Cooper for popularizing the term.[6] Thus, according to Goddard, r*dskin emerged in native languages in a specific region at a specific time to address a changing political landscape; it made reference to Native Americans distinguishing themselves from Europeans and Euro-Americans as members of distinct cultural groups affiliated with unique political entities.

These findings more or less fit in an emerging understanding of racial thinking in eighteenth-century North America, albeit in a slightly simplified fashion.[7] "At the start of the eighteenth century," according to Nancy Shoemaker, "Indians and Europeans rarely mentioned the color of each other's skin. By midcentury, remarks about skin color and the categorization of peoples by simple color-coded labels (red, white, black) had become commonplace."[8] Before this, religion or culture prevailed as means of classifying the other.[9] And when indigenous skin color did merit comment, chroniclers offered a variety of descriptions, including "tawny, brown, yellow, copper-colored, and occasionally red."[10] In Europe, color became more central after 1740, when Linnaeus published his classic study of human diversity that identified four major races distinguishable by color. Shoemaker suggests that in the British colonies, specifically in the southeast region of what would become the United States, some tribes began making reference to red men and red people, offering complementary terms and references to European as white men or white people, and these terms may have derived from indigenous political cosmologies in the region that pivoted around red/white or from other precolonial usage.[11] By the mid-eighteenth century both colonists and natives had begun using color to describe differences, and these differences became increasingly fixed and immutable across the century.

Alden T. Vaughn attributes emergence and fixity of color during this period to changing ideas and to growing conflict between settlers and indigenous people. Thus, while *r*dskin* may have been neutral, it emerged in a charged context, marked by friction, struggle over resources, and hardening distinctions across the colonies. In fact, the quick adoption of the word by Euro-Americans says more about prevailing political and ideological struggles and less about linguistics. "Once red became a viable designation, it seems to have satisfied everyone. To the Indians' bitterest critics, red could signify ferocity, blood, and anger; to their most avid supporters and to the Indians themselves, red could suggest bravery, health, and passion; to those who fell between the judgmental extremes, red could mean almost anything or nothing. In short, red was sufficiently flexible and ambiguous to meet the metaphysical imperatives of a society that did not wholly agree about the Indian's basic character or social and political fate."[12] This flexibility and fecundity had important consequences for how the word would develop over the course of the nineteenth century. It quickly became a term for all indigenous people, not just those who originally used it, and somewhat less swiftly it became a racial epithet. In this light, following Darren Reid, we should understand *r*dskin* to be "a product of the colonial experience . . . a label which evolved to accommodate an increasingly racialized European and European American view of the world which was imposed upon a broad range of peoples who only gradually developed a sense of a collective identity in response to it."[13]

Such complexity, of course, does not have a place in the origin story presently offered by the franchise and its fans, a story that stops two hundred years ago and effaces questions of race and power. To properly understand the word and how it became a the moniker of a professional football team necessitates an appreciation of this complexity, precisely because, in the words of Nancy Shoemaker, the team name "was not harking back to French-Meskwaki treaty councils. . . . It was harking back to 19th century use of the word."[14]

Colonial Violence

Critics of the team have long offered an alternate origin story, one that connects the term to the history of colonial violence, particularly the state-sponsored bounties placed on Native Americans. Baxter Homes (Cherokee) presents a detailed rendering.

> The story in my family goes that the term dates back to the institutionalized genocide of Native Americans, most notably when the Massachusetts colonial government placed a bounty on their heads. The grisly particulars of that genocide are listed in a 1755 document called the Phips Proclamation . . . ordering on behalf of British King George II for, "His Majesty's subjects to Embrace all opportunities of pursuing, captivating, killing and Destroying all and every of the aforesaid Indians." They paid well—50 pounds for adult male scalps; 25 for adult female scalps; and 20 for scalps of boys and girls under age 12.
> These bloody scalps were known as "redskins."[15]

Although the particulars vary from speaker to speaker, many American Indians know the key elements of this narrative: indigenous people were targeted, hunted, and killed; their bodies were prized and commodified; the process fragmented them, reducing them to a single fetish—the scalp—and these acts were part of larger genocidal projects. *R*dskin* was the keyword of this process and condenses the symbolic, cultural, and physical violence embodied by the term for many Native Americans today. As such, it lingers as a prime index of dehumanization and oppression.

It may be tempting to dismiss such readings as fantastic distortions in light of etymological and historical analyses. To my mind, this would perpetuate the violence this narrative describes, while missing the forest for the trees. Like Mairin Odle, I want to hear the larger truth, as this story and its tellers speak truth to power. "Redskin may not directly derive from scalp bounties, but that does not mean that scalp bounties were not both very real and very widespread. It also does not mean that contemporary people are wrong to draw associations between, on the one hand, a term that asserts the primacy of skin over all other identities, and on the other, a history of violence against Native Americans that treated them as objects and commodified their body parts."[16] Two sports, football today and bounty hunting then, united in trophy taking—skins, cultures, identities—dehumanization, dispossession, and death. This culture of violent anti-Indianism surely play a pivotal role in transforming *r*dskin* into a racial epithet.

Slur

Whatever the word's precise origins, countless American Indians have suffered the indignity and intimidation of being called a r*dskin by a stranger, classmate, peer, coworker, boss, police officer, or commanding officer. Often said out of anger, meant to target, and designed to hurt, the symbolic violence of the word multiples when coupled with adjectives like *dirty*, *lazy*, *stinking*, and *fucking*. It is very much a living slur. Today, *r*dskin* is widely regard as an epithet. Dictionaries define it as a slur, describing it as "usually offensive," "offensive slang . . . disparaging," "contemptuous," "rarely used today . . . perceived as insulting," and "old-fashioned . . . highly offensive."[17] Having a bit of caustic fun with defenders of the name, the columnist Robert Harding asked, "If it's not an offensive term, why isn't it widely used today? Why do we say and write 'Indian' or 'Native American' when we could use 'redskin?' If it's not derogatory, as Snyder and backers suggest, why not use it?"[18] Indeed, one does not use it as a synonym for an American Indian in any form of public discourse, and one would not use it as a reference to or description of a Native American in any context in contemporary life outside of sport; however, as the linguist Geoffrey Nunberg notes, "when it comes to slurs, 'context' isn't a decontaminant."[19] To offer but one reminder of this, from a sign outside a Sonic Drive-In in Missouri, December 2013: "KC Chiefs Will Scalp the Redskins; Feed Them Whiskey; Send 2 Reservation."[20] Here the slur anchors a chain of racist invectives, including genocide, trauma, alcoholism, and dispossession; dehumanization as the ultimate rallying cry for team spirit.

While calling out the slur may prove relatively easy today, even if many people would not universally or immediately recognize it as such, as this example would seem to emphasize, dating the emergence of the term as a slur has proven vexing. In efforts to do so, we should distinguish between when the usage of the term became a slur and when members of society began to understand that the term was a slur.

If Goddard is right about the earliest uses of the word, it enters English as a neutral noun, flowing from one set of indigenous speakers to American political, journalistic, and then literary discourse. In these contexts, it gains a foothold, popularized especially in the work of James Fenimore Cooper, particularly his Leatherstocking Tales. Like the n-word, the r-word moves from neutral term to epithet through a process of pejoration, a transformation that renders it a pejorative. I would hypothesize that whereas slavery encouraged this process for the n-word, increasing ethnic friction associated with westward expansion, open calls to dispossess and destroy indigenous communities, and the resistance of American Indians to Euro-American settler colonialism were the catalyst of this process for the r-word. The hardening racial thinking and the quickening of Manifest Destiny after 1850 likely accelerated its pejoration, a process that was surely well on its way to completion by the end of the Civil War, when the reunited nation intensified its conquest of the West. One confirmation of this may be found in newspaper articles from the second half of the nineteenth century, which increasingly relate the struggles to suppress and dispossess native nations through use of the term.[21] Another may be gathered from the absence of any positive uses of the term. Surveying usage of the word since the mid-nineteenth century, Bruce Stapleton found "no support" for the assertion that it was "ever commonly used to symbolize 'success, courage, pride, and achievement.'"[22]

In late 1890, Frank Baum, better known for *The Wizard of Oz* than his anti-Indian sentiments, affirmed the completion of the transformation when he gave voice to the white supremacy anchoring the epithet in a lament (of sorts) for Sitting Bull and the Sioux:

> The proud spirit of the original owners of these vast prairies inherited through centuries of fierce and bloody wars for their possession, lingered last in the bosom of Sitting Bull. With his fall the nobility of the Redskin is extinguished, and what few are left are a pack of whining curs who lick the hand that smites them. The Whites, by

law of conquest, by justice of civilization, are masters of the American continent, and the best safety of the frontier settlements will be secured by the total annihilation of the few remaining Indians. Why not annihilation? Their glory has fled, their spirit broken, their manhood effaced; better that they die than live the miserable wretches that they are. . . . We cannot honestly regret their extermination, but we at least do justice to the manly characteristics possessed, according to their lights and education, by the early Redskins of America.[23]

Here Baum celebrates genocide, underscoring the propriety of readings that link the term to violence, terror, and ethnic cleansing. His comments also presage the zenith of the slur, the usage of which peaked between 1892 and 1911, the two decades following the closing of the frontier and the massacre at Wounded Knee and the period in which popular culture images began to harden in Wild West shows.[24]

It is equally challenging to identify the precise point at which English speakers perceived the r-word as a pejorative. The decline in its use after 1911 provides one tangible indicator, suggesting the term had begun to fall out of favor. And even though the team name was selected in 1933, that roughly coincides with another marker of disuse: after 1931, Stapleton found only one literary use in his study.[25] An even better measure might be to examine the changing definitions of the word. Merriam-Webster's dictionaries offer a nice illustration.

1890: North American Indian—so called from the color of their skin
1898: A North American Indian—often contemptuous (*Collegiate*)
1910: "Often contemptuous" dropped

The disparaging quality of the term is highlighted at the height of the term's usage, and reference to the disparagement is subsequently removed. This may be "due to lack of space" or due to changing editorial priorities. After more than half a decade it returns:

1961: Usually taken to be offensive (*New International*, 3rd ed.)
1983: "usu. taken to be offensive" (*Collegiate*, 9th ed.)
2003: "usually offensive" (*Collegiate*, 11th ed.)

And once the sense of disparagement returns, it remains; the understanding of the word as a pejorative deepens and solidifies. This shift predates calls to end the use of the team name. It also underscores that for more than half a century the Washington professional football team has used a racial slur as its moniker.

Team Name

Wherever the word originated and whenever it became a slur precisely, sport kept the word alive. Indeed, media coverage in the late nineteenth and early twentieth centuries quickly adapted the language of the Indian Wars to their coverage of sports. They used it to represent the exploits of the athletic teams at American Indian boarding schools and to sensationalize their contests with elite, historically white institutions. Journalists and the public generally regarded indigenous people with a mixture of fascination, antipathy, pity, and nostalgia. The r-word became a familiar and still loaded term to refer to indigenous players and teams. When George Preston Marshall opted to change the name of his fledging team from the Boston Braves to the Boston R*dskins in 1933, he did so against this background. Although it is not clear exactly what led Marshall to make this decision, the immediate circumstances do offer some clues. The selection of a new moniker coincided with the relocation of the team from Braves Field to Fenway Park. Moreover, it occurred in association with the hiring of a new coach, William Henry "Lone Star" Dietz, who claimed to be Lakota and had played and coached at Carlisle Indian Industrial School during its heyday, when football games were pictured as a restaging of the so-called Indian Wars. And during his first year, Dietz, who had coached previously at Haskell Institute and won a Rose Bowl while at Washington State College, recruited four American Indians to the team as well: Orien Crow, Larry Johnson, David Ward, and Rabbit Weller.[26]

The franchise and its fans routinely explain that the name change was motivated by the best of intentions, meant to convey respect to American Indians, most often Dietz himself. The current owner, Daniel Snyder, articulated this perspective in an October 2013 letter: "As some of you may know, our team began 81 years ago—in 1932—with the name

'Boston Braves.' The following year, the franchise name was changed to the 'Boston Redskins.' On that inaugural Redskins team, four players and our Head Coach were Native Americans. The name was never a label. It was, and continues to be, a badge of honor."[27] Nearly a year later, on *Outside the Lines*, he affirmed this account, asserting, "Coach Dietz was Native American, he named the team. . . . The historical facts are the historical facts."[28]

To begin, press coverage contradicts this narrative, exposing it to be wishful thinking at best. The *Hartford Courant* ran a story on the name change in which Marshall clearly states, "The fact that we have in our head coach, Lone Star Dietz, an Indian, together with several Indian players, has not, as may be suspected, inspired me to select the name Redskins."[29] And the *Boston Herald*, reporting on the new team name, noted that "hereafter, the erstwhile Braves of pro football will be known as the Boston Redskins. The explanation is that the change was made to avoid confusion with the Braves baseball team."[30] Clearly, the "historical facts" do not support the claims that Dietz named the team or that the moniker was selected to honor Native Americans. Such assertions are, in the words of Linda Waggoner, "phony baloney."[31]

Marshall, a keen businessman, appears to have sought above all else to establish a marketable brand. He wanted to avoid confusion, which meant, upon relocating the team to a new venue in Boston, selecting a new name for the team, but perhaps one that was familiar to sport fans. In keeping with the conventions of the day, in which baseball and football franchises had team names that echoed one another (Chicago has the Cubs and Bears, respectively, Detroit the Tigers and the Lions), his search for a distinct yet familiar name was further limited, as Cleveland already had a baseball team named the Indians. *R*dskin*, then common in media and popular culture, may have seemed the best alternative. In this context, he may have seen hiring Dietz as an opportunity to leverage popular interest in Indianness and Dietz's association with the history of Carlisle to his advantage. In this frame, Dietz's hiring followed the brand, not the reverse preferred by supporters.[32]

And while Marshall and many in the public may have accepted Dietz as an American Indian, significant questions surround his claims. Indeed,

recent interpretations have suggested that he was an imposter who bor-
rowed the identity of a Lakota man to reinvent himself (see fig. 1). Born
in Rice Lake, Wisconsin, to parent of German heritage, Dietz's new-
found identity became something of a joke to those who knew him as a
youth. Poor record keeping combined with a nostalgic and nationalist
zeal for authentic Indianness and the popularity of playing Indian all
likely contributed his charade, a charade that allowed him to get an
education, find a wife, and start a career in coaching. If it had not been
for the First World War, no one may have ever known, but Dietz claimed
exemption as a "non-citizen Indian." Upon investigation, the Federal
Bureau of Investigation deemed this assertion to be fraudulent, leading
to his prosecution for being what the press at the time called a slacker or
draft dodger. A media spectacle surrounded the trial, which resulted in a
hung jury and a subsequent plea of no contest and thirty days in jail. After
his release, Dietz continued to pass himself off as Indian and to coach.
In retrospect, one may marvel that the public continued to accept him
as Indian and may wonder more at his capacity to rehabilitate himself
and his image.[33]

Dietz held tenure with the team for two years, garnering a record
of 11 wins, 11 losses, and 2 ties. He was fired rather unceremoniously,
highlighting the primacy of the brand, its independence from the coach,
and the preeminence of business and athletic success over latter-day and
fanciful ascriptions like honor. In 1937 Marshall moved the franchise to
Washington DC, where he further embellished the Indian motif begun
in Boston and endeavored to make it the team of the South. It appears
that neither he nor anyone else gave the origins of the team name much
thought for most of the next three decades of his ownership.

Logo

Compared to the word or the team name, less controversy surrounds the
creation of the logo used by the franchise. The team currently trumpets
the origins of its current iteration: "Our logo was designed by Native
Americans."[34] The franchise adopted it in response to overtures from a
former president of the National Congress of American Indians, Walter
"Blackie" Wetzel (Blackfoot), who wanted what he regarded as a positive

image of indigenous people associated with the team. He approached the owner, Edward Bennett Williams, unhappy with the more generic logos that the team had used since the mid-1960s, and worked with others in Indian Country to create a new version. For its first three decades, the team used in succession four artistic renderings of an American Indian man, shown in profile with braids and two feathers in his hair. For a brief period (during its 1965–69 seasons), it replaced this with a yellow and white illustration of a spear and then (during the 1970–71 season) used the short-lived logo that unnerved Wetzel so—a red *R* at the center of a circle with the familiar feather motif. Wetzel proposed a return to the earlier Indian-head design, returning apparently to the same inspirational source originally consulted—the Indian Head nickel. With the exception of the 1982 season, when the orientation of the figure was reversed and the size of the design increased, the version proposed by Wetzel has remained on the team's helmets, a prominent symbol of the franchise and a profitable feature of its NFL-licensed clothing and memorabilia.[35]

While there is little doubt about Wetzel's role in the inception of the current logo, accounts of its source operate much like other narratives surrounding the team and its traditions. It is very much an origin story that seeks to make sense of the present through a reiteration of the past, setting things today in their proper place by speaking of their beginnings. To tell this story, the team neglects the first four decades of its existence and holds under erasure its earlier Indian-head logos, preferring not to focus on this longer tradition. Moreover, the team legitimates itself through the enthusiastic endorsement and involvement of American Indian leaders, allowing it to suggest by extension, "this can't be racist or offensive, an Indian designed it." Wetzel was, of course, only one American Indian, but the team has him stand in for all American Indians, flattening the diversity of native experience and opinion to protect the brand. In effect, the team disappears other Native Americans. Of particular importance, the narrative excludes those opposed to the moniker and actively working to change it. The Wetzel logo origin story enables the team and its supporters, then, to continue to use Indianness for fun and financial gain; to vanish the larger, uncomfortable history of playing Indian; to claim indigenous support; to refute charges of racism;

and to erase opposition. Even as the organization insulates itself from anti-Indianism by invoking Wetzel, it reinvigorates a standing pattern of selective sampling (choosing to recognize only those indigenous people who agree with them), distortion (support written over opposition), and sowing division (pitting American Indians against one another).

As a partial representation, the team's account of its logo, of course, does not tell a complete story. It edits out or neglects to mention that in many ways the Wetzel design mirrors and updates its earlier logos. In fact, one might say Wetzel created an image in keeping with both the resurgent romanticism of the times and the team's established embellishments of Indianness. Indeed, as I explore in greater detail in the next chapter, Marshall consciously cultivated his brand, long before many of his peers: "His was the first pro-sports team to co-opt an American Indian identity with such fervor: The Redskins' halftime band marched in tribal regalia; the coach wore feathers on the sideline; and Marshall had an Indian-head logo printed across the center of their uniforms."[36] These traditions were very much in full effect in the early 1970s.

Significantly, it is not just that the modernized image reflected earlier versions or resonated with the team's traditions; it drew from the same source as had the earlier logos. The Indian Head nickel served as an inspiration to Marshall and, years later, Wetzel. In circulation from 1913 to 1938, it provided one of the most common images of American Indians when Marshall renamed his fledging franchise and as Wetzel came of age. Its designer, James Earle Fraser, who also famously sculpted *The End of the Trail*, had sought to convey something distinctively American with his use of the Indian head on one side and the buffalo on the other. At the time, most in the United States would have thought the pair authentic, if imperiled, representatives of nature and primitivism. The logo, like the nickel, allowed Americans to absorb indigeneity, laying claim to indigenous people's rightful inheritance while lamenting nostalgically their passing. Far from positive, the Indian-head logo appears in retrospect to be akin to a trophy taken and reintroduced into circulation to secure citizenship, celebrate racial superiority, and fashion identity.[37]

For Wetzel, both the nickel and the logo meant something else entirely. He saw something positive in the Indian head, perhaps one of the few popular images in his day that seemed to accord indigenous people a modicum of humanity. Of course, origin stories do not allow a consideration of complexity and contradiction, but rather they work to resolve them, quieting uneasy questions and uncomfortable conditions.

Opposition

To hear some tell it, the media, liberals, and/or a vocal minority have manufactured opposition to the Washington professional football mascot. Far from an indigenous movement, according to this line of thinking, it is a conspiracy of one sort or another. For instance, as the controversy began to escalate in 2014, the former Alaska governor and onetime U.S. vice presidential candidate Sarah Palin posted on Facebook that it was another of "the liberal media's made-up controversies [meant to] divide our country." And Billy Kilmer, a DC quarterback (1971–78), suggested, "Everybody's got to be so politically correct today. . . . I think it's all politically connected and I think it's festered by liberals against (Redskins owner) Dan Snyder, who's a conservative."[38]

As with the other origin stories examined in this chapter, this narrative seeks to defend the team while deflecting criticism. In doing so, it misconstrues the history of opposition and its significance. "By reframing the issue this way," explains Navajo-Yankton Dakota activist Jackie Keeler, "the Washington NFL team continues to make real, modern Native people to disappear, much as their mascot does. It's a continuation of the extinguishment of the Native voice and the appropriation of our identity and lands."[39] There is in fact nothing new about opposition to the team and its traditions. Writing in 1992, Clarence Page would note that American Indians and their allies had been pressing for change "for years."[40]

Indeed, at precisely the same moment that Walter Wetzel approached the franchise about its logo, American Indians across the United States had begun protesting the continued use of Indianness in sport, including team names, logos, and mascots. They won important early victories at Stanford University, the University of Oklahoma, and Dartmouth College, among others. Seeking to build on this momentum, a group of Native Americans pushed the Washington professional football team to make a change as well. On January 18, 1972, Harold M. Gross, director of the Indian Legal Information Development Service (ILIDS), sent a letter to the team's owner, Edward Bennett Williams, emphasizing that ILIDS regarded the team name to be a "derogatory racial epithet," akin to other racial slurs. "Born at a time in our history when the national policy was to seize Indian land and resources, and hunt down Indian people who stood in the way, the term 'Redskin' has been perpetuated through such media as western movies and television. Most often, the term is coupled with other derogatory adjectives, as 'dirty Redskin' or 'pesky Redskin' which is used interchangeably with the word 'savage' to portray a misleading and denigrating image of the Native American."[41] Even at this early date, Gross draws a tight connection between symbol and structure, underscoring the name's deep entanglements with a history of dispossession, destruction, and dehumanization.

At this point, Williams, also a practicing attorney, had some familiarity with the Red Power movement and its agenda, as a few years earlier Ethel Kennedy had recommended that LaNada Means (Bannock), a representative of the activists occupying Alcatraz, contact him about the possibility of defending the group. And he had reportedly given the group a color television on a previous occasion.[42] Williams appears to have taken Gross's letter seriously, agreeing to meet with American Indian representatives. In late March, LaDonna Harris (Comanche), president of Americans for Indian Opportunity and the wife of U.S. Senator Fred Harris; Richard LaCourse (Yakama), Washington bureau chief for the American Indian Press Association; Ron Aguilar, district representative of the National Indian Youth Council; Dennis Banks (Anishinaabe), district representative of the American Indian Movement; Hanay Geigomah (Kiowa/Delaware), director of youth programs, Bureau of Indian Affairs; and Laura Wittstock (Seneca), editor of the ILIDS Legislative Review, along with Gross and Leon Cook, president of the National Council of American Indians, met with Williams at the team's headquarters. Williams would later characterize it as a "listening session" and not a negotiation. He made no promises during or immediately after the meeting, but he did summarize it in a letter the next day to NFL commissioner Pete Rozelle.[43]

For their part, the assembled Native Americans had a clear set of demands:

Change the "derogatory racial epithet, 'Redskins.'"

Sponsor a campaign to get a new name.

Get rid of the pseudo-Indian dancing girls called "Redskinettes," as well as the team song, "Hail to the Redskins."

Actively encourage other professional sports organizations to cease the use of similar stereotypes degrading America's Indian people.

Needless to say, the franchise effectively weathered the resistance, refusing to entertain most of the activists' ultimatums. That said, it did make minor changes (discussed in greater detail in the next chapter), including altering the lyrics of "Hail to the Redskins" and ending the practice of dressing the Redskinettes in "Indian-style wigs."

The key arguments articulated at the time continue to shape debate over the team and its traditions. Echoing Gross, LaCourse told reporters that *R*dskin* was comparable to other slurs, like *Darky*, and that with its name, the team "keeps the cheap stereotypes of the Indian in circulation." Meanwhile, Williams, the team's owner, came to mock the opposition in the press, trivializing their claims: "This is getting silly. . . . Suppose blacks get together and demanded Cleveland's football team stopped calling itself the Browns, or ornithologists insisted that Baltimore was demeaning to birds because the name is the Orioles." More important, he suggested, was that the name was about honor and respect: "If there was anything involved but the glorification of the American Indian, we would change our nickname." Wittstock dismissed his claim, noting that "any commercial use of a race of people can't be glorification."[44]

Far from a media-driven conspiracy, opposition to the team and its tradition has deep roots in Indian Country. In fact, during its eighty-plus years in existence, the franchise has spent more time under fire than not (thirty-nine years without opposition and forty-two with opposition).

The Need for New Stories

Together, the various stories reviewed in this chapter are more than stories. Those who tell them put them to work, mobilizing them for particular ends, in the service of specific cultural and political projects.

While the etymology offered by many in Indian Country speaks truth to power, rightly highlighting the deep entanglements of symbolic and physical violence in U.S. settler colonialism (past and present), most of the narratives discussed here actually work to defend the status quo, clothing the use of Indianness and abuse of Indians as legitimate, even appropriate. In many ways, these origin stories equip the franchise and its fans with a mythology that reframes moral questions and social issues. The embrace of these stories, in turn, encourages forms of entitlement and thoughtlessness intent on facilitating the ownership of Indianness, the denial of history and power, and the preservation of privilege. At the core of these origin stories lies a refusal to acknowledge; according to Pauline Turner Strong, "This refusal to acknowledge the offensiveness of the Redskin trademark is both a legacy of colonialism and a contemporary form of racism."[45] In turning away from these legacies, from living history, these origin stories foster the perpetuation of harm. On the one hand, they allow other damaging distortions to flourish: "The problem with the name Redskins for a sports team is that it perpetuates the crippling myth that Native Americans, their lands, their culture, their sovereign powers, their very existence, are relics of the past."[46] On the other hand, they block efforts to come to terms with, or even overcome, historic injustices. If, as Linda Waggoner recently phrased it, "we inherit all the bumps and bruises and gashes and dis-eases that our parents and ancestors could not heal themselves," it is only by revisiting old narratives and telling the world and its pasts anew that we might begin to transform the present.[47] In many respects indigenous people and their allies have challenged the team and its traditions to open up just such a space of possibility.

Uses

3

In the 1940s, fans attending a professional football game at Griffith Stadium in Washington DC might purchase a copy of *Redskin Review* for a dime, chuckle at the little American Indian boy who found ingenious ways to best the opposing mascot—for example, by putting salt on the tail of the larger Eagle when Philadelphia came to town—and take in the Redskin Marching Band, decked out in flowing headdresses as they played "Hail to the Redskins."

A decade later, they might read the program featuring the same childish caricature or, later, a renowned indigenous leader, regally drawn; marvel at the wigwam erected atop the stadium; and delight at the halftime spectacle, including at times wild, dancing "Indians," or at least white men playing out their fantasies in that guise (see fig. 2).

In the 1960s, fans would travel to District of Columbia Stadium, later Robert F. Kennedy Memorial Stadium, enjoy the band and the fight song, and witness the Redskinettes—cheerleaders in short, "Indian-style" dress, pigtails, and feathered headbands—while reading from an Indian-themed game day program.

While some of the trappings of Indianness began to fade in the 1970s with the introduction of new lyrics to the fight song and more modern outfits , lacking any native motif, for the cheerleaders, was well as programs unadorned with caricatures, one could still sing along with the band in headdresses and, in 1978, see the birth of the super fan Chief Zee, an African American booster known for his faux headdress and fake tomahawk.

A decade after the initial protests against the team and its traditions, fans might hear Princess Pale Moon, described in television commentary at the time as "an authentic Indian princess," sing the national anthem, accompanied by the marching band, or hear repetition of any of myriad tired clichés associated with the team name and racial slur. This atmosphere is vividly captured in a video taken at the 1982 NFL Championship Game against Dallas, where signs hanging about RFK Stadium read, "Welcome to Little Big Horn" and "Scalp 'em live on CBS." The NFL Films production renders the game and the season in the dehumanizing metaphors the team name conjures: "As Danny White gets knocked out by Dexter Manley in that game, the narrator intones, "Not since Custer's last stand had Cowboys been so overwhelmed by Redskins!' Talking about the Redskins' championship performance that season, the narrator says, 'When the sun set in Pasadena, Super Bowl XVII became another feather in their headdress.'"[1]

Even as the franchise has sought to diminish the presence of sanctioned stereotypes in the wake of litigation brought against it over the past two decades, the fight song and band have remained fixtures, Chief Zee—who has become something of a folk hero—and more anonymous fans alike have played Indian at games, war whoops and tomahawk chops have rained down on opponents, and headlines like this gem from 1998 have still appeared: "Cowboys Scalp Redskins, 31-10; Improve to 3-2."[2]

Much has changed since the inception of the franchise: the team has played in three different stadiums in the DC metro area; the band was formed; the fight song was written and lyrics later changed and later still sanitized; the logo, as discussed in the previous chapter, has taken numerous forms; the Redskinettes were spawned, first as early versions of today's Poca-hotties and then without Indian references, invented Indian costumes, or racialized sexual fetish and with a new name, Redskin Cheerleaders. Three things, however, have not changed: the team name; the centrality of Indianness, even if it is increasingly held under erasure; and the denigrating ways in which the former has overdetermined the latter.

In this chapter I examine the ways the franchise and its fans have used and understood Native Americans. Throughout its history, Indianness has been the primary raw material for the team and its traditions, anchoring the brand and its power and profitability. After reviewing mascotting as a cultural practice, I take up embellishment, or the creation of the brand, and ambivalence, or the overlapping associations attached to the slur at the core of the brand. In conclusion, I reflect on how and why alterations of these uses matter.

Invented Indians

The use of names, images, and motifs associated with American Indians became commonplace in American sport during the first third of the twentieth century, making it ordinary, if not fashionable, to name the professional football team in Boston as first the Braves and then the R*dskins. During the early twentieth century, these key symbols and the rituals associated with them came of age with modern sport, and both crystallized in response to crises around masculinity and modernity, particularly a perceived softening of the American male and a more general feminization of American culture. Indianness offered white youth a means to recapture a more natural, truer manhood, as exemplified by organizations like the Boy Scouts. Indigenous masculinities, as imagined by Euro-American boys and men, then unfolded as a creative space of reinvention, a pliable and performative domain at once productive, pleasurable, powerful, and ultimately profitable. Indianness offered athletes, coaches, bands, boosters, and reporters a ready language of masculinity, a means to translate and transcribe fierceness, bravery, and honor while affirming the core attributes associated with whiteness and America, including freedom, independence, sacrifice, and strength.[3]

As a consequence, Native American mascots have very little to do with Native Americans. They do not, nay, cannot, represent indigenous men and women. Much like blackface, such inventions and imaginings, meant to represent a racial other, tell us much more about Euro-Americans and their perceptions, preconceptions, and preoccupations: how they understand themselves, how they interpret the world around them, and how they want others to see them. They reflect and reinforce the fundamental features of racial and gendered privilege in a settler society, particularly a sense of entitlement to take and remake without consent and to do so without the burden of history, the challenges of knowing, or the risk of penalty. Two examples clarify this interplay between race, gender, and power.

First, mascots have served as masks, allowing Americans, especially white men, the capacity to put on Indianness as if it were a costume. Photographs of students who portrayed Willie Wampum at Marquette University more than a half century ago capture this pattern. At the height of his popularity, the mascot, representing the school and its Golden Warriors, was a white male student dressed in fringed buckskins and donning an oversized papier-mâché head, sometimes with ridiculously large sunglasses or an oversized tomahawk. Images from the sideline have something of a carnivalesque feel, the football field as a kind of heterotopic space, a zone of frivolity and liminality made possible by imagined indigenous masculinity that empowered white male student athletes and a white patriarchal public sphere more generally. Arguably more telling are the backstage photos, in which the student performers pose partially undressed—for instance, with the exaggerated head beside them. Some may say the images offer no pretense and a simple summary of pleasure, power, and possibilities in a simpler moment, at a time when neither the assumptions of the settler state nor its supporting ideas about gender and sexuality were questioned or perhaps even questionable. Much the same, we will see, can be said about the Washington professional football team during this period.[4]

Second, at every Florida State University home football game, a white student playing at being Osceola, leader of the Seminole resistance to white encroachment, rides onto the playing field and throws a flaming spear at midfield. The proud freedom fighter electrifies the crowd and reaffirms hegemonic formulations of whiteness, masculinity, and Americanness. For the fans to go wild and FSU to stage the ritual entrance, all must forget or, more likely, not know that Osceola was regarded by many of his Euro-American contemporaries as a terrorist, and after he was put to death for having the temerity to defend his land and people, parts of his remains were taken as souvenirs.[5]

In this context, Native American mascots are not unlike trophies, remnants from a kill, longingly kept reminders of past glory, and continuing signs of the prowess and superiority through which Euro-Americans channel the strength and energy of those they (or, better said, their forebearers) have vanquished. Such conjurings, of course, depend on disfigurement and dehumanization, transmogrifications that have reduced an abject and imagined other to cypher and caricature. Warriors, Chiefs, and Braves have a generic appeal, embodying the ideals of white masculinity on the plain of battle and the field of play, namely, bravery, bellicosity, loyalty, strength, aggression, leadership, and camaraderie. Qualities amplified in more extreme monikers like Savages and Redskins, which replace nobility with intensity, animalism, terror, and brutality, are elements understood to be part of the masculine ideal as well, best understood perhaps as darker complements. Together, these renderings anchor character building and individual aspiration; bind teams and communities to one another, anchoring them in time and place; map the world and one's location in it; and bring social distinctions and cultural values to life.

Origins

The Washington professional football franchise began in Boston in 1932 and shared a name with the local baseball team, the Braves. A year later the team changed its name to R*dskins, and it relocated to the nation's capital in 1937. The franchise, the NFL, and many fans erroneously claim with increased frequency and volume that the team name honors American Indians, and they do so by making a connection to the fact that the moniker was selected during the brief tenure of coach William "Lone Star" Dietz, who identified himself as a Lakota. Much of the criticism of the team rightly directs attention at its traditions, particularly its name, its perpetuation of stereotypes, and its well-documented history of racism. The team name, as noted in the previous chapter, is a racial slur, which had contested origins before it became a derogatory and dehumanizing reference for American Indians. Like all such mascots, its iconography trades in ahistorical archetypes still common throughout popular culture. And, long before the NFL expanded to have teams in Atlanta, Dallas, and New Orleans, the DC franchise positioned itself as the team of the

South. It famously was the last NFL team to integrate and then only in response to federal pressure to do so.[6] As the owner George Preston Marshall, who also chose the name of the team, remarked at the time, in a manner eerily reminiscent of many modern assessments of race and power: "We'll start signing Negroes when the Harlem Globetrotters start signing whites."[7] The franchise has successfully put this ugly history behind it and built itself into one of the most valuable professional teams in the United States.

In many ways, as likely surprises no one, the R*dskins are all about men. Football is among the most pronounced articulations of hegemonic masculinity in the United States. The centrality of violence, domination, and conquest give material form to ideals like assertiveness, strength, decisiveness, hierarchy, and (self-)control. Indianness accentuates and extends their expression on the playing field and their emulation by countless fans in the stands and on the streets. In turn, women in the form of the cheer squad, the Redskinettes, which debuted in 1962, put gender norms and roles in stark relief. This gendered crucible plays a foundational role in the creation and contestation of the team name.

In common with many teams with American Indian mascots, the Washington professional football team emerged in a context that romanticized indigenous masculinity and celebrated white men playing Indian. Coach Dietz, neither namesake nor Lakota, who lived his adult life in white society as an American Indian, was in fact a fraud, taking the impersonation of indigenous people beyond the momentary rituals associated with scouting, fraternal organizations, and theatrical performances to craft a false persona.[8] That Dietz passed and so many (then and now) embraced him as an American Indian underscores the ease with which Euro-American men could fashion their identities as white men by taking and remaking elements of indigenous culture (regalia, names, stories, and so forth). The willingness of so many to continue to believe a lie communicates something very deep about settler society, namely the lasting force, value, and utility of stereotypes about Native Americans and the power and privilege non-Indians have enjoyed to use those stereotypes to stage themselves for the world.

Football is noteworthy for the manner in which it sanctions a largely homosocial, hypermasculine space. The original owner of the team, George Marshall, sought to attract women and families to the games, believing that the presence of more women would increase the attendance of men as well. To this end, he seized upon the marching band as the perfect set piece and recruited some 150 members to form it in 1937.[9] In the process, he sought to create a heteronormative ideal of sorts: the sporting spectacle, set to a bombastic soundtrack and dressed in feathers, gave purpose, order, and meaning to white team, white family, and white nation.

The hallmark of the team and its symphonic signature would debut the following year. "Hail to the Redskins" articulated many of the reigning ideas about race and gender. The song, with its line "Braves on the Warpath," celebrated and claimed indigenous masculinity for the team and its fans, encoding it, like the Indian head on the side of the team's helmet, as a trophy and a totem—romantic, stoic, brave, defeated, and repossessed. To underscore the intense savagery, at once desirable and detestable, it cast vanquishment of the opponent as scalping and employed broken English to drive the point home ("We will take 'em big score"). Again, white masculinity has secured and centered itself through projections of indigenous masculinity as race and gender, giving meaning to the team. And the later addition asserting that the team will "Fight for old Dixie" makes plain the shape and scope of whiteness. Importantly, "Hail to the Redskins" has changed over time. As Locke Peterseim notes,

> Where today's song cheers fans to "Fight for old D.C.!" ... "Fight for old Dixie!" played directly to the fans' Southern identity. And while the Redskins still use a racial slur for their team name, some words in the original fight song didn't do much to deflect accusations of racism. Where the song now says, "Beat 'em, swamp 'em, touchdown!—Let the points soar!" it once went, "Scalp 'em, swamp 'em—We will take 'em big score / Read 'em, weep 'em, touchdown!—We want heap more!" The lyrics were subsequently cleaned up in the '60s, after Marshall's Redskins were, notoriously in 1962, the last pro team to integrate.[10]

The racial slur remains but the reference to Dixie has faded away; the broken English has been edited, beautified much like the origin story and evolving rationale. One of course wonders why, if these elements can be reconfigured, the team name and associated iconography cannot.

Embellishment

George Preston Marshall clearly understood the importance of publicity and entertainment. He regularly worked the press to draw a crowd and routinely worked the crowd to intensify interest and sales. For instance, after drafting Sammy Baugh, who was a college standout at Texas Christian University, Marshall played up the future Hall of Fame quarterback's roots. Upon his arrival, Marshall handed Baugh cowboy "boots and a ten gallon hat." Confused, because he had not seen "anything like that before," Baugh asked the owner for an explanation. "It's showmanship," Marshall retorted. "Put them on for the pictures." The western mystique clearly left an impression on the DC press corps: "A reporter asked him about the boots. 'They hurt my feet,' Baugh complained. 'Son, is it true that you once killed a buffalo?' another reporter asked. 'Naw, I just winged him,' Baugh replied."[11] Marshall's use of the media to create buzz about his team, cultivate an image, and secure a market was ahead of his time. In contrast, his use of Indianness was very much in keeping with his time.

Marshall never understood R*dskins to be merely the name of a team; no, ever the showman and always the businessman, he always embraced it as a brand, a recognizable sign and marketable commodity that would encourage consumption, foster identification, and promote loyalty (see fig. 3). Indianness, an established reservoir of symbolic associations, proved irresistible for players, fans, and the franchise alike (see fig. 4). Arguably nearing the height of its resurgent popularity at the inception of the franchise, Indianness provided him with what at the time must have seemed like the perfect brand—at once flexible, highly fecund, and favored by the public. He used each of these elements to his advantage in developing his brand. In fact, he established and embellished them throughout his tenure as owner in order to make the franchise viable, visible, and valuable.

He did this in part by making game day a spectacle, bigger than a contest between two football teams, with every element saturated with an Indian motif. His initial logo featured the profile of an Indian warrior, reportedly inspired by the Indian Head nickel, which was still in circulation. He also choose team colors, burgundy and gold, meant to accentuate the redness of the moniker. And, as noted above, he created a band to attract a wider audience, dressing them in feathers. Late in his tenure as owner, the team would add cheerleaders, the Redskinettes, attaching to its tableau the perpetuation of sexualized stereotypes of American Indian women.

Moreover, according to the columnist Bob Considine, Marshall had the wisdom to listen to his wife, the former silent film star Corinne Griffith, who encouraged the team's relocation to the nation's capital, help design the uniforms, and wrote the fight song "Hail to the Redskins." Her initial rendition did not reference Dixie, as many claim, but it did play off popular clichés. It included several refrains that emphasized broken English, making a joke of the intelligence and linguistic acumen of American Indians. And throughout, it gave life to the stoic warrior in the team's logo, stressing his romanticized bellicosity as conveyed with reference to the warpath, taking scalps, and defeating the enemy. The song also made a magical transference, much like all of the traditions did, in which elements projected onto American Indians became the property of the team and its fans. So when the braves go on the warpath, they are the sons of DC who fight for DC.[12]

It was at halftime that these elements would get their fullest and most sophisticated expression. In the words of Considine, "A Redskin game is something resembling a fast-moving revue, with cues, settings, music, pace, tableaux and, hold your hats boys a ballet." Indeed, "once the game was under way," he continued, "the musical background was a big-piece swing band, mounted in a smart canvas tepee at the back of a section of bleachers. At the half time intermission smoke began pouring out of the top of the big tepee, a rhythmic tom-tom set up, and out on the field war-whooped a 150-piece band in Indian dress, playing 'Hail to the Redskins.'" Considine went so far to credit these embellishments of Indianness with saving the franchise from bankruptcy and making it a financial success, as it drew more than 350,000 spectators annually in the late 1940s.[13]

Although Marshall and Griffith were arguably the two of the more successful entrepreneurs to capitalize on Indianness in the twentieth century, their uses and understandings of American Indians were very much in keeping with the time. The team took its moniker and established its traditions in an era in which many professional and collegiate teams did the same, as the Western reached its zenith and countless Americans were socialized through youth groups and popular stories to embrace the vision of Native Americans that anchored the team. But one example comes from the franchise's inaugural season, when it faced the New York Giants en route to winning the league championship against the Chicago Bears. The *New York Times* ran a vivid account of the atmosphere surrounding the game, under the headline "Washington Is Capital of Football World as Redskins Swell 'Home' City's Pride": "A band of whooping Indians—the professional football Redskins Tribe—chased the politicians right out of the capital spotlight today. With the scalps of the New York Giants dangling from their belts, the Eastern Champions captured the city's imagination. . . . Night club and hotel orchestras turned from the moment's romantic melodies and went to town with swing arrangements of such Indian lyrics as 'Pale Moon' and 'Red Wing.' . . . [Myriad citizens] went about the city muttering: 'I saw 'em—the Redskins.'"[14]

Clearly, the Washington professional football team established its brand in an era at ease with stereotyping and in love with Indian-styled things, which people mistook for actual Indians. Marshall, in collaboration with Griffith, reflected the times and recognized that Indianness was ripe for exploitation and embellishment. While times have changed, the franchise has resisted efforts to rethink its brand or the centrality of anti-Indian racism to it.

Ambivalence

R*dskin is a slur: it denigrates and dehumanizes; it has a deep connection with organized killing and ethnic cleansing, including taking scalps and bounties; it may be one of the key words of conquest in the United States, imprinted on the national imaginary through journalistic coverage of the so-called Indian wars, dime novels, Hollywood Westerns, and, of course, football. The franchise and its fans see the history and significance of the term differently; they either do not know these sordid details or prefer to ignore them. This pattern of erasure, lack of reflection, and active disengagement, what I describe as thoughtlessness in the next chapter, has enabled supporters to render the team and its traditions in positive terms, to describe their actions and imaginings as respectful, honorable, and worthy of celebration. NFL commissioner Roger Goodell phrased it this way in the run-up to Super Bowl XLVIII: "Let me remind you, this is the name of a football team, a football team that's had that name for 80 years and has presented the name in a way that is honored—that has honored Native Americans."[15] Saying it is so does not make it so, for the Washington professional football team has offered numerous representations of Native Americans since its inception that work against this and similar declarations.

On the whole, its representations of American Indians have favored a more or less generic native, whether cartoonish or romanticized, a nameless indigene conforming to prevailing preconceptions and satisfying needs and desires arising outside of native nations. They have always been first and foremost what Robert Berkhofer described as the "white man's Indian," that is, an invention of settler society crafted with reference to its historical preoccupations and in response to contemporary social, political, and economic issues.[16] Almost exclusively, the franchise and its fans have favored American Indians frozen in time, most frequently, stuck in the past, caught in the historic periods emphasized by conflict and popularized by fiction and film, especially peoples from the Plains and Southwest. Moreover, with the exception of the cheer squad, which for roughly a decade dressed as Indian maidens (as imagined by whites), all of their Indians have been men, primarily warriors, braves, and chiefs, precisely the totems, tokens, and trophies that American society has most deeply coveted. Finally, they have displayed great comfort for decades in taking and remaking Indianness, tearing objects, people, and practices from specific contexts to create something new, meaningful, and enjoyable to them, typically without the consent or counsel of those from whom they have stolen. Looking across the past seventy-five years, one cannot help but conclude that, far from honoring indigenous peoples, these images and enactments share a propensity to distort, dehumanize, and disparage. They would on the whole be best read as stereotypical, racist, and even anti-Indian.

For all of their similarities, the ways in which fans and the franchise have imagined American Indians also exhibit a pronounced diversity. There is not a singular image, fixed and unchanging, but multiple images.

First, the team created and the fans embraced a range of images dedicated to extolling the virtue and virility associated with the warrior. The logo, despite its changes, has long featured a native warrior in profile, projecting a regal air. Many see the current iteration as a "positive" rendering of native peoples. A series of game day program covers from the 1950s derived from a shared stylistic and sentimental foundation, picturing tribal leaders like Geronimo, Sequoyah, and Chief Red Cloud, who would be familiar to virtually every fan, in black-and-white portraits. The romanticized renderings seen in the logo and on the program convey a nostalgia for a lost and defeated indigeneity, at once mournful and celebratory. They affirm the superiority of white civilization even as the franchise and its fans draw symbolic power from the native other.

Second, the team took elements from indigenous societies to create tableaus that resonated with the core brand and amplified its pseudo-Indian motif. For instance, the September 30, 1962, cover showcased a tomahawk and shield (see fig. 5). These were often hybrid creations that juxtaposed these elements with modern society, especially football. The November 17, 1963, program features a southwestern artisan making what appears to be jewelry with a football helmet in the foreground; the October 13, 1963, cover uses an eagle head and a football to make a totem of sorts (see fig. 6); and that from November 25, 1962, pictures a grand teepee erected on top of District of Columbia Stadium. Holiday programs provided a special treat, including the 1961 issue, which centered on a teepee adorned with a stocking and the team's signatures (see fig. 7). Two years later the program transformed Santa Claus into a native dancer. These images congeal as odd, impressionistic anthropological tableaus that seem intent on appreciating indigeneity, unaware of the appropriation and invention that bring them to life.

Third, the team produced a set of covers meant to be humorous. They

all have a small Indian youth as their protagonist, doing silly things to capture, outsmart, or otherwise defeat the opposing team, likewise rendered
through some exaggerated version of its mascot. For instance, he plucks
feathers from an eagle, attempts to trap a bear, or shoots his bow and
arrow from a tree at a 49er with guns ablazing on Pennsylvania Avenue.
Later, other humorous covers would feature a generic native man being
kicked over the goalposts by the Baltimore Colt. These images belittle
indigenous people. The Indian youth series infantilizes them, making
them less than fully human. They all transform American Indians into
a joke. And while seemingly in good fun, humor can be, as Freud understood, a psychic weapon.

One can see in these distinct imaginings a deep ambivalence for indigenous peoples and cultures, marked by an unnerving mix of reverence,
lament, humor, and disdain. Both the noble savage and the ignoble savage
make appearances in the team's pantheon, a reflection, undoubtedly,
of the complex and contradictory ways in which American society has
pictured Native Americans—as uncivilized heathens, children of nature,
bellicose threats, tragic victims, proud people, virtuous rebels, mighty
warriors, dirty savages, lazy wretches, and more. Above all, one finds in
examining programs and halftime performances a comfort in reducing
American Indians to a symbolic resource that can be mobilized at will,
without reflection or responsibility, for pleasure and profit.

Alteration

At the close of her bestselling memoir, *My Life with the Redskins*, Corinne
Griffith reflected on the place of the franchise in the nation's capital a
decade after arriving.

> Some years you win and some years you lose . . . but win, lose or draw
> there is always the same rush for season tickets in the spring; the
> same Indian "woo-woos" practiced and perfected in the summer; the
> same fraternal red feather to be gotten out and placed in the hatband
> at the first faint tinge of fall; the same thrill of the opening game;
> the same arguments on street corners with the final decision that all
> officials are blind; and the same dissenting opinions, accompanied

by demonstrations, of two famous Supreme Court Judges over the proper rendition of ["Hail to the Redskins"].[17]

Griffith, who played a leading role in creating the brand, speaks here of a simpler time, smoothing out the rough edges, as she emphasizes the unifying spirit and shared rhythms associated with the team. Her contribution to the team and its tradition, like her memoir, came before the integration of the NFL, before the freedom struggles of the 1960s, and during a time in which the entitlements of whiteness and the assumptions of settler society went unquestioned and American Indians remained an absent present, a tragic remnant and powerful resource. Neither she nor George Preston Marshall, not to mention thousands of fans at the time, likely gave much thought to either what American Indians thought about the team or how the team might affect living, breathing people across Indian Country.

Despite Griffiths saccharine remembrance, the Washington professional football team and its tradition have misused Indians and Indianness from the start. The franchise embellished a pseudo-Indian motif to exploit popular sentiments and expand its brand. During its formative years, the team did not have to reflect on its name, game day spectacles, or marketing. Management may have recognized a problem after Native Americans initially pushed for change and had a lengthy meeting with the owner to express their opposition in 1972, and it made minor, token modifications in response. And in the wake of renewed protests at Super Bowl XXVI and the filing of a lawsuit to strip the team of its trademarks, it was surely clear to the organization that it had to craft a more sensitive public image.

A 1993 letter from John Kent Cooke Jr., director of marketing for the franchise, to McDonalds about an upcoming marketing campaign underscores the heightened awareness and increased vigilance around the brand. Cooke, lamenting the pervasiveness of "political correctness," wrote to the fast-food giant, outlining appropriate uses of the team name, logo, and image. He issued the following guidelines:

No caricatures
No Indian Costumes or Headresses [sic]
No War Chants, Yelling, Derogatory Indian language (i.e.: "Scalp
the Cowboys")

Use of "Hail to the Redskins" must be Presented Tastefully
No Smart-Elect [sic] Language or Humor
No Insulting Language or Humor[18]

At least three things are clear from this letter. First, it repudiated the branding of the team during the Marshall era. Its edicts would have disallowed much of what the team did under the original owner to attract fans and enhance the profile of the team. Second, the team did not take this stance out of principle or to challenge the racist legacies of this earlier period, but rather to protect the brand. And third, it seems to tacitly acknowledge that the franchise's brand contributed to racist beliefs and behaviors.

At least since the early 1990s, the Washington professional football team, in coordination with the league, has sought to sanitize its image, editing out patently offensive material while accentuating renderings conceived of as positive, particularly the stoic warrior profiled in the logo. This shift builds upon earlier changes directed at the same end, such as changing the lyrics to the fight song and phasing out the pseudo-Indian uniforms worn by the cheer squad. In endeavoring to craft an honorable image of itself through an invented Indian, the team has sought to have it both ways: it has sought to retain a racial slur as a team name and to continue to profit from anti-Indian racism without being overtly racist, to use Indianness while denying harms, and to approve of others playing Indian to foster pride and team spirit. In subsequent chapters, I unpack the arguments advanced and actions taken in defense of the team and its traditions that allow them to remain viable and valuable and have enabled fans, the media, the players, and the ownership to feel good about the team and about themselves. In the process of unraveling these strategies, we will gain deeper insights into current uses and understandings of Indianness, form a clearer picture of racial politics today, and grasp how and why a brand rooted in a racist slur remains meaningful to so many.

Erasure

4

On December 28, 2014, nearly eighty-one thousand fans watched Dallas defeat Washington in its final game of the NFL season at FedEx Field. Amid the usual festivities, a group of fans known collectively as the Extremeskins, after the online discussion board of the same name that originally connected them, planned to tailgate en masse, as they did at every home game. In their announcement, organizers boasted of their unique qualities and the franchise's high regard for the group and its regular events. "The Extremeskins Tailgate has become an institution at Fedex Field, and it is because of all the members involved. The dedication, hard work and investments by folks year in and year out is second to none. This tailgate is getting bigger every year and is well respected because of our passion, our friendly welcoming environment and the charity we do. The Redskins organization has recognized our contributions and how we present ourselves and because of that, has recognized our tailgate as official Redskins Fan Captains. Lets continue to do our best as the best tailgate at Fedex Field!"[1] For the final home stand, in addition to the usual camaraderie, food, and fun, organizers announced plans to burn opposing quarterback Tony Romo in effigy and to raise money for charity. In particular, they wanted to generate $2,000 for Camp Fantastic, an annual event for children with cancer.

While this was a laudable end, organizers originally dubbed the event

"Scalp Out Cancer: Because Bald Is Beautiful." One might read this as a slip made possible by denial and ignorance: they did not understand the meaning of scalping nor did they appreciate its place in the violence and dispossession visited upon indigenous people or the legacy and symbolism of each for many Native Americans today. "Michael Kennedy, the event's coordinator, said the name is not meant to offend anyone, and he insisted that use of the term 'scalp' was neither a reference to the Indian mascot nor an insult." His denial begs credulity, however, suggesting this reading is too charitable. Indeed, the wordplay used by the organizers seems purposeful, part of a larger joke: "We're taking our hair all the way down to the skin" and "It will be Dallass [sic] Week, and what better way to celebrate it by scalping some people for a great cause!"² Either way, the name plays off a larger history (discussed in chapter 1). Its repetition and erasure speak to its continued force. Organizers came to see rather quickly that not everyone shared their sense of humor, changing the name of the event to "Shave Out Cancer" the same evening that news of it broke in the *Washington Post*. Even after the change, Kennedy wore a stocking cap bearing the original name on the day of the event, exposing the change as insincere at best.

Not surprisingly, the title of the event stunned many Native Americans. For instance, Kris Rhodes (Chippewa), executive director of the American Indian Cancer Foundation, remarked, "I'm just dumfounded. I have no words . . . It's just so incredibly ignorant." And Tara Houska (Anishinaabe), an attorney, noted with surprise and outrage, "That's insane. Really? They're that clueless? . . . That's incredibly offensive. That's the kind of thing that we're basically saying is wrong."³

Houska and Rhodes are right: clearly, organizers of the fundraiser do not get it. They, along with countless others who were in attendance at the game, who watched it on television, and who only casually follow football do not get the history and significance of the team name or its connection to the marginalization and dehumanization of indigenous people. The Extremeskins, the franchise, and, I would argue, most Americans have so fully embraced the national narratives and racial ideologies at the heart of American history, society, and identity that they act thoughtlessly, that is, they act without thinking, without considering their social location, without incorporating alternative interpretations, without listening to others, and often without question. Such thoughtlessness demonstrates the power of privilege and socialization as well as an associated underdevelopment of critical literacies. As a result, they exhibit a strong command of dominant ideas about race, culture, and history but have no capacity to question and limited interest in questioning the sincere fictions and prevailing mythologies through which they make sense of the world. For our broader consideration of the DC NFL franchise and its name, this thoughtlessness contributes to the active erasure of American Indians, even as it appropriates and invents elements of Indianness. It reflects and reproduces sentiments and actions that distort, dehumanize, and detest indigenous peoples and cultures, offering prime examples of anti-Indianism and anti-Indian racism.

In this chapter I consider the forms of erasure that make it possible to celebrate and defend the R*dskins, highlighting those practices that marginalize, silence, and trivialize American Indians and at the same time render imagery, names, and mascots (often wrongly) associated with them meaningful and moving to millions of Americans. In particular, I work through the deep connections between what I have termed thoughtlessness and anti-Indian racism. To begin, I return to the final home game of 2014, examining how it clarifies our understanding of anti-Indian racism. Against this backdrop, I detail various mechanisms embedded in U.S. society that encourage Americans not to know, not to remember, and not to think. In the end, I explore the possibility of pushing back against erasure, encouraging the cultivation of thoughtfulness to combat anti-Indianism.

Anti-Indian Racism

The continued use of American Indian imagery in athletics reminds us of the force of anti-Indianism in the contemporary United States. Anti-Indianism, according to Elizabeth Cook-Lynn (Crow Creek Sioux), has four key elements: "[First,] it is the sentiment that results in the unnatural death of Indians. Anti-Indianism is that which treats Indians and their tribes as if they do not exist. . . . Second, Anti-Indianism is that which denigrates, demonizes, and insults being Indian in America. The third trait of Anti-Indianism is the use of historical event and experience to place the blame on Indians for an unfortunate and dissatisfying history. And, finally, Anti-Indianism is that which exploits and distorts Indian beliefs and cultures. All of these traits have conspired to isolate, to expunge or expel, to menace, to defame."[4] Native American mascots clearly embody all of these elements. Invented icons displace embodied agents, encouraging individuals and institutions to ignore the presence of native nations as well as their position on such imagery. As tokens and trophies of conquest, such imageries diminish Indianness, dehumanizing and disempowering indigenous peoples.

Everyday Anti-Indianism

While it would be nice to think that the fundraiser was the worst example of anti-Indian racism to mark the final home game of the 2014 season, it is merely one piece of a larger tableau. In fact, it may be more disturbing to consider the ways in which the broader context normalized it. The Extremeskins felt comfortable with the wordplay around scalping because, as I outlined in the previous chapter, the traditions associated with the team and its fans have always relished amplifying their vision of Indianness for their own ends, whether that be profit, pleasure, or philanthropy. Moreover, these inventions and amplifications have so fully dehumanized indigenous people and so distorted history that a terrifying practice can be repurposed to raise money and build community in what purports to be a wholesome family environment.

Far from an aberration, then, the fundraiser reminds us that every aspect of this game day, like so many others at FedEx Field, persistently reiterates anti-Indianism: the ever-present logo, emblazoned on T-shirts and hats and across the field and built environment, as well as on programs and memorabilia; the endless repetition of the team name in cheers, color commentary, and conversations, across public-address announcements, and in radio and television coverage; the countless fans adorned in feathers, frequently headdresses, and face paint; the beaming and boisterous cheerleaders; and the marching band with its signature song, "Hail to the Redskins." Individually and collectively, these elements target, exclude, and injure Native Americans.

Navajo golfer Notah Begay summarized what is at stake at a typical R*dskins game: "I think it's just a very clear example of institutionalized degradation.... It undermines the very human foundation of the people itself.... It's about the culture, it's about the identity, it's about the history of our people." As a consequence, he continued,

> I don't ever see myself going to a Redskins game.... Or I should say, if I were to take my kids to a Redskins game, and we were to see a non-native dressed up in traditional regalia, with eagle feathers in a headdress, dancing around, basically mocking the culture and the tradition, it would be very difficult to explain to my children. And not only to my children, but children of many families across this country. I mean, this country was founded on the premise of equality and human rights and civil rights, and I don't know at what point we decide what our tolerance levels are for discrimination.[5]

For Begay, a R*dskin game is a hostile environment, not a joyous gathering place or a family friendly outing. It is a key example of institutionalized anti-Indianism that denies equal rights to Native Americans. The active erasure of indigenous humanity and the thoughtlessness anchoring it render the fundraiser fun and the final home game of the 2014 just another game, unremarkable save perhaps for the beating the team took on the field.

Extreme Anti-Indian Racism

The "Scalp Out Cancer" fundraiser coincided with a large protest against the team and its name. While most attending the game paid no attention to the protestors and did not engage them, others captured the scene on their smartphones. Worse were the fans who did engage and push back, giving voice to some the more extreme expressions of anti-Indian racism. As if to remind the protesters of their place, to construe them as inferior aliens encroaching on hallowed ground, some sang "Hail to the Redskins." Tara Houska recalls others yelling, "Go back to the reservation!" and "Go the f— home!" One fan went so far as to yell expletives at the assembled group of protestors, which included children, and to flip them the bird. As if to say, go away; leave us, and our Indian, alone. The open attacks also gave way to something like arguments: "It's nothing personal," one fan yelled. "You can't change history," said another. A man with a sticker of an Indian-head logo on his cheek said he didn't understand: "They should be honored." In other words, for many in attendance, what the protesters had to say was irrelevant—it's not about you; we won; get over it—and incomprehensible—how can they feel this way? In both its extreme and everyday forms, anti-Indianism cannot recognize or respect Native Americans, it cannot hear them speak or engage their perspectives, and above all else, it cannot see their humanity. As Houska reports, "Drunken fans rolled down the windows and screamed fake war whoops at our crowd. Most participants listened to the speakers, but some stood at the taped-off boundary line, attempting to hand out educational flyers to fans as they walked past. It was on this line that I heard one man say, 'Look, real Indians! Look at that one with the braids.' The dehumanization tied to Native mascots was on full display—we were not people to them, we were a sideshow, a historic relic somehow brought to life."[6] Their taunts mocked and minimized, diminished and dehumanized, working to somehow make the problem go away. They sought, furthermore, to silence the protesters, to eliminate their presence, to render them less threatening by converting them into unreal and inhuman tropes.

Vanishing the Indian

Anti-Indian racism disappears Native Americas. It expresses a will to vanish the Indian: whereas everyday iterations reduce indigenous people, cultures, and histories to a palimpsest on which to write and rewrite Indianness as they see fit, often through invention, projections, and mystifications, more extreme forms call for the exclusion and extermination of the indigenous other. At that final home game, we saw the former in the logo, the team name, the fight song, and fan antics; we encountered the latter in the verbal assaults, the calls for removal, and even the well-intentioned fundraiser.

Anti-Indian racism disappears Native Americans, replacing them with stories and stereotypes that simplify, flatten, and freeze them. As such, it renders false images and impose fraudulent identities, while silencing and speaking for indigenous people. It perpetuates the "symbolic extermination" of Native Americans, a process that often venerates imagined Indians, trapped in the past, while rendering indigenous peoples and their perspectives today invisible.[7] From popular culture to academic discourse, according to Ned Blackhawk (Western Shoshone), dominant uses and understandings of American Indians have placed in a space of impossibility: "Indigenous peoples remain fixed within static definitions of culture, imprisoned in notions of essentialism. As a result of the pernicious, self-perpetuating logic of timelessness on the one hand, and of primitivism on the other, these groups remain outside of history, and any changes or adaptations they have made become only further evidence of their demise."[8] This paradox facilitates the erasure of American Indians, encouraging invention and simulation in their purported absence: "Native interpretations and accounts of historical events are ignored or elided, while change over time in Native communities, the very basis of historicity, is taken as proof that they are no longer 'real Indians.'"[9] The team logo and traditions, no less than the imaginings and enactments of fans, confine indigenous people within a narrow time-space, emphasizing (a) history over the present, (b) generic Indianness over tribal or cultural specificity, and (c) Hollywood clichés instead of embodied individuals and expressed variations.

Anti-Indian racism disappears Native Americans. It actively works to terminate their sovereignty, liquidate their humanity, and devalue their cultures and histories. It has long grounded projects of extermination, appropriation, and invention. It provides a dehumanizing anchor for what Patrick Wolfe describes as "the logic of elimination." This logic holds that indigenous people must be disappeared. It has encouraged killing, ethnic cleansing, and forced removal but also has fostered efforts aimed at assimilation, education, and incorporation, projects intent to "kill the Indian and save the man.[10] This logic has proven fundamental, moreover, to the practices of appropriation and refashioning that made playing Indian powerful and pleasurable to generations of Americans. It provided the foundational premises for the team name, logo, and fight song, no less than the antics of Chief Zee and the "Scalp Out Cancer" event. Such acts of taking and remaking turn on a fundamental ambivalence—detesting embodied Native Americans and their claims to land, heritage, and identity and loving imagined Indians like the R*dskins and Pocahontas—rooted in the erasure of indigenous humanity, the suspension of recognition, and the denial of respect.

Misrepresentation

Misrepresentation may be the initial impulse to and basest expression of vanishing, pointing to the pervasiveness and power of anti-Indianism. Thoughtlessness has its roots in misrepresentation: dime novels and sophisticated literature, national narratives and commercial icons, anthropological analyses and sport cheers, Hollywood Westerns and textbook histories. "Widely consumed images of Native American stereotypes in commercial and educational environments slander, defame, and vilify Native peoples, Native cultures, and tribal nations, and continue a legacy of racist and prejudiced attitudes. In particular, the 'savage' and 'clownish' caricatures used by sports teams with 'Indian' mascots contribute to the 'savage' image of Native peoples and the myth that Native peoples are an ethnic group 'frozen in history.' All of which continue to plague this country's relationships with Native peoples and perpetuate racial and political inequity."[11] Misrepresentation dehumanizes as it erases and reinvents, giving Americans stereotypes and tropes in place of insight and understanding. The DC NFL franchise anchored and elaborated its false version of Indianness in this fertile soil and, in turn, reiterated it regularly until its imaginings displaced embodied American Indians, becoming at once more real, valuable, and meaningful. Consequently, as the longtime activist Michael Haney (Seminole/Lakota) observed, "As long as white America feels that Indians are not quite human, that we can be construed as mascots or caricatures or cartoon figures, then they will never deal with the issues of education and economic development for our people."[12] Indeed, it may be worse than all that: rendered less than human, American Indians still have a difficult time getting most Americans to see them, hear their perspectives, or take them seriously.

Naturalization

Misrepresentation fosters misrecognition, which, in turn, furthers mystification and dissociation. As Terrell Jermaine Starr observes, "The closest most non–American Indians have ever come to connecting emotionally with a Native culture was during a viewing of "Pocahontas." I know, she's a caricature and not a real Native American, but that's exactly my point. American Indians have been so marginalized in our society that all we know of them mostly consists of racist stereotypes and animated Disney characters. And when someone says there's something wrong with these images, we think, 'What's the problem.'"[13] Misrepresentation and misrecognition, a symbiotic pair, have longed encouraged thoughts and actions that impair and injure indigenous people, compromise non-Indians' understandings of and interactions with them, and undermine Americans' commitments to their ideals of inclusion, equality, and justice. In this context, most American take dominant formulations of Indianness and most accounts of the national past for granted, accepting them as natural facts rather than questioning them as social constructs, political projects, and cultural narratives.

As a result, Johnnie Jae (Jiwere-Nutachi/Chahta) concludes, these forces have naturalized anti-Indian racism. "Dan Snyder and supporters of the R*dskin moniker are the poster children for what happens when racism becomes so universal and ingrained into the values of our society that it becomes tradition, that it becomes invisible and normal." In such a context, anti-Indian racism does not appear to many as either anti-Indian or racism. Rather, it is accepted and acceptable. This arrangement, Jae continues, undermines empathetic reception of indigenous readings of the team name and its history, often encouraging defensiveness in responses that misconstrue the movement and its significance as "being 'PC', Liberal, or hating the 'white' man." Significantly, then, the natural-ization or normalization of anti-Indianism and racism hides both under convention and exacerbates efforts to challenge "the foundations that allow and promote racism against Native people."[14]

On Not Thinking

At the outset of this chapter, I suggest that the "Scalp Out Cancer" event exhibited a great degree of thoughtlessness. Its organizers did not reflect on the significance of their action; they refrained from asking what this might mean in the big picture (the history of scalping or debate over the team name) or what this might mean to American Indians. Much the same could be said of the fans who cursed at the protesters or dressed in feathers. They, like a significant number of Americans, displayed an inability or unwillingness to reflect on their location, utterances, or actions. Sadly, for some, such as the fan who flipped off the protesters, reckless disregard may even be a badge of honor. I would argue that the pronounced lack of reflexivity exhibited on any given Sunday at FedEx Field reflects underdeveloped critical literacy, causing many Americans to be unable to read uses of Indianness like one finds in DC in association with its professional team: they do not have the faculties to be thoughtful, to interpret the text (to say, what does this team logo or name mean?) or the context (what is Indianness doing in a sport spectacle played on ground from which Indians were removed?), and they cannot interrogate their relationships to the production and politics of the text and context. Worse, underscoring the work of erasure, when many Americans do read text and context they give primacy to their experiences and interpretations without appreciating or acknowledging their status as settlers who necessarily benefit from the displacement, dispossession, and dehumanization of American Indians.

At its worst, not thinking fosters defensiveness and reactionary tantrums like those endured by the protesters outside FedEx Field. The pundit and occasional presidential candidate Pat Buchanan provides a good example of this, a know-nothing platform for the twenty-first century. Responding to the resurgent criticism of the team name, he asks and answers his own questions: "And so what are we going to do here? Edit Jefferson's declaration, tear down the Jefferson Memorial, pull down Sherman's statue, dynamite T.R. off the face of Mount Rushmore? Or maybe just tell the Oneida crowd we know how excruciatingly painful it must be to have to hear 'Hail to the Redskins!' but are confident they have the moxie and the manhood to deal with it. Meanwhile, let's get back to the game."[15] Dialogue equals destruction; taking seriously the concerns of another demands defacing American history and (from his vantage point) its heroes; and enduring offensiveness demonstrates one's masculinity. In the end, mocking his critics, he returns to the game, what really matters to him. He rhetorically flips the bird at those who deign to question his team, which embodies for him manhood, family, community, and nation.

It is only by not thinking about the name that Buchannan can launch such a rant. As the *Onion* phrased it, "When you hear or say 'Redskins' in the abstract, it's completely harmless, but we've discovered that if you briefly pause to remember it's a racial slur for an indigenous group wiped out by genocide over the course of a few centuries, then, yeah, it's awful. . . . It has the potential to come across as a degrading relic of an ethnocentric mentality responsible for the destruction of an entire people and their culture, but that's only if you take a couple seconds to recognize it as something beyond a string of letters."[16]

On Not Knowing

Americans likely cannot think about the team name and its significance because they have never been taught about American Indians.[17] As Kevin Gover (Pawnee), director of the National Museum of the American Indian, notes, "Beneath the debate over the name of the Washington NFL football team is an underlying truth: the vast majority of Americans have a limited—and often mistaken—understanding of Native American history." They know of neither the diversity of native nations nor the basic principles of sovereignty. "There are," he continues, "566 federally recognized American Indian tribal governments in the United States. Yet, most Americans—even those occupying our economic and political centers—do not encounter Native Americans in their day- to-day lives. Perceptions are reduced to myths and caricatures and to the limited education retained from the American classroom."[18] In place of knowledge about indigenous cultures and histories, most Americans content themselves with misrepresentations.

Eni Faleomavaega, a delegate to the U.S. House of Representatives from American Samoa, echoes this conclusion, connecting it explicitly to anti-Indianism and erasure.

With the exception of schools in Indian country and collegiate Native American studies programs, the violent history associated with the term "redskins" is not taught in American schools. It is no wonder why the general public does not understand the reason this racial epithet is so offensive to millions of Native Americans across the nation.

It is this ignorance that perpetuates the hatred that an entire race has endured for centuries. It is this ignorance that allows people like Snyder and Goodell to pretend that the name of the Washington, D.C., NFL franchise actually honors the Native American people.[19]

In fact, the team, the league, and their media partners exploit the lack of knowledge to secure the status quo and increase their revenues.

For the artist Gregg Deal (Pyramid Lake Paiute), not knowing is distinct from ignorance. It is an active process of revision and forgetting. Speaking directly of the team, its name, and collective memory, he observes, "Americans are really short-sighted when it comes to history. No one wants to look past the 80 years of the Washington Redskins." Going deeper would be too painful and cause the core myths to begin to unravel. Or, as Deal puts it, "If you take a step further back, you'd realized that this is a country that's never rectified or reconciled any aspect of its relations with Native Americans. And then for someone to name a football team with a racial slur?"[20] In other words, ignorance adds insult to injury, compounding the mystification and trauma.

On Not Remembering

If not knowing enables not thinking, then not remembering lays the foundation for these other forms of thoughtlessness. Echoing and expanding on Deal's comments, the journalist Ray Cook (Mohawk) summarizes these interconnections.

> But it is too much to swallow when the American sports fans say that the team name Redskins is used to honor us. They are trying to hide their history, rewrite it, redefine it. That is wrong. The sports profession and their devoted fans can't be allowed to go Orwellian with double speak. Where was the country's honor for us at Sandy Creek or during Sullivan's Campaign? They cannot be allowed to forget about themselves and how over a brutal history they got what they have today. A country's worth of stolen Indian land built upon with African and Asian slave labor.[21]

One might argue, then, that only by Americans not learning and not being conversant with the past do the national narratives and cultural myths of the United States persist. In a very real way, these processes allow the unsettling aspects of the settler state to stay settled. Not remembering deflects attention away from the appropriation of indigenous land and culture, from the ongoing occupation of tribal lands, from a history of dispossession, dislocation, and death. It allows for a triumphal rewriting of these foundational elements of the American experience such that one may feel empowered to silence those who speak the truth about the past, as one editorial about the team name remarked: "One of the problems with being conquered is you don't get to write the rules. You were conquered."[22]

Clearly, as this effort to foreclose memory, dialogue, and engagement underscores, repetitions of the team name and constant circulation of associated imagery and traditions erase the past, give comfort to many who enjoy the fruits of forgotten injustices, and reiterate the dehumanizing violence associated with them. Thus the r-word, according to Chief Kirk Francis, chairman and chief of the Penobscot Nation, is "not just a racial slur or a derogatory term," it is also a "reminder of one of the most gruesome acts of . . . ethnic cleansing ever committed against [our] people."[23] The sportswriter Howard Bryant offers an even more chilling description: "Drive through New England. Or Oklahoma. Or New York. Don't think about the People, the Native American populations that first inhabited these places. . . . The People are largely gone. Replaced by statues."[24] Sport mascots have likewise vanished and replaced indigenous people. . In this context, remembered thusly, the team name can be read as a placeholder for and marker of (an incomplete) genocide that makes the United States, the NFL, the franchise, and even football possible; the legacies and legitimacy of all four must be questioned if the history of that genocide is acknowledged.

Against Erasure

Thus far, I have examined the shape and scope of anti-Indianism radiating from the DC NFL franchise, its name, and the ongoing defense of it. I have emphasized an array of cultural practices that contribute to the erasure of indigenous cultures and histories and promote the dehumanization of American Indians. In this closing section, I identify three instances of pushing back against erasure and countering anti-Indian racism. These encounters and interventions encourage thoughtfulness: the development of critical literacies, or the capacities to read text in context and against the grain; the faculties to listen and reflect; and the propensity to reclaim and rethink.

Defamiliarization

Anti-Indian racism persists in part because it is normalized, taken for granted, and familiar. One cannot challenge it if one does not see it or know it is there. Arguably the first, crucial step is to denaturalize it. The sports journalist, historian, and activist Dave Zirin offers an anecdote relating his epiphany:

> Like many people in this area, I have cheered for this team. I also once had a gig analyzing games as a fill-in anchor on Comcast Sports Net and never gave a great deal of thought or inquiry into the history of the name or how it affects people in the twenty-first century. I started looking into it more after a young girl of Native American ancestry saw the logo on a media folder in my bag and asked me fearfully why "the man's head had been chopped off." To paraphrase Arundhati Roy, once you know the history and hear the voices of those who have to live with the way these images define their lives and their place in this country, it is extremely difficult to pretend you haven't.[25]

The young girl disrupted the naturalness of the logo, prompting Zirin to see the team name and imagery anew. He could not unsee it. Not every denaturalization or reframing will be so powerful or transformative, but as subsequent chapters relate, once the familiar becomes strange, people have a different relationship with the name, logo, and imagery, often rethinking or even rejecting them.

Dialogue

In my earlier account of the final game of the 2014 NFL season, I highlighted the ways that fans lashed out at the protesters. These actions included silencing, speaking for, talking over, calling for removal, name-calling, and obscene gestures. While many fans remained anonymous and invisible, one man, the one who flipped off the protesters, became immediately infamous on social media, with an angry image of him circulating on Twitter. Although he might have remained the face of resentment and rage, the fan, known now as Rick, accepted an invitation to meet Joe D. Horse Capture (Gros Ventre), an associate curator at the National Museum of the American Indian–Smithsonian Institution, for coffee. Although details are sketchy, the two appear to have had a real heart-to-heart conversation. Rick apologized, and Horse Capture reported that the two "nearly hugged . . . it was that kind of thing." A short report on the encounter features a photo of the two side-by-side, smiling.[26] How lasting the transformation will be is an open question, but it suggests that embodied interaction, talking, and, above all else, listening are crucial to breaking down misunderstandings, overcoming misrepresentations, and opening a space of recognition and respect.

Remembrance

Throughout this chapter, I have highlighted the ways in which misrepresentation, not knowing, and not remembering work to dehumanize indigenous people, literally removing them from the past while replacing them with false imitations. Caricatures may make for good marketing campaigns and embolden team spirit, but they only distort and diminish those they purport to represent. Key to challenging such erasures is learning about Native Americans, understanding their complex histories, and appreciating how race and colonialism affected their lives and our own. The historian Claudio Saunt offers a pointed example of what this might mean for the NFL franchise in our nation's capital. In reviewing the team's webpage he notes obvious omissions that reveal its true commitment to indigenous people and that most visitors would not notice because the removal and replacement of American Indians has been so complete in our imaginary. "The team's official history page includes a description of Darrell Green's goal-line stop in the 1987 NFC Championship Game and a feature on the franchise's 80 greatest players but not a word about the native peoples who lived where the team plays today." Saunt then proposes a rewriting that would record the native nation displaced from the land on which FedEx Field stands and from popular memory as well.

> The website could describe the epidemic disease, dispossession, dispersal, and survival of Maryland's Piscataway people. In 1623, Virginia colonists invaded Piscataway country and, in the words of the colony's governor, "putt many to the swoorde," despite the Indians' best efforts to appease the newcomers. A generation later, the Piscataway were forced onto reservations and subjected to colonial law. Disease and alcoholism became widespread, and at least a few individuals were forced into slavery to toil on one of the Chesapeake's many tobacco plantations. In 1701, the surviving Piscataway abandoned the region altogether, settling on a reservation in Pennsylvania. Yet, a core identity persisted among Piscataway families, and in 2012, the state of Maryland formally recognized two Piscataway bands. Their history, like that of other indigenous Americans, is complex and belies the stereotyped, featureless warrior that appears on the Washington team's helmets.[27]

While one would not expect the franchise to embrace this proposal, it highlights the gap between erasure and inclusion, recognition, and reflexivity, between anti-Indianism and humanization.

In the end, defamiliarization, dialogue, and recollection all offer important alternative to vanishing. They emphasize the importance and value of thoughtfulness.

Sentiment

5

Although best known as a hard-nosed, All-Pro tight end and later coach of the 1985 Chicago Bears, Mike Ditka, now an analyst for ESPN, has strong feelings about the Washington DC NFL franchise and the controversy swirling about it. In an interview on the subject with the former journalist and self-styled team historian Mike Richmond, "Iron Mike" let loose in his typical brash style:

> What's all the stink over the Redskin name? It's so much horsesh*t. It's incredible. . . . It was said out of reverence, out of pride to the American Indian. . . . This is so stupid it's appalling, and I hope that owner keeps fighting for it and never changes it, because the Redskins are part of an American football history, and it should never be anything but the Washington Redskins. That's the way it is. . . . This was the name, period. Leave it alone. These people are silly—asinine, actually, in my opinion. . . . Really, I think it's tradition, it's history, it's part of the National Football League. It was about Sammy Baugh and all the guys who were Redskins way back then. I didn't think that [Vince] Lombardi and [George] Halas never had a problem with it, why would all these other idiots have a problem with the name?[1]

Ditka's take on the team name resonates with the official position of the team, public comments made by owner Dan Snyder, and the opinions expressed by fans and supporters: the name represents tradition and conveys respect, while efforts to change it are ridiculous at best.

On one level, Ditka exhibits the thoughtlessness discussed in the previous chapter. "This is so much horsesh*t." His words, however, also reveal the importance of feelings, affect, and identity to the ongoing struggle, which often override the lack of knowledge, memory, and reflexivity. For many, this is personal; it is deep, often unconscious, even ineffable. The name speaks to them in powerful ways, evoking memories, experiences, and passions. Fans get attached to the name; they identify with the team; they internalize the rituals and traditions associated with both. Together, name, team, rituals, and traditions come to represent goodness in the world: core values, prized relationships, and lasting connections, including honor, community, childhood, family, and possibility. Together, they proclaim something to those who invoke them that is undeniably good, yet inexplicably imperiled. Oddly, these personal associations have become refuges in a changing world; they have become a prime means to legitimate and defend the team and its name. This emergent structure of feeling merits attention, then, both for what it says about uses and understandings of Indianness and for what it reveals about cultural politics today. At the same time, if the affective aspects of words and symbols merit serious reflection, as I believe they do, then we must also attend to their often unseen and largely unintended consequences. That is, the team and its name, along with its imagery and its traditions, not only affect fans, they also have real influence on those they purport to venerate, namely American Indians.

In this chapter, then, I explore the sentimental and psychological dimensions of the controversy. I emphasize the emotional connection many fans have with the team, its name, and its traditions, while detailing the use of attachment and intentionality to defend them and defer criticism. Against this background, I consider recent scholarship on the harms associated with such mascots, especially for Native Americans.

On Not Feeling Racist

The contemporary United States presents scholars of race with a noteworthy paradox: most Americans do not think of themselves as racist, and yet racial stratification, exclusion, and injury remain pronounced. Eduardo Bonilla-Silva has suggested that we live in a moment character-ized by racism without racists. By extension, most people associated with the DC NFL franchise, who support it, cheer for it on any given Sunday, wear its stylized designs about town, or sing its fight song, do not feel that they are racist. While this derives from the patterns of erasure described in the previous chapter, it also reflect a shifts in prevailing conceptions about what constitutes racism, where it comes from, and how it manifests itself. In large part, Americans subscribe to a limited, individualized, and ahistorical notion of racism that stresses intention and affect.

In this framework, they believe the defeat of Jim Crow and the associated achievements of the civil rights movement, the rise of multi-culturalism, and the increasingly multiracial face of popular culture have ushered in a new, more enlightened era of color blindness. This frame-work proposes that racism is antiquated, a relic of the past, and that it is now an individual feature, even a failing, and not a core element of the American experience. It recognizes five forms of racism. First, it focuses on *bad intentions*, ideas and actions anchored in malice and prejudice, meant to express animus, foster exclusion, or target other races. Second, this framework isolates *bad ideas*, suggesting that lack of education, out-dated ideologies, and ignorance all encourage people to do racist things or think racist thoughts. Third, it associates racism with *bad attitudes*, most commonly prejudice, bias, and hate. Fourth, it often ascribes racism to *bad choices*: mistakes, errors in judgment, and other ill-advised or unin-formed actions. Finally, it locates each of these indicators or expressions of racism in *bad actors*, most notably deviant groups, like Klansmen and neo-Nazis, and so-called bad apples who blend into acceptable society.

This limited conception allows Americans to identify racists but leaves them with an impoverished model of racism, making it difficult for many Americans to interpret and engage its long history and persistent legacies. Significantly for our discussion of the affective elements of the ongoing controversy over the DC NFL franchise, this model attributes racism to individuals, while ignoring sociohistorical structures; it looks to the past, neglecting the present; it stresses intention and affect over and against consequences and effects; and it restricts racism to individual

maliciousness and ideological errors. Ultimately, this model gives supporters of the team, its name, and its traditions an important out, creating a
context in which intentionality and positivity work to let them off the hook.

Emphasizing Affect

A small protest greeted visitors to Lucas Oil Stadium in Indianapolis on
November 30, 2014. As fans filed passed, eagerly anticipating the game
with the visiting squad from the nation's capital, one frustrated Washington supporter shouted, "It's just a name. Get over it."[2] While this is not
an uncommon response to the opposition, it runs counter to the strong
defense of the name and the connection that many fans have with the
team. Indeed, most fans feel strongly about the team, its name, and its
traditions precisely because they evoke such strong feelings in them. I
believe these feelings are genuine, which often complicates efforts to
discuss the origins of the name, the history of anti-Indian racism, and
the prospect of change. While acknowledging this sincerity, I think it is
important to note as well that sentimental and psychological dimensions
have proved increasingly vital as a means to defend the name and to
legitimate the franchise's use of it. In this section I want to emphasize the
affective elements, at once stressing how fans feel and the sociopolitical
use of such feelings in the ongoing controversy. To this end, I analyze
their emphasis on attachment, intention, and remaining positive.

Attachment

At the franchise's 2014 summer camp in Richmond, Virginia, Sean Labar
sold handmade t-shirts emblazoned with the phrase "Keep the Name."
Owner Dan Snyder purchased a number of them from the loyal fan. Like
many of his peers, Labar expressed a deep affection for and connection
to the team: "I've always been a Redskins fan, and always identified with
the pride that was associated with the name. . . . I grew up singing Hail
to the Redskins and watching Chief Zee get the crowd excited. There is
just so much history that is associated with the name."[3] His attachment
formed when he was a child, grew through his exposure to the team's
traditions, and crystallized around its history and values. Many fans
share a variation of this core narrative.

The actor Matthew McConaughey offers a strikingly similar reminiscence: "Longhorn in college, but Washington Redskins in the NFL. . . . I grew up watching westerns with my father; I was always rooting for the Indians instead of the Cowboys. My favorite food was hamburgers growing up; they had a linebacker, no. 55, Chris Hanburger. And then John Riggins. When you're 4 years old, that's why you really commit to a team, for reasons like that. It goes way back."[4] Westerns lurked in the background for the future cinema icon, who identified with the Indians, a reminder that the team and its significance always resonate with other popular narratives and representations of Indianness. Furthermore, for McConaughey, star players cemented his connection to the team, a connection made all the more powerful because he grew up in Texas.

And Daniel Snyder himself hits many of the themes found in the recollections of Labar and McConaughey. He recalled in a letter to fans,

Like so many of you, I was born a fan of the Washington Redskins. I still remember my first Redskins game.

Most people do. I was only six, but I remember coming through the tunnel into the stands at RFK with my father, and immediately being struck by the enormity of the stadium and the passion of the fans all around me.

I remember how quiet it got when the Redskins had the ball, and then how deafening it was when we scored. The ground beneath me seemed to move and shake, and I reached up to grab my father's hand. The smile on his face as he sang that song . . . he's been gone for 10 years now, but that smile, and his pride, are still with me every day.

That tradition—the song, the cheer—it mattered so much to me as a child, and I know it matters to every other Redskins fan in the D.C. area and across the nation.

Our past isn't just where we came from—it's who we are.[5]

For Snyder, his attachment formed in childhood—at birth, really—was nurtured at games, and became fully formed in and through his father. The name, the team, and the traditions have long been something more than a word, a group of men playing a game, and a set of symbols and rituals. Snyder has a deep and transcendent bond with his father, with the past, with his childhood and so much more through the brand, logo, song, and name.

Denise Perry, like most longtime fans, can relate quite well to Synder. To her, the team and its name "represents the Washington family, team spirit and the unifying atmosphere of match days. She understands there are negative connotations too but adds: 'Calling it anything else would take away from the meaning and history of the Redskins I grew up with. If the owners ever considered a change, I would join the protests.'"6 In fact, her attachment is so deep that she would fight efforts to change the name. Her affective investment trumps knowledge and thought, fostering an unabiding passion for and commitment to the team.

The attachments so many fans have to the team and its traditions, and the ways that sentimental associations bind them to the name, make change an especially challenging prospect. Indeed, the sportswriter Michael Tomasky believes that efforts to retire the name threaten to crush how many fans imagine themselves, understand the world, and recount their life histories. Referring specifically to the team owner's personal investment in the team, Tomasky notes, "If you're Snyder's age (born 1964), you grew up going with your friends over to the schoolyard that's about a short par five up the road from where I'm typing these words pretending to be Billy Kilmer and Larry Brown and Roy Jefferson and Chris Hanburger. And to you, the Redskins name was drenched in glory. Changing the team name would amount not merely to capitulating to liberal-harpie critics; it would take the fantasy he's living and kill it cold."7 Thus, for many fans change brings with it certain violence. And while largely affective, change would strike at the heart of who they are and what makes the world good.

Staying Positive

Supporters of the DC NFL franchise accentuate the positive. They repeatedly highlight the goodness of the team, its name, and its traditions. At the same time, they regularly push back against or deflect interpretations that imply that their cherished symbols and stories may be racist. Above all else, they seek to stay upbeat and retain a positive disposition. NFL commissioner Roger Goodell embodied this frame of mind in his response to a letter from members of the U.S. Congress who wrote him suggesting that the team name is demeaning and should be changed: "The Washington Redskins name has thus from its origin represented a positive meaning distinct from any disparagement that could be viewed in some other context. . . . For the team's millions of fans and customers, who represent one of America's most ethnically and geographically diverse fan bases, the name is a unifying force that stands for strength, courage, pride and respect."[8] In other words, despite what you may have heard, the name is positive. It embodies ideal we wish others to emulate: "strength, courage, pride and respect." And moreover, its use is not meant to be disrespectful or to offend.

In a 2014 interview on *Outside the Lines*, Daniel Snyder echoed this sentiment, expanding on its central tenets: "It's just historical truths, and I'd like them to understand, as I think most do, that the name really means honor, respect. . . . We sing 'Hail to the Redskins.' We don't say hurt anybody. We say 'Hail to the Redskins. Braves on the warpath. Fight for old D.C.' We only sing it when we score touchdowns. . . . And, and, it, it's a positive."[9] It's positive. We praise them. We don't hate. It is about respect. These core phrases become something of a template to at once express deep sentiment, claim to place indigenous people in an esteemed position, and offer a solid defense of the continued use of the team name and traditions.

Like Snyder, many supporters clothe this argument in the language found in the team song and familiar from much of popular culture: we are warriors celebrating the greatness of indigenous warriors. Loren Smith said as much in an editorial in March 2013: "The Redskins name is a salute directed at the warriors who protected many American Indian tribes. The fact that racism, war and murder have taken such an enormous toll on Native Americans throughout American history does not diminish the bravery of the Indian fighters of long ago. It would be a shame, and in fact an insult to their memory, for the Redskins' name to be consigned to the scrap heap of history."[10] The R*dskins become a kind of mnemonic device that insists we remember indigenous people and enable supporters to dissociate themselves from ongoing racism.

Accentuating the positive (not unlike Disney did in *Pocahontas*) allows supporters to simultaneously claim to honor indigenous people and to be good, honorable people. Joe Theismann, a former quarterback for the DC franchise, recently came out with a strong endorsement for the team: "I was very proud to play for the Washington Redskins, and I did it to honor native people in that regard. I think sometimes people perceive words in their own particular way. What happens, what Mr. Snyder decides to do is totally up to him. I can just tell you that when I put that uniform on, and I put that helmet on with the Redskin logo on it, I felt like I was representing more than the Washington Redskins. I was representing the great Native American nations that exist in this country."[11] Of course, as a casual fan who remembers when he led the team, I cannot say I ever heard Theismann speak of Native Americans, let alone claim he took the field to venerate them.

Intention

While fans have long had attachments to their teams, certainly since the founding of the team, they have not always spoken of their intentions or what they have meant to convey through a name, song, or symbol. Over the past quarter century, this has become key to defining one's connection to the team and in turn to defending that connection and the team itself. The positions of the NFL and its DC franchise, as stated in the previous section, ground themselves in intention. They echo a stance taken by the previous owners on the team in the face of mounting criticism in the early 1990s. John Cooke, the son of then-owner Jack Kent Cooke and the team's executive vice president, for instance, spoke to the rising objections: "Over the years, it's come to represent the best of the culture—bravery, organization, the whole works. The name Redskins means football in Washington. We honor Native Americans. We believe that."[12] Their actions and imagery, he contends, convey honor and are meant to honor indigenous people; by extension, there is no hate, animus, or racism here.

More recently, Lanny Davis, a team advisor, has made two separate statements reaffirming and elaborating on this foundational premise. In the first, like Cooke, he emphasizes history and tradition, while reminding his audience of the true intentions of the team. "If people are offended, we should be respectful of that, care about that, and tell people we care about that. But also say, we just have to say to you that this is an 80-year old name, we sing 'Hail to the Redskins' to honor the Native Americans, and it's not a term of disrespect."[13] Davis has added a new wrinkle here, in keeping with the need to stay positive, namely respect. The team not only respects American Indians, it respects its critics as well. He reiterates this element in his second statement: "We at the Redskins respect everyone. . . . But like devoted fans of the Atlanta Braves, the Cleveland Indians and the Chicago Blackhawks (from President Obama's home town), we love our team and its name and, like those fans, we do not intend to disparage or disrespect a racial or ethnic group."[14] Significantly, here he also makes more sweeping and comparative statements. The DC NFL franchise is like other teams with Indian mascots, whose sincerity and intentions have not been questioned, and its fans display deep affection and attachment. Love, respect, and good intentions all underscore the innocence of the team, work to absolve of it of wrong, and otherwise defuse any allegations of racism.

Not only those invested in the team advance such sentimental claims. Jerry Jones, owner of the rival Dallas Cowboys, employed a similar logic when asked about the team and its traditions: "I don't want to weigh in on it, other than the fact that I know that it was intended initially and is today to be complimentary." Subsequently, he elaborated:

> I know that it's not in any way meant to denigrate the Redskins, or the Washington team, or what it represents. It's like *Cowboys* to me. And I think we should all feel that way about it. It's a great part of the tradition of the league. And I don't want to be insensitive, but I sure think that if the Redskins and [Daniel] Snyder want to keep that, then they should keep it. . . . I think it's pretty pointed that this name is one of pride; this name is one of competition; this name is one of a lot of great things that have happened with this franchise. And [it] should be looked at that way.[15]

Following Jones's reasoning, the name cannot be read as racist because it embodies pride, competition, tradition, the league, and more, and it was meant to cast American Indians in a positive light.

Even critics will commonly concede the that supporters have no ill will and do not mean to disparage or offend American Indians. In his famous editorial observation that aired at halftime of the game featuring Washington in Dallas, Bob Costas noted, "Let's start here. There is no reason to believe that owner Daniel Snyder, or any official or player from his team, harbors animus toward Native Americans or wishes to disrespect them. This is undoubtedly also true of the vast majority of those who don't think twice about the longstanding moniker."[16] In other words, their love of the team and tradition, not racism or anti-Indianism, motivate their allegiance and action, and that should not be held against them. This is a trap of sorts, which accepts the framework of defenders in hopes of undoing it.

Such an acquiescence, however, threatens to dilute or even dismiss the racial foundations of the team name and traditions, accepting a more limited, individualized conception. As the anthropologist Pauline Turner Strong argues, "This refusal to acknowledge the offensiveness of the Redskin trademark is both a legacy of colonialism and a contemporary form of racism. As critical race theory has shown, it is not only the intent of a racist act that matters but also its impact or effect. Those who 'love' the Redskins' name may not intend to be disrespectful, but reducing the matter to one of intent trivializes the concerns of American Indians who perceive the name as a profound societal expression of disrespect, disparagement and dehumanization."[17] In the end, emphasizing affect (identity, attachment, intent, positivity, and so on) minimizes racism and racial power. Worse, the strategic deployment of sentiment discussed herein discourages reflection and change, while fostering harm. When affect obfuscates effect, it allows the consequences of racism to persist and its perpetrators to hide in plain sight.

Appreciating Effects

In 1974, shortly after moving to Washington DC, Suzan Shown Harjo (Cheyenne and Hodulgee Muscogee), former president of the National Congress of American Indians, president of the Morning Star Institute, and lead plaintiff in the initial trademark challenge case, attended a home football game in the nation's capital. She recalls, "We're football fans and we can separate the team name from the game, so we went to a game. And we didn't stay for the game at all, because people started—someone said something, 'Are you this or that?' So, we started to answer, then people started like pulling our hair. . . . And they would call us that name and it was very weird for us. So, we just left and never went to another game." Harjo said her experience at the Redskins game "solidified" her opposition to the team's use of Indianness. "It wasn't just namecalling, it was what the name had promoted. . . . That's the example of what objectification is. You strip the person of humanity and they're just an object and you can do anything."[18]

Harjo's experience more than forty years ago echoes the events described in the previous chapter; it also corresponds to accounts offered by others active in the movement.[19] All confirm how hurtful attending a game can be. Increasingly, psychological research corroborates these anecdotes, indicating that the impacts associated with Native American mascots not only occur at games but also register consciously, or manifest themselves immediately. These studies, according to the psychologist Wendy Quinton, demonstrate that "regardless of their intention, these mascots do not honor American Indians, but instead bring to mind negative thoughts associated with them as a group of people [and encourage people] to negatively stereotype other ethnic groups as well."[20] Together, they direct our attention away from intention and attachment to effects as the best measure of the scope and significance of anti-Indian racism.

Stephanie Fryberg and her colleagues have shown in a series of studies that mascots and other stereotypical images hurt American Indians. In particular, they have found that when exposed to such imagery, American Indians have lower regard for themselves, a depressed sense of community worth, and a more negative assessment of future possibilities.[21] Similarly, Angela LaRocque and her colleagues found that Americans Indians had higher levels of psychological distress after exposure to Native American mascots than their white peers had.[22] Moreover, psychologists have concluded that such imagery blurs the distinction between imaginary Indian caricature and embodied indigenous person, activates negative stereotypes of Native Americans, and encourages negative assessments and bias directed at American Indians and members of other marginalized ethnic groups as well.[23] Importantly, according to the psychologist Michael Friedman, "even a positive image, if it's stereotypical, will lead to psychological distress, lower self-esteem, lower sense of achievement."[24] Recognizing "the catastrophic effects of prejudice" associated with Native American mascots, in 2005 the American Psychological Association issued a position paper denouncing them.[25]

Clearly, whatever the intention, mascots hurt, underscoring the deep impacts of anti-Indian racism as well as the history and power anchoring it. Anti-Indianism, like all racisms, is not an individual aberration but a systematic and systemic bundle of relations. Thus, as these studies affirm, an image or name is never just an image or name. It concentrates and conveys much more. At the very least, the affective force of symbols and stories associated with American Indian mascots, including those surrounding the NFL franchise in the nation's capital, reflect and reinforce a pattern of dispossession, dislocation, denial, and death. In keeping with the patterns of erasure described in the previous chapter, they depend on taking and remaking: "How would you feel if you had your home taken away from you and then watched as your identity was stolen for profit? It's adding insult to injury."[26] Put another way, they revisit violence and violation on American Indian individuals and communities, establishing a context of certain harm: "Because sports fans have the power to play Indian without the consent of American Indians, relations between both groups are negatively affected."[27]

"Cumulatively," according to DeShanne Stokes, "these studies show in horrific clarity what supporters of the Red*kins—Native and non-Native alike—seem not to realize: that ethnic mascots are integrally intertwined with their offensive team names, and together they have the effect of perpetuating institutionalized racism."[28] Dean Chavers (Lumbee), the director of Catching the Dream, a scholarship fund for Native Americans, links American Indian mascots to bullying in schools: "The Indian kids get stomped on, get called names, get beaten up, but if they fight back they're the problem. . . . There have even been instances where trucks have been shot at after basketball games."[29] Outside of schools, others have asserted that such uses and understandings of Indianness contribute to the disturbingly high level of violence and hate crimes directed at indigenous people in the United States.[30] And more broadly, "the effects of systematic prejudice and discrimination against Native Americans can be best illustrated in that Native American/Alaska Natives have among the highest suicide rates in the country. The rate of suicide among Native Americans has risen 65% in the past decade alone."[31]

Realizing Respect

In 2006 Kateri Joe (Swinomish) reflected on an impending professional football game between Washington and Seattle: "It's like we're slipping back in time. The fans with the war paint on their faces, the feathers, the bad costumes—I mean, don't they know how that looks and makes us feel?"[32] Most of them do not know how the name, logo, and associated rituals affect American Indians. They know how the symbols make them feel; they know how they want Native Americans to feel; they know how Native Americans should feel. Rarely, however, do they know how Native Americans do feel. In large part, this because they do not ask, because they do not interact with Native Americans, and often such encounters, at protests outside of games, for instance, foster defensiveness, not listening or engagement. In addition, they cannot conceive of the team, its name, and its tradition as racist: they are not hateful; they are positive, reverent, and venerable; they are meant to respect, to pay tribute even. These interpretations correspond to prevailing framings of racism that individualize, decontextualize, and demonize it, reducing it to antipathy and prejudice, antiquated ideas and intentional actions. From this conventional, even dominant, perspective, they hear calls to change the name because it is racist as nonsensical, or, to recall Ditka's assessment that opened this chapter, as "silly—asinine actually."

When exposed to scrutiny, placed in context, and opened to study, the affective aspects of the name and associated imagery and antics become more troubling. Such a reframing forces an acknowledgment that the uses and understandings of Indianness associated with the team negatively affect American Indians and other racialized groups. The words and symbols hurt, causing measurable harms, which over time and through repetition inflict psychological trauma. Significantly, these effects are not necessarily immediate or conscious, nor are they limited to a dominant pivot in the controversy—offensiveness. As Brian Cladoosby (Swinomish), president of the National Congress of American Indians, has recently emphasized, "Until the team's name is changed, every week during football season American youth around the country—whether Native American or not—will watch Washington football fans dressed as 'savage' Indians and wearing 'redface' and conclude that it's acceptable to defame and mock Native people. This will create another generation of Americans who think Native peoples are less than others, are characters and caricatures out of the past and are not due the rights promised to all."[33] At the very least, the psychological studies and personal testimony discussed in this chapter should prompt the NFL, the franchise, and the public to rethink not only the moniker, its past, and its future but also how to conceive of and combat racism in an effort to prompt inclusion, equality, and justice.

As a starting place, the owner, the media, and fans might work toward realizing respect. And in doing so, they might follow the lead of Jordan Wright, granddaughter of George P. Marshall. Wright, of course, has a very personal connection to the team and even endorsed its name more than a quarter century ago. "She knows what people expect her to say: The team's history matters. She also knows what she believes: The name needs to change. 'It's about respect,' Wright said . . . from her Alexandria home. 'If even one person tells you that name, that word you used, offends them, then that's enough. That *should* be enough.'"[34] It should be enough to move conversation and action from how we think others should feel or how we want them to feel to how they actually do feel. In this light, the first step toward realizing respect may well be change.

Black/White

6

In November 1996, Clem Ironwing (Lakota) spoke before a committee established by the Wichita Unified School District to deliberate the continued use of R*dskins as the mascot of Wichita North High School. He spoke of the place of the word in his life, connecting it to broader efforts to assimilate Indians and eradicate Indianness—kill the Indian, save the man, as it were—and highlighting deep-seated anti-Indian racism.

The word Redskin was taught to me at a very young age, and this is the meaning it has for me.

I am a Native American. I grew up on an Indian reservation. As a child, the United States Government and the Catholic Church came into our homes, took us away from our families, and forced us into Catholic boarding schools. There was no choice to be had in this matter, you had to go. The Catholic Church with the blessings of the United States Government took it upon themselves to determine that we were savages, and needed to be transformed to fit into their society.

When my hair was cut short by the priests, I was called a "redskin" and a savage. When I spoke my native tongue, I was beaten and called "redskin." When I tried to follow the spiritual path of my people, I was again beaten and called a "redskin." I was told by them to turn my back on the ways of my people, or I would forever be nothing but a dirty "redskin."

The only way "redskin" was ever used towards my people and myself was in a derogatory manner. It was never, ever, used in a show of respect or kindness. It was only used to let you know that you were dirty and no good, and to this day still is.[1]

From Ironwing's testimony, there can be little doubt what the term conveyed, its dehumanizing force, and its repugnant core. It is black and white, really: *R*dskin* is a racial slur.

That same year, John Kent Cooke, son of Jack Kent Cooke, at that time the owner of the DC franchise, sat for a deposition in the initial lawsuit challenging the team name and trademark. His account, as one might anticipate, is more opaque and evasive. Much of the questioning turned on the younger Cooke's understanding of race and language. In particular, the deposition takes up a series of racial slurs, from *w*tback* and *g*ok* to *J*p* and *k*ke*. While he acknowledges having heard these words, he often is uncertain whether the words disparage those to whom they refer. Similarly, he has a narrow understanding of *R*dskin*:

Q: Sir, what does the word Redskin mean to you?
COOKE: It means the Washington Redskins football club.

Q: Does the word Redskin mean anything else to you?
COOKE: No.

. . .

Q: Sir, does the name Washington Redskins mean anything about native Americans?
COOKE: The Washington Redskins are named after or are associated with native Americans.

Q: Sir, do you believe that the Washington football team intends to honor native Americans?
COOKE: I believe that the Washington Redskins are to play football in the National Football League and represent the Nation's Capitol. In so doing, they, because of their name, reflect the positive attributes of native Americans. . . .

. . .

Q: Do you yourself, view the word Redskin insofar as it refers to native Americans as an offensive usage?

. . .

COOKE: I don't know.

Q: When you say "I don't know," are you telling me, sir, that you hold no belief as to whether the word Redskin, when used to refer to native Americans, is offensive?

COOKE: I don't know if it is offensive to native Americans. I just simply don't know, sir.

Cooke's ignorance, feigned or not, labored to get the team off the hook and to trouble any easy association between the team and racism.

When the inquiry shifted, however, he expressed certainty about another racial slur.

Q: Sir, do you consider the word nigger disparaging?

COOKE: It is to some people . . .

Q: To what people, sir, is the word nigger disparaging?

COOKE: I don't know, I would suppose it would be to blacks, particularly, also to—if you're describing blacks, it's disparaging to them. If you take the other part of my definition of being insulting [made previously], it would be insulting also to me.

Q: Why is it insulting to you?

COOKE: Because I believe it is a disparaging epithet to describe black Americans . . .

Similarly, Cooke expressed discomfort with references to skin color, which, much like physical size or eye color, would be inappropriate as forms of address, not because they would be hurtful but because they would be "uncivil."[2]

For Cooke, *r*dskin* has no racial referent, cannot be construed as a racial slur, and would be best seen as an honorific. Significantly, he makes no reference to the origin stories so common in ongoing efforts to defend the team and its use of the name. At the same time, he finds *n*gger* to be an objectionable slur, all about race, and best kept out of everyday discourse.

While we might reasonably conclude that his universal reading of the n-word and his more limited and limiting interpretation of the r-word—particularly when contrasted with Ironwing's statement—derives from his feelings about the litigation, his personal experience, and his desire to defend the team, I would argue that it points to something deeper as well. On the one hand, it highlights the ways in which racial thinking in the United States has come to pivot around the interface of blackness and whiteness, especially key histories of oppression, slavery, Jim Crow, and the civil rights movement. I will refer to this as the black/white paradigm for understanding race and racism. On the other hand, the questioning and the testimony both point to the shifting mores around racial thinking and expression that push back against overt iterations of racism, including name-calling. I will describe these new mores as new racism. In this frame, Cooke's distinction also points to a context in which the moral, political, and social significance of the n-word is more universally known, accepted, and policed and, perhaps largely because of the patterns discussed in the previous chapter as anti-Indianism, the r-word is deemed to be more acceptable, or at least less problematic.

In this chapter, then, I map the broader racial politics shaping the struggle over the team and its name. In particular, my discussion explores the dominance of the black/white paradigm. It details the ways in which this paradigm shapes public perceptions of *n*gger* and *r*dskin* and high-lights the manner in which activists have drawn on this paradigm to secure traction and visibility for their movement. My discussion begins with a brief review of the shifting contours of racism in post–civil rights America before considering the centrality of the black/white paradigm and its utility for ongoing resistance efforts.

New Racism

New racism describes shifting attitudes toward race and racism in the wake of the civil rights movement in the United States, including a commitment to color blindness, a decline in legal or de jure discrimination, and a withering of biological racism. And yet racial stratification persists, in areas including access to resources, citizenship, mobility, education, employment, wealth, health, and life expectancy. In other words, while the ways in which individuals and institutions think and talk about race and racism have changed, the materiality of racism remains constant. Amy Ansell, Patricia Hill Collins, Eduardo Bonilla-Silva, and others have assembled a theoretically sophisticated and critically engaged approach to recent reconfigurations of race, describing the current racial formation as new racism.[3]

Structured by emergent global economic flows and transnational webs of power, mass media and spectacle play an increasingly important role in the manufacture of consent; according to Collins, they "present hegemonic ideologies that claim that racism is over. They work to obscure the racism that does exist and they undercut antiracist protest."[4] In this context, social life is raceless and racism is an aberration that interrupts this appearance. A racial epithet, overt discrimination, and pronounced bias, typically by individuals, intermittently rips through this idealized status quo. This vision of social life holds under erasure not only the ways in which racial stratification reproduces but also more accepted and naturalized forms of racism. The embedded forms of anti-Indianism discussed in the previous chapter would be key examples.

Moreover, three features, Ansell contends, have proven crucial to the solidification of this conjuncture and its capacity to reproduce racial hierarchy in this context: "(1) a sanitized, coded language about race that adheres to, more than it departs from, generally accepted liberal principles and values, mobilized for illiberal ends; (2) avid disavowals of racist intent and circumvention of classical anti-racist discourse; and (3) a shift from a focus on race and biological relations to a concern for cultural differentiation and national identity."[5] The application of a set of overlapping frames and strategies dematerializes the reigning forms of racial stratification, legitimizing notions of fairness, freedom, opportunity, equality, democracy, and America. The increasing visibility of people of color in the media, popular culture, and sport has proven fundamental to efforts to advance new racist formulations of racial progress. The defense of the DC NFL franchise and its name offers prime examples of the emergence of coded language, the emphasis on intentionality, and the celebration of culture, often phrased as respect, honor, and tradition.

Finally, Bonilla-Silva conceives of color blindness as a primary building block of the racial ideologies that support and extend the reigning racialized order of things.[6] Like all ideologies, he continues, color blindness works because it offers a set of frames to account for and make sense of race and racism. Specifically, he suggests that within a the context of new racism whites employ four frames: abstract liberalism, an ethos blending individualism, a rhetoric of equality, and choice; naturalization, or the assertion that "racial phenomena . . . are natural occurrences"; cultural racism, the appeal to culture to explain difference; and minimization, or efforts to reduce or dismiss the continuing significance of race and racism.[7] These shifts in the means and meanings of racism have encouraged creative and troubling redeployments of (anti-Indian) racist discourse while limiting the means to combat it in public culture. Perhaps most importantly, they have reinvigorated the black/white paradigm, first because it takes the civil rights movement as the key break in racism and second because much of its attention to the core contradictions focuses on the persistence of black injury and exclusion and the reconfiguration of white racial attitudes. As a consequence, anti-Indian racism often goes unnoticed as racism, an unrecognized and even unnamable presence in social life.

An Inexcusable Utterance

By all accountants at the time, the country music star Kenny Chesney gave a masterful performance in Philadelphia in June 2013, at once powerful and intimate. Nevertheless, save for those in attendance, the concert either remained unknown or quickly faded from memory—that is, until a brief video surfaced at the end of July. The clip featured a drunken and enraged Riley Cooper, a wide receiver for the Philadelphia Eagles, exclaiming, "I will jump this fence and fight every n*gger here" when denied backstage access, which apparently had been granted to some other members of the team who had credentials. Once the clip was made public, a predictable spectacle swiftly engulfed the outburst, with fans, players, and pundits expressing outrage, indignation, and embarrassment, along with excuses, explanations, and equivocations. Cooper apologized to the public and his teammates, the Eagles condemned him and fined him an undisclosed amount, mandating he attend counseling, and the NFL denounced the outburst while reiterating its commitment to diversity but took no further punitive action.

Cooper's diatribe was the latest in a series of very public utterances of the n-word in the first half of 2013: the celebrity chef Paula Deene lost her gig on the Food Network and a series of endorsement deals when it was revealed she had used the term; the radio personality Rush Limbaugh, who seemingly reveled in courting controversy once more, asserted his right to employ it amid George Zimmerman's trial (since African Americans were); and the comedian Tim Allen lamented the ways in which individual sensitivities and identity politics around the word had negatively affected the entertainment industry, disenfranchising white performers like himself. No, Cooper was not alone. In fact, to read comments expressed by his defenders via tweets and online posts, one might conclude that for a large segment of white America such language is not only ubiquitous but also understandable, maybe even acceptable. Cooper, along with Deene, reveals the deep tensions at the heart of the post–civil rights era in the United States: race no longer matters in society committed to (the idea of) color blindness, but racism thrives beneath the surface. His outburst illuminates what happens when the codes and mores deemed acceptable in private become public, or, as Leslie Houts Picca and Joe R. Feagin would say, it illuminates what happens when backstage behaviors find their way to the center of social life.[8] Moreover, Cooper underscores the conceit and privilege anchoring whiteness today. Like Allen's and Limbaugh's, his use of the n-word pivots on a perceived slight, a felt hurt, an imagined loss of entitlement, which can be reclaimed by seizing on the invective and putting things, bodies, and subjects back in their proper place. Defenders of Cooper (whom, his apology and actions after the public revelation suggest, he would prefer not to speak for him) underscore the force of this structure of feeling. Thus, while undoubtedly minor and ephemeral, the incident offers a fairly sad commentary on the regular workings of race and power.

Significantly, reducing the outburst to white privilege, the afterlife of white racism, and the familiar dance of white-black relations in the early twenty-first century overlooks other crucial dynamics. Indeed, for all of the talk about what was said and what it means, the underlying patterns remain undiscussed.

Even as fans, players, administrators, the league, and sports media expressed outrage about the utterance and its import, they took for granted, repeated, and even celebrated another racial slur—*r*dskin*, which happens to be the moniker of the NFL franchise located in the U.S. capital and the longtime rival of the Philadelphia Eagles.[9] To put it plainly, this is a double standard. It is black and white. One word is read as a racial slur, and only a racial slur, and must not be uttered, even as the structures of violence, degradation, and inequality remain entrenched in society; the other word, despite linguistic, historic, and psychological evidence, is framed as anything but a racial slur and can be used in marketing, media coverage, and fan cheers. The former word is taken to be a reference to the bad old days of racism, best forgotten, a reminder of the unresolved history of slavery and the social death that rendered blacks as property to be exchanged and exploited. The latter word is defended as a tradition, an ideal—or so it is claimed in the so-called time after race, the raceless present—and, more, a trademark, a valuable piece of property from which Dan Snyder, the league, media conglomerates, and countless others make obscene profits through distortion and dehumanization.

Banning a Bad Owner

On April 25, 2014, *TMZ Sports* broadcast a recording of Los Angeles Clippers owner Donald Sterling ranting to his friend V. Stiviano. Made the previous fall, the tape captured Sterling lambasting Stiviano for posting on social media a photo of her with a black basketball player and instructing her not to bring African Americans to Clippers games. Reaction was immediate and intense. Superstar LeBron James denounced the owner and his comments, stating emphatically that "there is no room for Donald Sterling in our league" and demanding that NBA commissioner Adam Silver "make a stand." Other players echoed James and the Clippers coaches, and players threatened to boycott upcoming games, while sponsors terminated agreements with the team and the National Association for the Advancement of Colored People rescinded its plans to give Sterling a second lifetime achievement award. Sports media raged, pundits offered blistering critiques, and even President Obama condemned Sterling. In less than a week, on April 29, 2014, Commissioner Silver took decisive action: he banned Sterling for life and set in a motion a process to sell the team to a new owner. Sterling, who had made his fortune in real estate, had a checkered history, marked by earlier efforts by the NBA to terminate his ownership, a series of lawsuits alleging racial discrimination and sexual harassment, and repeated boorish behavior.[10]

Sterling's utterance became a media spectacle and a moral crisis. Like Cooper's, Sterling's words were construed as an aberrant transgression that sparked a public panic. And his punishment reestablished the status quo. All the while, the anti-Indian racism associated with the DC NFL franchise, part of that status quo, persisted; Daniel Snyder remained in good standing with the NFL; and Roger Goodell never initiated any action against him or the team. For his part, star defensive back Richard Sherman doubted the NFL would take similar action if given a chance: "Because we have an NFL team called the Redskins. I don't think the NFL really is as concerned as they show. The NFL is more of a bottom line league. If it doesn't effect their bottom line, they're not as concerned."[11]

It is black and white, really, a clear double standard. As the psychologist Michael Friedman phrases it, "By promptly removing Donald Sterling and imposing a fine, the NBA has shown us that racism is unacceptable and must be addressed swiftly and decisively. Native Americans are the only group of people in this country that are forced to tolerate a derogatory racial slur as the name of a professional sports team. The NFL and Washington organization must follow the NBA's example." Thus he highlights this discrepancy and demands intervention not simply to punish a transgression but to right historic wrongs and their legacies: "They must change the team name and mascot and finally set about healing a wound that has been festering for decades."[12]

The columnist Clarence Page rightly argues that the decided difference in the responses of the NBA and the NFL turns on the greater demographic presence of African Americans in the United States and the power that accords them (however limited that might be in the big picture). "If the

NFL was two-thirds Native American instead of two-thirds black, we wouldn't be having the same conversation. But it is a sad, cynical reality of today's racial etiquette that respect goes to those who have not just sympathies but numbers, money, votes or some other leverage with which to wield real power."[13] This "cynical reality" may be far worse than Page imagines. As Dana Lone Hill (Lakota) asks, "Donald Sterling might not have wanted his mistress to bring black people to Clippers games, but Dan Snyder wants all his fans to celebrate—and even chant—a racist slur against an entire class of people. Which is worse?"[14] In other words, whereas Sterling's racism threatened to cost the franchise and the NBA revenue, Snyder's racism continues to generate revenue for his franchise and the NFL. Demography, politics, capital, and ideology all reiterate the distinct ways anti-black and anti-Indian racism operate in the United States and how individuals and institutions enact and interpret them, reaffirming the centrality of the black/white paradigm with particular significance for the ongoing debate over the R*dskins.

Using the Black/White Paradigm against the R*dskins

Observers have long noted the glaring contradiction posed by the R*dskins in a league that declares its commitment to diversity and in a nation that prides itself on being postracial. Comedy has proven invaluable for highlighting it. At the 2014 ESPY Awards, the host, Drake, remarked, "Now look, some rough words in football this year. . . . Riley Cooper said some things. Richie Incognito said some things. I just want to stress that there's no room for racism in the NFL—unless you own a team in Washington DC. Then it's a go."[15] Almost a quarter century earlier, the comedian Chris Rock quipped, "The Washington Redskins? That's not nice. This ain't cool. That's a racial slur. That's kind of like having the 'New York Ni**as' . . . 'Denver Dykes', man."[16] Rock's satiric analogy echoes more serious formulations made by opponents of Native American mascots.

Indeed, in the early 1970s, racial metaphors emerged as an important rhetorical and political strategy. Precisely as Native Americans were questioning the imagery and antics associated with the DC NFL franchise, indigenous activists across the United States drew comparisons between popular uses and understandings of American Indians and those of other racial groups. It emerged in struggles against Stanford University, the Atlanta Braves, and the Cleveland Indians. For instance, Jeffrey Newman, assistant director of the Association for American Indian Affairs, in a broader critique of Chief Noc-a-homa, the onetime mascot of the Atlanta Braves, lamented the presence of the Washington R*dskins, noting they "wouldn't think of calling a team the 'Blackskins' or the 'Yellowskins'."[17] Around the same time, Russell Means turned to racial analogy to advance his argument against mascots. "Take the Washington Redskins. . . . Redskin is a derogatory name . . . what if we called them the Washington Niggers, or Washington Rednecks, or Washington Pollacks?"[18]

Racial analogies may be even more effective in visual media. A number of editorial cartoonists have drawn amusing and unsettling images. Thom Little Moon (Oglala), for instance, in 1995 encouraged readers of *Indian Country Today* to reflect on the appropriateness of Chief Wahoo, the mascot of the Cleveland Indians, by drawing two children pondering the question "Which one is the mascot?" as they look at four portraits. One is of Chief Wahoo, labeled "Indians"; the second, dubbed "Blacks," features the same smiling visage, darkened, with a large afro and pick comb in place of Wahoo's feather; the third, named "Jews," renders a smiling Hasidic Jew complete with yarmulke; and the final image, labeled "Chinese," has slanted eyes and a goatee. A year later, in December 1996, Little Moon presented two football helmets with stereotypical images, one for the Washington Blackskins and the other for the Kansas City Zulu Chiefs, asking, "Would African Americans like being mascots?" And the National Coalition against Racism in Sports and the Media has fashioned a moving poster that features pennants for imaginary sports teams—Fighting Jews, Blacks, Latinos, Orientals, and Caucasians, alongside the real pennant of the Washington Redskins.

Opponents of the R*dskins continue to draw on the black/white paradigm to unsettle the continued use of the racial slur and underscore its significance. The Lakota journalist Tim Giago reiterates the truism in an editorial, writing, "The 'R' word is as insulting to Native Americans as the 'N' word is to African Americans and yet most Americans never question its repeated use."[19] WNBA great Shoni Schimmel (Umatilla) connects the hurtfulness of the word to deeper issues.

> I would change the name of the Redskins mainly for the Native American people as a whole. . . . It's about respect for the Native American race, especially to not promote the racism carried over from the past. It was racist to be called a "redskin" back in the day, so what makes it OK today? There isn't a team called "whiteskins" or "blackskins"—how would that go over with the world?
>
> Just because what our people went through was hundreds of years ago doesn't mean we forgot what happened, forgot what our elders went through. Changing the name would help give us, as Native Americans, the same equality that every other race wants.[20]

Here she foregrounds racism and respect, calling for recognition and respect as a foundation for empowerment. Schimmel, like others who have employed this strategy, makes her point in part by underscoring the absurdity of the analogy: Who in their right mind would say *n*gger*? Who would name a team the blackskins? Of course, no one would do either of these, which is precisely the point. If you would not do this, why do you continue to use *R*dskins* in any context?

It is worth noting that arguably the most watched and debated use of this strategy occurred when Bob Costas called out the franchise and NFL on Sunday Night Football.

> Still, the NFL franchise that represents the nation's capital has maintained its name. But think for a moment about the term Redskins, and how it truly differs from all the others. Ask yourself what the equivalent would be, if directed toward African-Americans, Hispanics, Asians, or members of any other ethnic group.
>
> When considered that way, "Redskins" can't possibly honor a heritage, or noble character trait, nor can it possibly be considered a neutral term. It's an insult, a slur, no matter how benign the present-day intent. It is fair to say that for a long time now, and certainly in 2013, no offense has been intended. But, if you take a step back, isn't it clear to see how offense might legitimately be taken?

While his commentary initially sparked much discussion, this has faded. Meanwhile, the team name persists, as does the predominance of the black/white paradigm.

Beyond Black and White?

Nearly twenty years after Clem Ironwing related his personal experience with racism as embodied in the r-word and John Kent Cooke sought to limit the meaning of the term in his deposition, too little has changed in the upper reaches of the NFL. To take but one recent example, in an interview with *Outside the Lines*, Adolpho Birch, the NFL's senior vice president of labor policy and government affairs, restated the position of the league: "We believe the team is a source of pride and it reflects the traditions of that organization and its fan base, which is very diverse . . . but we also understand and respect that people can have differing opinions." When asked, "Is the team name a slur?" Birch responded, "The team name is not a slur. The team name is the team name as it has been for 80-plus years. And what we need to do is get beyond sort of understanding this as a point-blank situation and understand it more as a variety of perspectives that all need to be addressed, that all need to be given some weight, so that at the end of it we can come to some understanding that is appropriate and reflects the opinions of all."[21] While Birch acknowledges differing opinions, in keeping with the contours of new racism, he stresses positivity, heritage, and respect. His circular argument, moreover, restricts the meaning of *R*dskins* to the franchise, limiting the scope of racism and keeping it very much within the bounds of the black/white paradigm, and reaffirms the status quo and, by extension, the anti-Indianism undergirding it.

Thus, while many opponents of the continued use of the racial slur in the NFL had hoped that the scandal surrounding Donald Sterling and the NBA's response to it would have forced the league to take action, prevailing racial politics (and shifting public attention) worked against this. In fact, as I have argued in this chapter, the centrality of the black/white paradigm, as reconfigured in response to the civil rights movement, not only has limited conceptions of what constitutes racism but has also shaped forms of resistance. And while the black/white paradigm remains entrenched in how the league and the public interpret and engage racism, the increasing prominence of racial politics in collegiate and professional football may provide a foundation for intervention and alteration.

In the wake of police violence in Ferguson and New York City that resulted in the deaths of African American men (Michael Brown and Eric Garner, respectively), athletes used the playing field to express solidarity with African American communities and to protest the events. For instance, the St. Louis Rams entered one home game with their hands in the air, referencing the widely held belief in the metropolitan area that Michael Brown had his hands up at the time of his shooting death, while individual athletes wore T-shirts during warm-ups that read, "I can't breathe," the last words of Eric Garner. More recently, in response to a fraternity singing a racial song at the University of Oklahoma, the football team (a multiracial unit) staged a walkout to protest the event and demand an improved racial climate on campus.

Players may hold the key to shifting public perceptions of the team name as well. Unlike in the NBA, where the majority of players were targeted by Sterling's racism, only a handful of Native Americans participate in the NFL. Thus any action would have to involve transracial coalitions and cross-racial identification of oppression and injury. Significantly, the latter is present among some players.

A decade ago, Mike Wise found that a number of players had reservations about the term and some believed it to be overtly racist.

It's hard for me to understand because our people weren't treated like that. . . . But if that's how [American Indians] feel, it's something that needs to be dealt with. (Joe Salave'a)

I understand the people who may have those complaints. . . . If I can assist them in any way, I would. . . . I don't tell people I play for the Redskins. . . . I just tell them I play for the 'Skins. When I sign autograph items, I do the same thing. I put 'Skins. It's my thing. I'm not saying everyone else should do it, but that's what I do. (Ray Brown)

I use to look at them [protesters] and think, "Why don't you guys do something else with your time?" Now I look at them and think they're right. I mean, if you look at that logo and you really think about the name, it is racist. (Chad Morton)[22]

More recently, former DC players have shared similar sentiments. Champ Bailey noted, "When you hear a Native American say that 'Redskins' is degrading, it's almost like the N-word for a black person. . . . If they feel that way, then it's not right. They are part of this country. It's degrading to a certain race. Does it make sense to have the name?"[23] And Bobby Mitchell, who was among the first black players to join the franchise in the 1960s, spoke with ambivalence: "When I hear 'Redskins,' I still feel the same way about it as I did when I came here and [during] all our glory years. It's just that now, when you say 'Yeah, yeah, Redskins!' you say, 'Yeah, yeah . . . [voice trails off] Redskins.' You can't help it, you know? Because as a black man, I understand what the Indians are saying. I understand. So, I don't know how this will work out."[24]

Might the mutual recognition voiced by these athletes be enough for subsequent action? Might their familiarity with the force of racism in the black/white paradigm be a catalyst to subvert it? Perhaps, but it may be best to temper expectations, for it must be acknowledged that salaries and sponsorship deals both work against sustained political resistance, undermining the possibility of a unified front as emerged in the wake of Sterling's comments. Moreover, while players may be important allies, the obligation to challenge and undo the deleterious effects associated with the team, the slur, and their intertwined histories rests upon those who have the greatest stake in the perpetuation of racism—anti-black, anti-Indian—and its myriad other forms, namely whites.

It is ultimately those who own the team, control the league, and profit from the possessive investment in whiteness, particularly fans, who have long enjoyed a sense of entitlement to Indianness, who must take the leading role in subverting the black/white paradigm and ending one of the prominent iterations of anti-Indianism. In the process, they might convey the respect so many of them claim the name currently bestows on indigenous people. Or, to borrow from Kina Swayney (Cherokee) and put in language that invokes and rewrites the black/white paradigm: "Throughout recent history, state governments and other teams have changed flags and names because they were found to be offensive to Black Americans. We are entitled to the same respect. Our self-identity is the core of who we are and how we move into the future as a people worthy of respect."[25]

Ownership

7

In the early 1990s, when the critique of the Washington professional football team and tradition had begun to gain real traction, its owner, Jack Kent Cooke, took a defiant public stance: "I have spoken to many, many Indian chiefs who say they have no objection whatsoever to the nickname. As far as I'm concerned, it's a dead issue. I'm not even interested in it. The name of the Redskins will remain the Redskins."[1] Nearly two decades later, in late spring 2013, as the ongoing controversy over the team name intensified once again, its current owner, Daniel Snyder, spoke with equal intransigence: "We'll never change the name," he said. "It's that simple. NEVER—you can use caps."[2]

Separated by twenty years, these comments underscore the long history of opposition and activism as well as the intense reactions they have elicited—a mix of organizational entrenchment, personal frustration with public criticism, and a desire to protect a profitable brand. Reflecting on Snyder's position, Joel Barkin, a spokesman for the Oneida Nation, went further. He highlighted the significance of sentimental attachments, echoing my earlier reading: "With Snyder, that brand, even though the name is racist, that brand means everything to him." It evokes his childhood, his relationship to his father, everything. In this frame, this connection has greater value to Snyder than what the team, the name, or the logo may mean to others. Barkin imagines him saying, "My connection to this team is worth more than you, an American Indian, being offended."[3] While one might read here an emphasis on ego, a not-so-veiled suggestion that the owner is selfish, insensitive, or narcissistic, I think it points to something deeper, expressed by both Snyder and Cooke. They have no interest in other perspectives and feel no particular need to factor them into their thinking. This open hostility, in turn, closes off the dialogue and discussion, refusing their viability, rendering the name "a dead issue," and otherwise negating the possibility of engagement. Although Cooke and Snyder have amassed wealth and power that few will ever match, their position derives from neither of these sources. In fact, one hears many variations on it from supporters of the franchise, ranging from advice to "get over it" because there are more important issues, it is an honor, or even one has a right to say racist things to more overtly racist threats like the following tweet: "I swear to god if the Redskins Change [sic] their name I will be the most racist fucker ever out there towards Native Americans #HTTR #RedskinsPride."[4] In these discursive moves, embattled owners and everyday people alike endeavor to exert control over the racial slur, claiming it as their own. In doing so, they seek not only to quiet debate but also to stabilize racialized power in a moment of crisis.

Knowingly or unknowingly, then, as Snyder, like Cooke before him, and countless fans use such rhetoric to dismiss critics and defend the team, they assert the privileges and prerogatives of whiteness. "Whiteness is simultaneously a practice, a social space, a subjectivity, a spectacle, an erasure, an epistemology, a strategy, an historical formation, a technology, and a tactic. Of course, it is not monolithic, but in all of its manifestations, it is unified through privilege and the power to name, to represent, and to create opportunity and deny access."[5] Indeed, while the brand, consumption of it, and identification with it turn on (invented) Indianness and a larger history of appropriation, exclusion, and extermination, in many ways, the team and its traditions reveal much more about Euro-Americans and the crisis of hegemonic whiteness than they do about indigenous peoples. I sketched elements of this broader cultural formation previously, including not having to know about others and their perspectives, not having to learn about the past, not having to think, the presumed capacity to speak for others, and the insistence on one's intentions over and against their impact on others. These are all examples of racialized privilege in a settler state that allows individuals to make claims of belonging to larger communal groups and to imagine themselves as raceless, national, cultural, and sporting citizens.[6] While scholars in cultural studies and critical race studies have rightly highlighted the ways in which political and economic forces invest in whiteness, rendering it a special form of property, here I want to direct attention to the entitlements that whiteness grants whites and white society.[7] I have as my target, then, ownership and its racial significance. I examine the ownership of the team, the more general practice of owning Indians, and efforts to unsettle both claims on Indianness. At root, in this chapter my reading of the controversy circles around the racial entitlements of those vested in the team and its traditions. I begin with a consideration of the articulations of whiteness and ownership in the regimes of George Preston Marshall and Daniel Snyder, as well as more mundane enunciations. Against this background, I consider legal action brought to strip the franchise of the protected status and profitability of its brand.

Unbearable Whiteness

George Preston Marshall made the R*dskins. He chose the name; he moved the team to the nation's capital; he played off popular fascination with all things Indian to cement his brand. During his time, the sportswriter Shirley Povich noted, he was known for two things: being "one of pro football's greatest innovators and its leading bigot."[8] He gained renown as an innovator for his showmanship, media savvy, and business acumen, all of which foreshadowed the NFL that would emerge in the years after his death. He secured his reputation as a bigot for his effort to make his franchise the darling of Dixie and his associated refusal to integrate it, a decision that some regard as a business decision and a frame of mind that many were pleased to see pass with him. "For the 24 years when he was identified as the leading racist in the NFL, he simply stared down the criticism of his refusal to sign a black player. It was the only subject on which the voluble Marshall never expressed a public opinion, never resorted to a quip. But he bristled when [Povich] reminded him in print that 'the Redskins colors are bur[g]undy, gold and Caucasian.'"[9] His race politics led some to describe the team as "the Confederates of the NFL."[10] With its rise in the 1950s, the civil rights movement increasingly made the franchise a source of controversy.[11]

Seeking to raise public consciousness and press the broader movement for equality and inclusion, the National Association for the Advancement of Colored People protested at the annual meeting of NFL owners in Philadelphia in 1957. In response, the assembled owners "unanimously passed a resolution honoring" their embattled peer: "George Marshall, having completed 25 years in professional football, is the greatest asset sports has ever known with his honesty, integrity, and his perfect frankness in expressing what he believes."[12] More than half a century later, the resolution and the rhetoric sound eerily familiar, as if the NFL has broken out this old playbook to defend the prerogatives of ownership and, by extension, uphold racism in the face of mounting public criticism. Marshall had other supporters as well. As the federal government pressed the team to integrate in 1961, members of the American Nazi Party picketed in support of segregation as the franchise hosted its longtime rivals from New York. Dressed in full regalia, a small band carried signs reading, "Mr. Marshall Keep the Redskins White!" "Fight Communism, Fight Race Mixing," and "Integration Is not Black and White. It's Red."[13] With friends like these, even in the early 1960s, one need not search for enemies.

Bowing to public opinion and an ultimatum from the Kennedy administration, less than a year later, Marshall relented, signing three African American players in advance of the 1962 season.[14] To some, the government interference, underlying social engineering, and what would be described today as political correctness were too much. "A man from Tennessee said he believed America was headed for dictatorship 'when a football owner is forced to put a nigger on his team.' Another disgruntled correspondent told [Secretary of Interior Stewart] Udall that if race, instead of ability, was used as a criterion for team membership then the game and society would be doomed 'to mediocrity and eclipse!'"[15] Their words and positions have an odd resonance more than fifty years later as the franchise and fans labor to defend white racism, traditional values, and the independence and autonomy an owner should enjoy in a free society. Marshall's defiance and public support of segregation then necessitated government intervention, underscoring that similar action may be needed again to change the name and disrupt the racial entitlements of ownership now.

Calling Marshall a bigot says a great deal about the history of the team, the league, and sports generally in the United States. The focus on Marshall simultaneously inserts the team in a black/white frame, allowing for a heroic chapter in the larger struggle for civil rights, and securely confines racism to the past, affirming the prevailing myth and mystique of a postracial society. Significantly, Marshall was recognized and is remembered as a bigot for his antiblack racism, not his anti-Indian racism. During his life, he never had to defend the team name. It was a moot point. And once the team was integrated, something funny happened: the African American community in Washington DC came to love the team as fervently as did the whites. In effect, one of the entitlements of citizenship granted to African Americans by the civil rights movement was the capacity to take and remake Indianness, to reimagine themselves as part of something bigger by owning Indians.[16]

Unacknowledged Whiteness

Whereas Marshall left his mark as an entertainer, innovator, and bigot, Daniel Snyder has distinguished himself through his deep attachment to the team, his entrepreneurial zeal, his micromanagement of the franchise, and what some see as an inflated, if overly sensitive, ego. And while segregationist sympathies no longer inform the business decisions and guiding principles of the franchise, it does benefit from the structures and legacies of white racism.

Two key foundations bear special mention because of they are ever-present yet absented from most discussion of the controversy. First, in common with other spaces in the United States, the team trains and plays on occupied land. "The Washington football team, for example, plays on land taken by sword from the Piscataway tribe."[17] Neither it nor its fans, not to mention the media, with few exceptions, engages or even acknowledges this. For many years the team simultaneously embellished its connection to iconic American Indians and furthered the erasure of native nations by holding its training camp in Carlisle, Pennsylvania, home to the legendary boarding school where Jim Thorpe and Lone Star Dietz once played.[18] Second, the franchise anchors itself in "the most pernicious and enduring kind of American exploitation—racism in service to capitalism, the truly shameful principles upon which the nation was founded."[19] Empire and exploitation, capital and conquest form the unspoken and unexamined foundations of racialized entitlements today, making the anti-Indian racism central to the team and its traditions profitable and pleasurable for so many.

The ongoing enrichment of Snyder and those with whom he does business derives in large part from the willingness of politicians and the public to subsidize racism. The state of Virginia offered more than $6 million to entice the team to relocate its training facility from Maryland: "The Old Dominion will give the Skins $4 million; Loudoun County (home to the team's headquarters) will give them another $2 million, and Richmond will kick in $400,000."[20] And when it came time to build a new stadium, what became FedEx Field, the state of Maryland provided more than $70 million of the total $250 million cost.[21] For all of this, Snyder remains intransigent and the public seems comfortable to reward the pernicious articulations of racism and ownership. That said, it may be that a new stadium will prompt Snyder to change the name.[22]

Vinny Cerrato, Snyder's longtime associate and the former executive vice president for football operations for the team, recently offered his assessment of Snyder's position, underscoring his sentimental attachments: "So this is all about principle. This is about his dad. This is about his childhood. . . . It's not about the money. . . . Dan's got a ton of money. He'll fight this." He continued, elaborating on the possibility of change:

> I said this when this first started a year ago or whatever, I said the only way I see him eventually changing the name is if—IF—he gets a new stadium out of it, downtown, where old RFK was. And he builds a stadium bigger than [Jerry Jones's], which he would do, bigger and better than Jerry's. He gets a Super Bowl. All that. I said that's the way that maybe he would change the name. Getting the property, getting

the land, getting a good deal from the city to make concessions to change the name. I don't know. But to me, he's going to continue to fight this.[23]

Perhaps then, it is all about the money. And while one might find hope in these remarks, sensing the end of a racial slur, the prospect and the process reflect and reinforce racial hierarchies. Arguably worse, they point to a moment in which Snyder may be doubly rewarded for his past racism, receiving both public praise for advancing tolerance and largess for his business enterprises. Clearly, Snyder has full possession of the racial slur, benefiting financially from its continued use, and, if Cerrato is to be believed, he is holding it hostage, awaiting the appropriate ransom to release it. Thus he retains title over the racist term, and by extension over public uses and understandings of indigenous people. In so doing, he authorizes the racialized entitlements associated with playing Indian and profiting from Indianness and delegitimates the claims of American Indians to dignity, humanity, and sovereignty.

Unremarkable Whiteness

While Marshall and Snyder remain exceptional for their wealth and influence, they share with fans, media analysts, policy makers, and myriad others, past and present, an embrace of everyday whiteness, a set of beliefs and behaviors that reiterate and reinforce the racial order, often unconsciously. These acts and ideas reflect an assemblage of relationships, roles, and routines anchored in a history of racial rule, marked by the elaboration of white supremacy and the normalization of settler conquest and colonialism. Anti-Indianism, as outlined throughout this book, has proven itself to be among the more pervasive and powerful expressions of this set of arrangements. Of equal importance has been the development of its obverse, which some have termed white privilege, or the unearned advantages associated with being white in the United States. Peggy McIntosh has famously described white privilege as an invisible knapsack that provides Euro-Americans with an unseen, unacknowledged, and unearned complement of tools, comforts, securities, rewards, and opportunities in everyday life. This racialized toolkit has taken shape over time and operates in a systematic fashion. Thus its manufacture, use, and significance derive not from individual effort, animus, affect, or intention but from a sociohistorical system of racial rule.[24]

Allan Johnson has argued that three features distinguish systems of privilege: dominance, identification, and centeredness. In the context of white privilege,

> white-dominated . . . means the default is for white people to occupy positions of power. . . . [Not that] all white people are powerful, only that the powerful tend almost always to be white . . . White-identification means that the culture defines "white" people as the standard for human beings in general . . . Several things follow from this, including seeing the way they do things as simply "human" or "normal," and giving more credibility to their views than to the views of "others." . . . White-identification also encourages whites to be unaware of themselves as white, as if they didn't have a race at all. . . . White-centeredness is the tendency to put white people and what they do at the center of attention—the front page of the newspaper or magazine, the main character in the movie.[25]

Following Johnson, we might think of white privilege in the United States as a system that normalizes white supremacy and settler colonialism: it encourages Euro-Americans to look upon prevailing uses of Indianness as part of the natural order of things, disconnected from questions of race, power, and history; it allows fans to take and remake Indianness without pausing to reflect on ethical or political questions and in turn to take umbrage when nonwhites question them or make plain the ways radicalized power shapes cultural practices; it prompts supporters of the mascot to place themselves and their traditions at the center of the controversy and in many cases to push back in intense and often hostile ways. White privilege grants them title to Indianness, and much of the debate revolves around defenses of that entitlement or derives from their sense of their entitlement.

Discussing the struggle over the R*dskin tradition at Lancaster High School in suburban Buffalo, Beth Kwiatek wrote an editorial expounding on these themes: "To be white and have white privilege is to stand up in a room full of people, look directly into the eyes of brown-skinned people and tell them what is and what is not racism. White people can ignore history. White people can ignore experts. White people can ignore their neighbors. . . . Whiteness is a relationship. And it is a relationship of power."[26] This is what many supporters of the name did in their failed attempt to retain it in Lancaster, and this is what many supporters of the Washington professional football team do in response to critics. They invoke their white privilege: they deny, distort, and delimit, manipulating and manufacturing claims to justify their actions and legitimate their continued use of Indianness.

In upstate New York, in the nation's capital, and throughout the United States, white privilege, following Kwiatek, "allows the supporters of 'Redskins' to argue that the word can be a racial slur, but in this moment it is not. In other words, to be white is to assert that ugly, insulting and racist slurs can be separated from their intention, history or definition."[27] The franchise routinely advances such arguments. As Daniel Snyder noted in an interview with ESPN, "A Redskin is a football player. A Redskin is our fans. The Washington Redskins fan base represents honor, represents respect, represents pride." That is, it is not first and foremost an American Indian, but even if it were, we intend to honor indigenous people with the name. It is not a racial slur in this reframing, it is, in the words of the owner, "a positive. Taken out of context, you can take things out of context all over the place. But in this particular case, it is what it is. It's very obvious."[28]

The team attorney Robert Raskopf went further in an interview with a DC-area sports talk radio show when "asked if he would call a Native American a 'redskin' to his or her face." He replied, in part, "That's not what this case is about. It's what *our* word means. . . . If you look at those dictionaries that are in this case, in evidence, every one of them defines 'redskin' as . . . 'a North American Indian.' It's *how* you use it, it's not *whether* you use it. You need to put the word in context. . . . It may or may not be used disparagingly. . . . The Washington Redskins, have made something honorable and successful and imbued that into this brand, there's no way that anyone can say that we use that mark disparagingly."[29] Counterfactual and convoluted at best in his argument, Raskopf, like his boss, labors to whitewash the team and its traditions. He justifies the franchise's title to Indianness by eliminating history, context, and the interpretations of embodied American Indians, grounding his entitlement to speak and silence, use and refuse, take and remake in the accepted discourse of white-dominated, white-identified, and white-centered society. His racialized prerogative here mirrors the general position of the team to dictate what matters and how it matters, echoing a oft-repeated refrain, here in the voice of the current owner: "We understand the issues out there, and we're not an issue. . . . The real issues are real-life issues, real-life needs, and I think it's time that people focus on reality."[30]

Owning Indianness

A common belief in the contemporary United States, often unspoken and unconscious, implies that everyone has a right to use Indians as they see fit; everyone owns them. Indianness is a national heritage; it is a fount for commercial enterprise; it is a costume one can put on for a party, a youth activity, or a sporting event. This sense of entitlement, this expression of white privilege, has a long history, manifesting itself in national narratives, popular entertainments, marketing schemes, sporting worlds, and self-improvement regimes. From the Boston Tea Party and Boy Scouts to the prevalence of redface in Hollywood Westerns and the preoccupations of hipster fashion today, Americans have long created and re-created themselves by playing Indian.[31] In fact, one might argue that the foundational articulation of whiteness and the foremost enunciation of white privilege can be found in the taking and remaking of Indianness: the act of laying claim to indigenous culture, language, and identity, the assertion of ownership of Indians (often in the form of simulation and invention).

The R*dskin brand, as documented in earlier chapters, may be among the purest expression of such ownership, converting Native Americans into property.

As with military worship, fashion choices and product loyalty, many sports fans tether their identities to a specific brand and thus to a type of commerce they only passively influence. These attachments can benefit consumers psychologically, but rarely economically, for they manipulate us into assuming illusory feelings of control.

Indian mascots are more serious than soft drink preferences, however. They are products of an American will to name what has been conquered and to maintain power through a refusal to reconsider traditions of naming. Replacing Indian mascots such as the redskin with more benign characters represents a threat much greater than a change of name or color. It indicates a shift of consciousness from one of colonial privilege to the imminence of tribal autonomy.[32]

Ritualized re-creations, fanciful imaginings in song, dance, and cheer, and commercialized conjurings of them make genocide profitable for the franchise and pleasurable for countless fans. At the same, such acts of commodification and consumption depend on erasure, on not thinking, knowing, or remembering. Empowered thusly, (white) Americans can simultaneously lay claim to Americans Indians and all associated with them and disclaim the force, violence, and harm central to them. In this frame, one of the most powerful ways of challenging the white privilege and racialized entitlement anchoring the franchise and animating its fans is to question their ownership of the team name and Indianness as protected by trademark and legal statutes.

Against Entitlement

On June 18, 2014, in a 2–1 decision, the U.S. Trademark and Patent Office Trademark Trial Appeal Board (TTAB) voided trademarks associated with the Washington DC NFL franchise because it found the team's name to be "disparaging."[33] The TTAB ruling was recently upheld on appeal.[34] The board reached its conclusion, according to Bruce Handy, writing in *Vanity Fair*, in light of three patterns: "(a) the fact that in virtually all English-language dictionaries the word is labeled 'often offensive,' 'often disparaging,' 'contemptuous,' or, at the very least, 'not the preferred term' (thank you, *O.E.D.*); (b) the fact that the term has virtually disappeared from newspapers and other media outside references to football; and (c) the fact that prominent Native American organizations and a sizeable proportion of individual Native Americans find the term offensive."[35]

The ruling, which followed precedent established by TTAB over the past two decades that had dismissed a range of trademark applications using the name, including "Redskin Hog Rinds," on the grounds that it contained "a derogatory slang term," predictably was met with adulation by opponents and outrage by supporters.[36] Whereas an editorial in the *Washington Post* labeled it "a victory of tolerance," a piece in the *Wall Street Journal* lamented the overreach of big government, invoking especially troubling racial metaphors to recast the decision and invert its historical significance: "But now even the lowly patent clerks are following liberal orders and deputizing themselves as George Custers to drive the Washington Redskins out of America."[37] And for much of the day, the decision lit up social media, spawning #newredskinnames, which was a trending topic for a time.[38] Focusing on the celebratory tones, raging resentment, and partisan politics palpable in immediate reactions, we might easily lose track of the larger import of the decision, while overlooking its limitations and dangers.

It is best not to think of the ruling as an end point. It instead moves the struggle to the next phase, fostering reconfigured dialogues and debate while opening new fronts for action and reaction. Indeed, the neither the name nor the brand will cease, and even if appeals uphold the decision, the franchise will retain rights, if more limited and less profitable. The organization said as much in its press release: "We've seen this story before. And just like last time, today's ruling will have *no effect at all on the team's ownership of and right to use the Redskins name and logo.*"[39] This is certainly not the end. Nevertheless, the finding is a hopeful sign or, better said, another positive development for those opposed to the name. It adds to growing political pressure and the increasingly audible voices of dissent. In other words, the fight will continue with increased visibility and heightened momentum.

Much of the coverage, but happily not all, has centered on the ruling by TTAB and its propriety, the impact on and reaction of the franchise, and the minutiae of intellectual property law. The media has disappeared American Indians again, often burying, if not altogether erasing, them. Many readers of media accounts will not learn the identities and actions of the five Native American plaintiffs, Amanda Blackhorse, Marcus

Briggs-Cloud, Philip Gover, Jillian Pappan, and Courtney Tsotigh, who courageously brought the case to TTAB, nor will they be given a fuller understanding of the long history of opposition to the team and its name, an opposition that dates back more than four decades and fits into a larger pattern of empowerment.[40] Indeed, as important as this ruling is, it is not the first time TTAB has taken up the question. In fact, it comes over two decades after Suzan Shown Harjo (Cheyenne and Hodulgee Muscogee), Raymond D. Apodaca (Ysleta del Sur Pueblo), Vine Deloria Jr. (Lakota), Norbert S. Hill Jr. (Oneida), Mateo Romero (Cochiti Pueblo), William A. Means (Lakota), and Manley A. Begay Jr. (Navajo) filled suit against the NFL, seeking to nullify associated trademarks.[41] Then as now, TTAB ruled in favor of the plaintiffs.[42] Thus the TTAB finding is significant, but not new; it was decades in the making. And while played out in mainstream contexts and the whitestream media, its energy and urgency come from Indian Country.

In bringing *Blackhorse et al. v. Pro-Football, Inc.*, the plaintiffs sought to make visible the history and significance of the name and the socio-economic complex that grew up around it. This meant, during the trial and in the court of public opinion, disrupting taken-for-granted precepts and practices, both the evolution and more contemporary manifestations of a racial slur, which, like many denigrating words, began as one thing and mutated over time, adapted to conquest, killing, and ultimately the creation of the United States. After the fact, those targeted became talismans, those hunted and hated became honored in some perverse twist of nostalgia and triumphalism. The legal action direct attention at the racial entitlements fundamental to the team and its traditions, questioning the legitimacy of the brand and the practices and privileges of owning Indians more broadly.

Today, the spectacle of any given Sunday—branded sportswear, family gatherings, tailgating, face painting, war whoops, "Hail to the Redskins," fond memories, and the best of intentions allow fans to forget that history, simultaneously rejecting and reenacting racism. In response to the ongoing protests and in the wake of the decision by TTAB, fans and the organization play Indian and play the victim; they speak of their hurt and pain; they defend their tradition. Indeed, they simultaneously speak for American Indians in the abstract and recuperate a victim slot. They are at once entitled to the power to name, endowed with claims on Indianness, and aggrieved and violated. Online comments, of course, will express such sentiments with greater vitriol, unaware that the mix of rage and resentment, entitlement and erasure, reiterates the very forms of racism, privilege, and narcissism they purport to refuse.

Whereas the NFL, the franchise, and fans have sought to maintain the status quo, the plaintiffs in *Blackhorse et al. v. Pro-Football, Inc.*, in common with those in *Harjo et al. v. Pro-Football, Inc.*, sought to call attention to the slur and its history, gain moral traction, disrupt the brand and its profitability, and reinforce the legal archive documenting anti-Indian racism. These two readings and their desired ends reveal two competing visions of race and racism: defenders of the name emphasize the intention behind the imagery and nomenclature, equate racism with prejudice and hate, and prefer to read the name as an isolated text; while critics highlighted impacts and effects, understand racism to be a structural and historical phenomena, and insist on placing the name and associated practices in social and historical context. This deep division suggests that it will take more than a judicial ruling to affect real change around American Indian mascots, alter public perceptions of Native Americans more generally, and fully humanize indigenous people. That said, the case and the ruling highlight the ongoing importance of ownership, the significance of unsettling it, and the possibility of dismantling one assemblage of anti-Indianism and white privilege by challenging its legitimacy in court.

For supporters, this is a hopeful moment. And without taking anything away from that, I think it important to note two things easily forgotten in the aftermath of *Harjo et al. v. Pro-Football, Inc.* First, on appeal, the courts reversed the decision issued by TTAB on a technicality known as laches, a legal doctrine that demands plaintiffs assert claims to their rights in timely fashion. Such a finding ignores the historical structures that worked against an earlier finding, while denying the associated trauma. It also laid the legal foundation for *Blackhorse et al. v. Pro-Football, Inc.*, in which a new generation of plaintiffs not bound by laches could target trademarks registered after 1968. Second, oppositional momentum stalled for a time. Both are possible again now. Dan Snyder, owner of the DC franchise, has vowed to never change the name, and the organization has already indicated plans to appeal. While it may be best to never say never, a protracted legal battle lies ahead. Perhaps more important will be its reverberations in the court of public opinion. To put it in the form of a question: will exposing the racist foundations and dehumanizing force of ownership push back against entitlement sufficiently, or will it further entrench supporters intent on defending their white privilege and the possession of Indianness?

The White Problem

Whatever the ultimate outcome of *Blackhorse et al. v. Pro-Football, Inc.*, its focus on racism and ownership underscores the problem of unrecognized and unexamined whiteness at the core of the team and its traditions. As Steven Salaita phrases it, "I instead would like to argue that the redskin has little to do with actual Indians and almost everything to do with the peculiar disquiet of a whiteness perceived to be in decline."[43] It offers a direct challenge to racial entitlement and lays bare the investment in, defense of, and lingering longing for white supremacy embodied by the team name.

There was a time when policy makers and pundits openly debated what they termed "the Indian Problem," by which they meant, How can we govern, assimilate, and otherwise transform these people we have dispossessed and dislocated in the expansion of the United States? Not surprisingly, in a context marked by the open celebration of imperialism and the overt expression of white supremacy, they saw native nations as the problem, an impediment to progress and a burden to be borne by a rapidly modernizing country. Of course, in retrospect, one can recognize that the problem was actually a white problem: Manifest Destiny, settling the frontier, wars against indigenous people, scientific racism, and on all resulted in removing and killing, taking and remaking, exploiting and excluding, transferring wealth and appropriating resources, and so on. Racism plus entitlement led to death and destruction. These were not the problems, no—for many Euro-Americans witnessing the results, then, the problems were the survivors and what they were going to do with them.

In many ways, today something similar is at play, but instead of talking about it, too often attention focuses on whether the name is offensive or respectful, turns on trademark rights and First Amendment rights, and pivots around questions of heritage and intention. Each of these framings prevents us from seeing the white problem at the heart of the controversy. As the anthropologist Alan Boraas notes, "The term redskin is offensive to many Native Americans and Americans. It's an intentional use of a slur by the non-Native power structure to subjugate and marginalize. Use of a derogatory name sends the message 'we can use a name that offends you and you can't do anything about it.' The name reflects an attitude of dominance and superiority and that's racism."[44] This is the white problem restated, ultimately reiterating its core elements. Racism plus entitlement: the capacity to take and remake, the prerogative to brand and bully, the privilege to own and erase, and perhaps above all else, "the desire of the colonizer to maintain control of the historical and contemporary narratives of their encounter."[45] In recognizing the heart of whiteness, we see with Autumn White Eyes (Lakota): "It's not me [as an indigenous person] they are honoring; they are honoring themselves for doing such a good job on killing all the Indians."[46] Read in this light, to not alter the traditions of the Washington professional football team necessitates not only removing a stereotype but working through and against anti-Indian racism, white privilege, and the legacies of conquest, including genocide, dispossession, and cultural appropriation.

While the ruling in *Blackhorse et al. v. Pro-Football, Inc.* may trouble the articulations of racism and entitlement, addressing the problems associated with whiteness will demand a will to be accountable for white supremacy and its histories, a capacity to acknowledged the structural foundations of wealth, power, and identity, and a desire to confront a broader system of privilege centered around, identified with, and dominated by whites and whiteness. The first steps on this path to address the white problem include recognizing the value and validity of others, a willingness to listen, and a capacity to change. Euro-Americans have unique opportunities and special obligations to pursue such ends.

1. William Henry Dietz poses in regalia, 1915. Photo by Artopho Studios. From WSU Historic Photographs Subject Files (PC4b6), Manuscripts, Archives, and Special Collections (MASC), Washington State University Libraries.

2. (*above*) Players at training camp, August 28, 1937. Players in the air are (*left to right*) Wayne Millner (Notre Dame), Pug Rentner (Northwestern), and Nels Peterson (West Virginia Wesleyan). Courtesy of the Library of Congress, # LC-H22-D-2247.

3. (*opposite top*) George Preston Marshall posing with twins, 1954 publicity photo. Courtesy Star Collection, DC Libraries.

4. (*opposite bottom*) Halftime, November 14, 1954. Photo by Abbie Rowe. Courtesy of the National Archives, NAI: 520197.

5. Program cover for game on September 30, 1962. Author's collection.

6. Program cover for game on October 13, 1963. Author's collection.

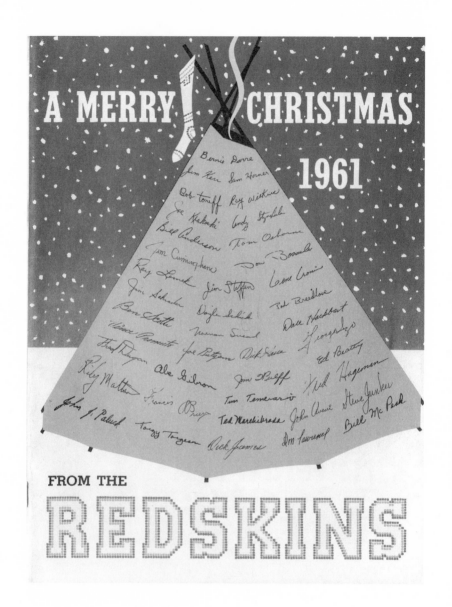

7. Program cover for game, December 1961. Author's collection.

8. *Redskin.* Performance art piece by Gregg Deal,
September 27, 2014. Used by permission of the artist.

9. (*above*) Protest at Super Bowl XXVI, Minneapolis, 1992. Used with permission from Doug Nemanic.

10. (*opposite top*) Not Your Mascot protest, Minneapolis, November 2, 2014. Photos © Fibonacci Blue. Permission via Creative Commons.

11. (*opposite bottom*) Not Your Mascot protest, Minneapolis, November 2, 2014. Photos © Fibonacci Blue. Permission via Creative Commons.

12. "Redskins, Honor the Treaties First," by Marty Two Bulls. © Marty G. Two Bulls.

Simulation

8

In August 2014 artist Gregg Deal gave a talk on his life and work as part of the Creative Mornings lecture series in Washington DC. Deal, perhaps best known for his ongoing work *The Last American Indian on Earth*, began with a brief introduction: "I am a husband and a father. I am an artist, an activist, and a member of the Pyramid Lake Paiute Tribe." He proceeded to discuss the influences and objectives shaping his art. The ever-present instance of imaginary Indians and their very real impacts have occupied much of his work, prompting him to find ways to call attention to and challenge such representations.[1]

Roughly six weeks after his lecture, Deal was a r*dskin. That is, he staged a performance art piece, dubbed *Redskin*, in which he drew on his experience living in the Washington DC area for fifteen years and on comments posted online and via social media to dramatize the scope and significance of anti-Indian racism at the heart of the ongoing struggle over the team name and associated traditions (see figure 8).[2]

For Deal, the piece marked an important departure from his earlier work, which had often relied on irony and humor to alter perception and prompt action. With *Redskin*, he sought instead for a more confrontational approach, which would render in a more realistic fashion the force of anti-Indianism. In particular, Deal wanted to focus on microaggressions: small, often unnoticed insensitivities and insults of every day that work to exclude and dehumanize. "A good example is someone coming along and saying, 'Well, you don't look Indian,' and then [they] turn around and say, 'Well, my great-great-grandmother was part Cherokee.' In that one statement, they've managed to invalidate me and validate themselves, all based on romanticism and based on their own sense of authority."[3] To this end, the piece featured Deal, seated, in matching black Dickies shirt and pants, and four "antagonists," representing fans and team name supporters. Together they brought to life established arguments and familiar scenarios, including:

> Red Face: Non-Indians dressed with "Indian war paint" and "fake headdress" try to convince Deal their actions honor him.
> "You're just not Indian enough": Antagonists evaluate Deal's identity, speaking critically about his conformity to stereotype (e.g., "You don't look Indian to me") and explaining the ways they perceive his identity as a Native person.
> Redskins: Antagonists sing the team song "Hail To The Redskins," preach about honor, and list other arguments and "facts."[4]

Although originally slated for eight hours, the performance came to a close after only four, because of the intensity and negativity, because "it was emotionally exhausting."[5]

In both of these instances, I hear Deal stating quite clearly, "I am not that stereotype. I am not your Indian. I am not a R*dskin." In his presentation and his performance piece, he calls attention to the ways misunderstandings and misrepresentations of American Indians have become more real, more meaningful, and more important than embodied indigenous people and, in turn, have laid a foundation for sincere fictions in defense of imperial inventions, doubling the force of anti-Indianism. In effect, Deal highlights the simulations that anchor the DC NFL franchise and their workings in American public culture, with *Redskin* pointedly employing simulation to expose the workings of simulation. In a subsequent address at the National Museum of the American Indian about his work, Deal noted that while he and his collaborators had staged the event, it had palpable reverberations for the audience in attendance and, the next day, for the participants, who had lingering distress in the aftermath.[6]

In this chapter, I turn to the fabrication of support. I explore the place of simulation in the defense of the Washington football team, while troubling a series of false claims on and about Indianness advanced by the owner and organization. In particular, I consider three efforts to legitimate the team and its traditions: (a) visible, public connections between the franchise and respected American Indians, (b) the embrace of pretendians, or individuals who play at being Indian, and (c) the establishment of the Original American Foundation. Each of these strategies endeavors to shore up support for a false rendering of American Indians by creating the illusion of support among real American Indians. Such undertakings, not surprisingly, receive a critical reception in Indian Country. Throughout, I foreground such counter-readings, exploring the ways in which they unmask the insincere fictions of the organization and return attention to key issues elided by simulation, namely history, context, and power.

The Power of Association

The Washington professional football franchise, like most sport teams in the United States, draws on symbolic connections to fashion itself and make statements to its players, fans, and opponents. Together, the name and logo operate as a totem, allowing those invested in the team to draw power from imagined Indianness: references to bravery, strength, honor, excellence, and even violence all speak to the symbolic force this invented talisman. George Preston Marshall encouraged the elaboration of Indianness to increase market share and enhance the nascent brand. As discussed previously, he achieved this through stereotypes and tropes familiar to audiences, through devices that embedded the brand in the rituals of game day and in the personal lives of fans, and by accentuating the Indianness of his team, which, after all, initially had a smattering of indigenous players and a coach who purported to be an Indian and reveled in playing Indian. Even as the foundational metaphors have come under fire, fans and the franchise have held tight to them. According to Courtland Milloy, "Team owner Daniel Snyder has taken to conjuring Indian support—trotting out fake Native Americans and manufacturing facts about the glorious origin of a team name widely regarded as a racial slur."[7] Indeed, Snyder and his organization have worked hard to identify and expand their connection, knowing that the appearance of authentic connections to American Indians has a pronounced capacity to legitimate the team name and deflect criticism of it.

In the summer of 1999, against the background of litigation, namely *Harjo et al. v Pro-Football, Inc.*, representatives of the franchise traveled to South Dakota, courting indigenous support for the moniker. "Snyder's lawyers," according to Suzan Shown Harjo (Cheyenne and Hodulgee Muscogee), "were dispatched to Indian country to find relatives of Lone Star Dietz, the team's long ago assistant coach." While it is unclear whether they found their quarry, their efforts and objectives fit a broader pattern. For Harjo, it constitutes "a modern-day version of the white man trading trinkets for Manhattan. The chief-makers gave away jerseys, jackets and hats sporting the team's name and asked for signatures on a paper saying the R-word is an honor."[8] To this day, the franchise continues to play chief maker, finding and fashioning American Indians' support.

On November 25, 2013, the DC NFL franchise choose to mark Native American Heritage Month and pay tribute to U.S. veterans at FedEx Field by presenting four Navajo Code Talkers during a commercial break in the first quarter of their game against San Francisco. The Code Talkers occupy a special place in American cultural memory because they used their native languages to help secure the Allied victory in the Second World War. The event allowed the franchise to simultaneously honor revered heroes from the Greatest Generation, underscore its professed respect for American Indians generally, and legitimate the embattled name. After all, the ceremony asserted, here are four true warriors, four real Indians; if they do not have a problem with the team or its name, surely there is not a problem. For their part, the Code Talkers appeared to buttress this assertion, indicating that the team name was "a symbol of loyalty and courage—not a slur."[9]

Viewing the event as cynical at best, critics mocked Snyder, suggesting that the ploy revealed how desperate the organization had become. The sportswriter Dave Zirin knocked the owner for excusing his anti-Indian racism by saying, "Some of my best friends are Navajo Code Talkers."[10] The activist Amanda Blackhorse (Navajo) echoed this reading: "The Code Talkers deserved a more genuine honor, not just 30 seconds of media time so the Washington team can sugarcoat their racism." Moreover, pushing back against the effort to delegitimize the movement, she continued, "There are thousands upon thousands of Natives and non-Natives who support our efforts to eliminate the racist team name. . . . Using four Navajo elders does not justify what they are doing. . . . The name is still inappropriate and disparaging toward Native American people."[11]

More recently, on October 12, 2014, a date many in the United States recognize as Columbus Day, Washington traveled to Phoenix to play Arizona. Even though it was an away game, the franchise seized on the occasion to deflect criticism of the team and distract from the largest protest scheduled to convene outside the stadium that day. Snyder invited Ben Shelly, outgoing president of the Navajo Nation, to join him in the owners' box to watch the game. The two were featured prominently in television coverage of the game and in photos published after its conclusion. In addition, according to news reports, the franchise paid for roughly 650 American Indians, including members of the Navajo Nation and Zuni Pueblo to attend the game, providing tickets and transportation. These individuals also received much attention from the media. Shelley and Snyder together with the hundreds of Native Americans conveyed strong support, official and grassroots, for the team, shoring up its beleaguered image. Indeed, the team successfully overshadowed the protest against it and kept the media from focusing on the overwhelming opposition to it in the Navajo Nation and among indigenous people in the region generally. For instance, viewers of the game would not learn that the Navajo National Council voted 9–2 to oppose the team name, that the Diné Medicine Men's Association passed a resolution against it as well, urging lawmakers to act to prompt change, and that Arizona state representative Jamescita Peshlakai proposed legislation designed to pressure the team and league to change the name.[12] As with the Code Talkers, association with American Indians legitimated the team and its traditions while marginalizing critics.

Pretendians

Since its inception the Washington football team has reveled in playing with Indianness. On the one hand, it has exploited popular images, stereotypes, and clichés associated with American Indians to craft a distinct brand, experience, and identity. On the other hand, its initial coach, who spent his adult life pretending to be Indian, was embraced for his embellishments. Today, the organization and many of its supporters often defend the former by invoking the latter. In the face of ongoing protests, many fans still relish playing Indian and the team still has a fondness for frauds, charlatans, and pretendians.

Princess Pale Moon

In the ninth week of the 1991 NFL season, Washington defeated Houston at RFK Stadium, bettering its record to 9-0. While remembered by many as part the team's championship season, capped by victory in Super Bowl XXVI, the game was noteworthy because a woman named Princess Pale Moon sang the national anthem and the American Indian Movement made a point of protesting the game and her role. Vernon Bellecourt (Ojibwe), the spokesman for the group, charged, "She wants to be an Indian, but she's just masquerading. We're totally opposed to her singing the anthem."[13] Pale Moon, born Rita Ann Suntz, dubbed herself "America's contemporary Pocahontas."[14] And while she had claimed Cherokee, Ojibwe, Choctaw, and Blackfoot ancestry at different times, she never became an enrolled member of any recognized tribe. As a consequence, according to Don Allery, the former deputy director of the National Congress of American Indians, "She could just as well claim to be Queen of England."[15] Her claim to a royal title was, of course, a fantasy, for as Suzan Shown Harjo (Cheyenne and Hodulgee Muscogee) pointed out in 1985, "Indians don't have princess[es]. . . . It's a scurrilous designation."[16] Suntz sang the national anthem at two Republican national conventions, marched in Ronald Reagan's inaugural parade, toured Europe as part of the USO, and had a part in the 1976 Summer Olympics in Montreal.[17] She had also performed at previous games, including at least one occasion that featured a group of Miss Indian USA contestants as part of halftime entertainment. Floyd Crow Westerman (Dakota) dismissed her as a sham, noting that the way she had "co-opt[ed] these young Indians to be used for something like that is to add insult to injury."[18] Worse, Suntz was not only an ethnic fraud, but she leveraged her claims to Indianness as a front for the American Indian Heritage Foundation, an organization noteworthy for shady practices that resulted in it being banned from soliciting funds in Virginia, New York, and Michigan and for its role in the establishment of American Indian Heritage Month in 1990.[19] Following her banishment from the 1992 World's Fair in Spain, Suntz faded from the scene, later reappearing online in support of her charity.

Chief Stephen Dodson

While the franchise dissociated itself from one wannabe nearly a quarter century ago, in the past few years it has embraced new pretendians. In the spring of 2013, Washington resident Stephen Dodson was featured on the team website under the headline "Native American Chief Talks about Redskins." In its "news item" and accompanying video, the team describes him as "a full-blooded American Inuit chief originally from the Aleutian Tribes of Alaska" who "represents more than 700 remaining tribe members." Dodson subsequently defends the name and normalizes the r-word, refuting assertions of its use as a racial slur.

"People," he asserts, "are speaking for Native Americans that aren't Native American. . . . They're misrepresenting the Native American nation." In the process, Dodson omits or erases the large number of American Indian advocates, intellectuals, and leaders who have condemned the team, while misconstruing the more than five hundred recognized native nations as a singular entity. Against this backdrop, he continues, "We don't have a problem with [the name] at all; in fact we're honored. We're quite honored. . . . It's actually a term of endearment that we would refer to each other as. . . . When we were on the reservation, we would call each other, 'Hey, what's up redskin?' Redskin' isn't something given to us by the white man or the blue eyes, it was something in the Native American community that was taken from us. . . . We respected each other with that term."[20] Dodson hits almost all of the key arguments marshaled in defense of the team and its traditions: it's an honor; it's not racist; we use it; we created it; we convey respect for other Indians when we use it.

The sportswriter Dave McKenna has deconstructed Dodson's claims, finding that he is too good to be true. Dodson is "neither a full-blooded American Inuit nor a chief in any formal sense of the term." While "Chief" is a nickname for Dodson, apparently bestowed on him in the military, he does not understand the political designation nor appear to appreciate that such a term does not exist among indigenous Alaskans. When asked about this subsequently by McKenna, Dodson offered a rambling explanation that undercut both his testimony and the claims made by the team: "I'm the son of a chief. I'm at the shaman level, a different type of chief. You're born into it, and the shaman chooses you. The shaman chose my father. I was born into it. The Dodson family, I'm the head of that family. The chief of that family. It's not easy to explain."[21] Moreover, in his interview on the website, Dodson blurs the Aleutians and Inuit as well as their distinction from American Indians, a term they do not apply to themselves. In addition, they do not attend powwows or live on reservations.

Clearly, Dodson is neither a chief nor an Indian. Yet his claims remain on the team website as of this writing in spring 2015, buttressing their claims. And Roger Goodell invoked Dodson and his comments to highlight indigenous support for the team name and dismiss charges to the contrary raised by U.S. senators.[22]

Mark One Wolf (aka Mark Yancey)

Chief Stephen Dodson, like Princess Pale Moon, has faded from view, save for the team webpage recording his support. More recently, another pretendian has emerged to take his place, Mark One Wolf. A slippery character, One Wolf has a number of aliases, including Mark Yancey, Mark Suzuki, Mark Yan, Kram Yecnay, Mark Yazzie, and Dalaa Ba'Cho, and has claimed a series of tribal affiliations, including Cherokee, Shinnecock, Chiricahua Apache, Mexica, Navajo, and, in a 2007 court record, "Native American/Alaskan." He is an outspoken supporter of the team name, who for a time enjoyed something of an esteemed status at training camp. In fact, when initially questioned, he stated, "The team is satisfied with my credentials." However, not only is there no proof that One Wolf is who he claims to be but his numerous alias and changeable affiliations underscore how flexible he thinks Indianness is and how hard he will work to try to achieve it in the minds of others. Toby Vanlandingham (Yurok) has gone so far as to dub him "the 21st-century version of William 'Lone Star' Dietz," lacking, of course, the success on the gridiron or in the court of public opinion. Like all ethnic frauds who pass as American Indian, One Wolf erases indigenous people, silences their voices, and undermines their efforts to advance projects meaningful to them and their communities. This point was emphasized recently when One Wolf resurfaced in upstate New York in support of a high school with an American Indian mascot. On this occasion, newspapers referred to him as an Indian because he claimed to be one, accepting the lie for the truth and allowing a poser to trump tribal sovereignty and established protocols for substantiating such claims.[23]

The Washington football teams loves pretendians. It seems especially fond of those who support the team and have a title that conveys esteem and prominence instantly. It does not trouble itself with fact-checking, redskinsfacts.com notwithstanding, or with shifting affiliations claimed by those playing Indian. The appearance of authority and authenticity matters far more, precisely because it anchors the illusion of Indianness and gives added importance to the endorsement. Much like its association with important American Indians, simulation, or to speak most plainly, fraud, bestows power on the franchise, offering it a means to defend itself, dismiss critics, and continue to profit from its use of Indianness.

Questionable Charity

In late March 2014, Daniel Snyder reported on his ongoing engagement with Indian Country in an open letter to "Everyone in our Washington Redskins Nation." He described how he and members of his staff had "traveled to 26 reservations across twenty states to listen and learn firsthand about the views, attitudes, and experiences of the Tribes." He spoke with pride of the support for the team, quoting Mary L. Resvaloso, chairwoman, Torres-Martinez Desert Cahuilla Indians: "There are Native Americans everywhere that 100% support the name." He lamented the myriad social ills they encountered, seemingly noticing them for the first time. And he committed himself to "making a real, lasting, positive impact on Native American quality of life—one tribe and one person at time." To this end, he announced the establishment of the Washington Redskins Original Americans Foundation (OAF), which would direct "meaningful and measurable resources" to "provide genuine opportunities for Tribal communities. With open arms and determined minds, we will work as partners to begin to tackle the troubling realities facing so many tribes across our country. Our efforts will address the urgent challenges plaguing Indian country based on what Tribal leaders tell us they need most. We may have created this new organization, but the direction of the Foundation is truly theirs."[24]

By all appearances, the appointed leadership reinforced the envisioned collaboration and outreach. Snyder named Gary L. Edwards (Cherokee), former deputy assistant director of the U.S. Secret Service and chief executive of the National Native American Law Enforcement Association (NNALEA), to lead OAF. In doing so, he declared, "I think we have the right leader in Gary Edwards." Much like the team's efforts to associate with esteemed Indians and passable pretendians, Edwards's past leadership left something to be desired. Namely, the Bureau of Indian Affairs terminated a $1 million contract awarded to NNALEA after federal investigators found the group's work "unusable."[25]

Whatever else its accomplishments may be, OAF has made some pretty powerful claims on "the real," especially in the form of authentic Indianness, to project sincerity and manufacture goodwill. Specifically, it locates the problems and partners "out there" in Indian Country, in tribal communities, on reservations, in "troubling realities" and "urgent challenges," not in Washington DC, the team name, anti-Indian racism, the voices of advocates, or the concerns of pan-Indian organizations. As Snyder put it, "They have genuine issues they truly are worried about, and our team's name is not one of them." Thus, this is not about us; it is all about them: Indian problems, Indian partners, Indian leaders, and a genuine Indian as its titular head. OAF softens the image of the team's owner, provides important cover for the organization, and lends legitimacy to its efforts, marking a stark divide between the team and its traditions and "real problems," while leveraging authentic Indianness to defend the embattled name.

Not surprisingly, critics were quick to question the charity. Both the animated comedy series *South Park* and the satirist Stephen Colbert lampooned OAF, while pundits lambasted it. Almost immediately, social media lit up in response to the announcement. To call attention to what they saw as corporate efforts to buy support for a racial slur, indigenous activists tweeted images of themselves with currency taped across their mouths and the accompanying tag "#not4sale."[26]

In a similar vein, the golfer Notah Begay (Navajo) described OAF as "a gimmick" meant "to offset some of the public disdain for the name of [Snyder's] football team" and to let the team and the NFL off the hook for their continued anti-Indianism.[27] Representative Betty McCollum (Minnesota), the cochair of the House Native American Caucus, echoed these sentiments: "Snyder wants to keep profiting from his team's racist brand and use those profits to attempt to buy the silence of Native Americans with a foundation that is equal parts public relations scheme and tax deduction."[28] And the longtime critic Suzan Shown Harjo noted that whatever good might come from the organization was undermined by its dehumanizing intentions and impacts, making it an injurious blending of "assault and bribery." Indeed, she continued, "I'm glad that he's had a realization that Native Americans have it tough in the United States. . . . All sorts of people could have told him that, and have been trying to tell him that for a long time. . . . Will (the foundation) do much of anything? No. But it probably won't hurt . . . except that it will continue the cycle of negative imaging of Native American people in the public arena."[29]

In the end, despite, or perhaps because of, its simulation of support, compassion, and uplift in response to charges of defamation, denigration, and dehumanization, OAF's claims on "the real"—real Indians, real Indian problems, real Indian support, and making a real difference—quickly became contested, rendering it a questionable charity. As Jim Enote (Zuni), director of the A:shiwi A:wan Museum and Heritage Center, phrased it, "While the foundation's name appears charitable, I question whether it is genuinely altruistic because it grew from an unwillingness to understand and acknowledge the damage the Redskins mascot causes to Native American identity."[30]

Divide and Conquer

In his announcement of OAF, Snyder trumpeted its accomplishments to date, including the gift of more than three thousand winter coats to the Lower Brule Sioux Tribe and the donation of a backhoe to the Omaha Tribe.[31] Other initiatives include giving funds to build a playground and sponsor a rodeo team for the Chippewa Cree Tribe.[32] In contrast with many of the more critical readings of OAF, a number of Chippewa Crees were pleased with the organization's efforts. Tribal Chair Rick Morsette, who has "no problem with the name," praised OAF for helping tribal youth. And Mike Sangrey noted, "If us accepting the money makes [Snyder and the team] sleep better at night, then fine, I wish them a good night's sleep. . . . What matters is our kids get to enjoy a new playground. And how can that be bad?"[33]

OAF has split other communities. In the Monument Valley School District, one of the lowest ranked and most underfunded in the state of Utah, for instance, the donation of $30,000 caused division. Monument Valley High School principal Spencer Singer expressed gratitude for the influx of funds: "The support means a lot for us. . . . It's hard to fundraise on the reservation. We don't have a lot of businesses to ask for donation type things so to have that help for funding the program is a good thing. . . . They are helping kids academically. . . . And for us it's huge and we really appreciate what they are doing."[34] At the same time, school board member Nelson Yellowman had a more sour reaction: "It is derogatory. . . . It makes me wonder if this is a way for the NFL team to retain their team name."[35]

Still others, like the Las Vegas Paiute Tribe, spurned OAF's advances.[36] Similarly, the Ft. Yuma Quechan Tribe turned down an offer from the organization to underwrite a skate park and donate iPads for use in a native-language program. Tribal member Kenrick Escalanti, president of Kwatsan Media, Inc., explained the decision: "We will not align ourselves with an organization to simply become a statistic in their fight for name acceptance in Native communities. We're stronger than that and we know bribe money when we see it."[37] Adrienne Keene (Cherokee), a vocal critic of the abuse of indigenous peoples and cultures, put it more bluntly, referring to the offer as blood money, reflective of a deeper pattern of marginalization and exploitation:

> But let's go back to the money, and let's think about the choice here—a choice that Native peoples in this country have had to make over, and over, and over throughout our history. We have deep and pressing needs in our communities. We have tribal members freezing to death, we have students unable to learn because their schools are falling apart at the seams, we have suicide rates 3.5 times higher than national averages. Because of centuries of colonialism, our communities have limited options. We are bridled by geographic location, federal red tape and bureaucracy, poverty, and any other number of factors. Then, outsiders come in. They offer us cash, in exchange for natural resources, for land, for mining rights, for oil—and our leaders and communities are faced with a lesser-of-two-evils choice.[38]

While the Ft. Yuma Quechans stood up to OAF and refused to repeat this ugly imperial history, many tribes and their citizens find themselves in a bind: turning down a gift will ensure the persistence of their impoverished, marginalized, and disempowered conditions; accepting the gift offers some measure of relief, a small opportunity for improvement, if not empowerment. OAF, then, according to Rick Cohen, "wants Native Americans to take the charitable money in return, at a minimum, for turning a blind eye to the racially disparaging team name."[39]

In the end, Snyder has reengaged a familiar strategy of divide and conquer. "It's the old colonial playbook," according to Jennie Stockle (Cherokee and Creek), "basically turning Native Americans against each other on this issue. This kind of charity forces us to make a choice to accept the funding or to claim our identity as Native people. We don't deserve a life where we should be forced to make that choice."[40]

Gyasi Ross (Blackfoot) outlines the very real impacts of OAF's intrusion into Indian Country:

> It's not an accident that he's picking our most economically vulnerable communities—money talks in those places. . . . Dan Snyder's Original Americans Foundation is going into the most impoverished

Native communities and presenting shiny things in exchange for perceived or real acceptance of the Redskins name/logo. That presents
an interesting conundrum. Obviously Dan Snyder's foundation is
engaging in ugly and predatory economics, seeking to pick off Indian
Country's most vulnerable communities with pennies on the dollar.
That's bad. Yet, these brothers and sisters have to eat. They should
be able to eat. They should be able to take care of their kids and pay
their bills as long as they're doing it legally. They should be able to
do those things without criticism.[41]

In essence, OAF fractures Indian Country and splits indigenous communities for its own ends. It uses money and goods to buy the support
of some American Indians while ignoring the dissent voiced by others
and, all the while, securing goodwill from the broader public for its philanthropic efforts and the simulated endorsements they produce.

Reclaiming the "Real"

While some may read OAF as a gimmick, a public relations ploy, and an
open expression of exploitation, numerous indigenous people understand
it to be the reiteration of a history of broken promises, insincere exploitation, and claims of Indians and Indianness. OAF revivifies American
imperialism and its distorted renderings of "the real."

Referring to OAF's work in Monument Valley, Ryan van Bibber also
reminds us of the connections between capital and the management of
the so-called Indian problem:

Soldiers once rode through here at the behest of railroads and mining
companies, promising Indians a better life if only they would take up
farming on the reservations, or a bayonet if they refused. Suits from
Peabody Coal came here promising jobs and a way out of the cyclical
poverty of reservation life in exchange for what little water the land had
to give and a long list of easily ignored health risks. The BIA's promise
was to smooth out the problems caused by centuries of exploitation.

A $2 billion NFL team named the Redskins and the owner's Original
Americans Foundation is just part of the same cycle.[42]

Similarly, Peter d'Errico asserts that OAF has its roots in a particular "missionary commercial zeal" central to efforts to colonize North America and convert its inhabitants, to show them the light and the way of truth. Entitlement and righteousness guided earlier efforts, grounding claims to property and propriety in a Christian ethos and often robing them in a language of uplift and charity.[43]

Brian Cladoosby (Swinomish), president of the National Congress of American Indians, presses further. He reframes OAF as a reformulation of treaty discourse that not only racializes and exploits indigenous peoples but works to remake "the real" as well:

> In our past, Native communities have received blankets, coats, trinkets, donations and the uninvited sympathy of those who see us only as an inferior people. These contributions can be helpful, but they are like putting a Band-Aid on a broken leg—they do nothing to solve the underlying problem. We have learned to be suspicious of gifts that stem from selfish interests, come wrapped in claims of generosity and serve to distract from the real problems at hand. . . . Snyder's foundation will do little to address the problems that the R-word brand compounds daily: racial inequality and a lack of understanding of the place of native people in our society, especially youth.[44]

Cladoosby underscores the connection between anti-Indian racism, the establishment of OAF, its denial of the importance of the team's name, and its efforts to identify what constitute "real" problems to embodied American Indians.

Indeed, following the Ojibwe author David Treuer, we would conclude that Snyder does not merely want to use OAF to define what constitutes a real problem, manage public opinion, or buy indigenous support, he also wants to define what constitutes an authentic Indian and acceptable uses of Indianness. "The unstated mission of the Washington Redskins Original Americans Foundation is clear: In the face of growing criticism over the team's toxic name and mascot imagery, the aim is to buy enough goodwill so the name doesn't seem *so* bad, and if some American Indians—in the racial logic of so-called post-racial America, 'some' can stand in for 'all'—accept Mr. Snyder's charity, then protest will look like hypocrisy." Treuer, for his part, like numerous other Native Americans today, will, of course, have none of this: "Mr. Snyder refers to 'our shared Washington Redskins' heritage. To be clear: There is no 'our' that includes Mr. Snyder. And there is no 'Redskins' that includes us."[45] In a very real sense, Treuer, Cladoosby, and countless other American Indians have sought to reclaim control of "the real" in their refusal of OAF and their resistance to the team more generally, contesting their preference for illusions and inventions as well as their comfort in decontextualization and dehumanization.

A year after the announcement trumpeting its launch, OAF had gone silent. It seemingly had joined Princess Pale Moon and Chief Dodson in obscurity. After extensive research, the sportswriter Ronald Guy could find no recent record of activity noted nor updates on its webpage, and he received no response to his queries of the organization: "OAF appears to be either idle or the most stealth philanthropic organization in history. If the former is true, it is sad commentary on 'Skins of Washington and the NFL . . . and there's no reasonably available evidence to think otherwise."[46] Indeed, the rapidity of its demise is especially striking given the importance ascribed to it and the commitment it represented, but then perhaps it not only cynically sought out the simulation of support to quiet dissent but was itself a simulation of actual concern and engagement as well.

No Illusions

At the close of his talk in August 2014, Gregg Deal briefly discussed another performance art piece that centered on simulation, *The Traditional Washington Redskin Honor Ceremony*. Staged in association with the opening of one of his art shows, it featured "a white man on display wearing a team jersey and hat," encoding a set of preconceptions about whiteness, sport fandom, and the team.

He was drinking beer, eating chips and watching a football game all the while cheering on the team. This piece . . . was meant to flip the fetishizing and objectification of indigenous people over to the fans. It was also a great illustration to how incredibly ridiculous the argument of 'honor' is in this situation. I can't imagine any team that cheers for a touchdown and starts singing 'Hail To the Redskins' is thinking about the systematic genocide of indigenous people, or the Native woman who froze to death last winter because she had no heat in her house on the reservation. Honor deserves respect.[47]

Deal has returned to satire, repurposing simulation to question accepted beliefs and behaviors. The inversion shifts attention to the team and its traditions, problematizing whiteness, and reframes them within tropes long intent to capture Indianness—tradition, ceremony, and even *R*dskin*. This morphing unsettles the claims of the franchise and its fans, rendering them hollow fictions. Honor, like the pretendians, thus resituated, appears as little more than a profitable projection and comforting fantasy in which select Indians can be bought, packaged, and managed—supported so long as they support the team and its traditions.

While the organization would like its simulations to quiet dissent and quell the ongoing crisis, they may be having the opposite effect, as evidenced by the impeachment of Gari Lafferty, chairwoman of the Paiute Tribe of Utah, for accepting funds from OAF.[48] The continued reliance on partial, purchased, and produced support only encourages further interrogation of intent and impact, while clearing a space for resistance and rebuttal. Ultimately, each new pretendian and every initiative like the Original Americans Foundation will prompt a chorus of voices exclaiming, "I am not that stereotype. I am not your Indian. I am not a R*dskin."

Opinion

9

The sportswriter Rick Reilly gave voice to the feelings of many as the controversy over the Washington football club escalated once again at the start of the 2013 NFL season. "I guess this is where I'm supposed to fall in line and do what every other American sports writer is doing. I'm supposed to swear I won't ever write the words 'Washington Redskins' anymore because it's racist and offensive and a slap in the face to all Native Americans who ever lived. Maybe it is." His defiant tone and evocative resentment surely resonated with many team supporters and numerous other fans. Reilly then pushed deeper. "I just don't know how to tell my father-in-law, a Blackfeet Indian," who, Reilly insisted, despite his objections to the KC Chiefs name, would have "a hard time" see the team and its traditions as dehumanizing: "It's an issue that shouldn't be an issue, not with all of the problems we've got in this country." And the columnist expressed concern about how to break the news to American Indian high school students "that the 'Redskins' name they wear proudly across their chests is insulting them." Drawing on a personal anecdote, an outdated and flawed poll taken nearly a decade earlier, and three high schools in Indian Country, Reilly concluded that this is not an Indian problem: "White America has spoken. You aren't offended, so we'll be offended for you.... Trust us. We know what's best. We'll take this away for your own good, and put up barriers that protect you from ever being harmed again. Kind of like a reservation." For Reilly, it is really quite simple: some Native Americans have expressed a counterintuitive and supportive opinion; therefore, the argument against the name has no foundation or no standing, and the status quo should prevail.[1]

Of course, as Dave Zirin highlights, Reilly overstates his case, and he does so by creating a straw dog: while some in the media have argued against the team name, even indicating they will no longer use it, on the whole, writers, radio hosts, and analysts, along with major television networks, continue to support it and profit from it; opposition to the team and its traditions dates back more than forty years and has its origins in actual Native American political leaders, advocacy groups, and tribes. Furthermore, according to Zirin, Reilly misreads history. Like many Americans, he forgets the history of dislocation, dispossession, removal, and ethnic cleansing, reminding readers that "if your team name exists only because there was a genocide, then you need a new team name." To this we might add that his rhetorical effort to project anti-Indianism onto white critics misconstrues the history of anti-Indian racism and, through a weird inversion, seeks to render those working to empower indigenous people and decolonize U.S. society as the source of harm.[2]

To make his case, Reilly misrepresented his father-in-law, Bob Burns, and his position on the R*dskins. After the publication of the column, Burns wrote a rejoinder, noting his "passionate" commitment to "the true history of how our people have overcome the trauma of 150 years of attempts to erase the Blackfeet people." He described how accepted accounts of the past often misremember, bestowing honor where it does not belong and forgetting who and what are important. He spoke with pride of his efforts to preserve and present more faithful renderings of the Blackfeet. Not surprisingly, Burns expressed "dismay" at how his son-in-law represented him and his views, suggesting Reilly's account "portrayed him as an 'Uncle Tom' in support of this racial slur." As he noted, "What I actually said is that 'it's silly in this day and age that this should even be a battle—if the name offends someone, change it.' He failed to include my comments that the term 'redskins' demeans Indians, and historically is insulting and offensive, and that I firmly believe the Washington Redskins should change their name." Indeed, for Burns, the word embodies the "colonial times when our men, women, and children were hunted" and informs the "racism and hatred our people continue to experience."[3]

Clearly, Reilly manipulated Burns for his own ends, exploiting his words to advance a contradictory position. One might conclude that he abused his authority and leveraged his privilege with reckless disregard: he spoke for Native Americas. His writing and his whiteness made their words meaningful. His editors turned a blind eye, neither clearing a space for Native Americans to express themselves nor offering an apology or retraction when they did so in another outlet.

In this chapter, I turn my attention to American Indian opinion. I offer an overview of its diversity and interpret the ways it is used and misused. It is particularly important to understand both of these elements in order to establish a full understanding of the ongoing controversy and its significance. For many, opinion has become the single most important measure of the struggles surrounding the DC NFL franchise and its use of Indianness. It has come to trump all other dimensions. Like Reilly, many find the seeming contradictions posed by supportive voices and the apparent equivalent uses to simultaneously justify the team and its tradition and undermine movement against them. To get at these themes, I revisit territory explored in my analyses of sentiment and simulation. Here I am especially interested in the manipulation of Indianness to create meaningful and manageable endorsements of the team. Whereas simulation emphasizes the ways in which the organization and its supporters fake, buy, and otherwise counterfeit indigeneity in support of the team and its traditions and sentiment focuses attention on the affective attachments of white constituencies, here I concern myself with Native American attitudes and what people make of and do with them. In marked contrast to simulation, which plays with Indianness and trades on manufactured authenticity, opinion wraps itself in fact and acts serious.

I begin with an overview of the complex, counterintuitive, and even contradictory attitudes expressed by American Indians on the team and its traditions. On this foundation, I provide a critical review of opinion polls on the subject, detailing the oft-cited 2004 National Annenberg Election Survey and its problems as well as more recent efforts to gauge Native

American attitudes. Next I consider, in turn, the search for equivalent uses of R*dskins* in Indian Country, the tendency to trivialize oppositional perspectives, and the architecture of silence that works to undermines dialogue and dissent.

It's Complicated

Walter "Blackie" Wetzel, former chairman of the Blackfeet Nation and onetime president of the National Congress of American Indians (1960–64), had a great fondness for the Washington professional football team. In fact, according to his son, "He loved every part of the Redskins." Wetzel, as discussed in chapter 1, played an instrumental role in developing the logo emblazoned on the team's helmet. Like his dad, Donald Wetzel Sr. takes great pride in the team, deepened because of his family's connection to it; however, Blackie's nephew Bill Wetzel disagrees with his uncle and his grandfather, believing that "anybody still fighting for it, they're on the wrong side of history." Not surprisingly, the two have decidedly different understandings of how connecting Blackie to the team name affects his legacy. The former sees it as an honor, while the latter thinks Blackie's association with a slur denigrates his memory.[4]

Although the Wetzels have a unique association with the team and its history, one the franchise regularly highlights, in some ways they remind us how complicated popular opinion on the subject is, even, or perhaps especially, among American Indians. Indeed, Native Americans are not of one mind on the team name or sports mascots more generally. Some American Indians embrace and support the team and its traditions. This seeming contradiction delights the franchise and its fans, who employ it to deflect criticism and defend their ongoing use of Indianness, while perplexing pundits and scholars, who often seem unsure what to make of it. So, are there Native Americans who support the name? Yes. A better questions might be, how could there not be some American Indians who support it? Some are fans; some don't think about; some have a family connection; some feel honored. More importantly, in a society that offers so few images of American Indians, that so regularly and thoroughly communicates anti-Indianism, and that has so fully erased living indigenous people in favor of imaginary versions of them, why wouldn't some number of Native Americans come to accept, endorse, and even identify with the Washington professional football team and its traditions? It is neither the first, deepest, or only contradiction of its kind. For instance, American Indians, despite their history, have long had one of the highest rates of enlistment in the U.S. military and routinely express a high level of patriotism.

Feelings and opinions on the matter in Indian Country, then, not only vary but display pronounced complexity and palpable slipperiness. As Bill Wetzel observed, "The best you can say is many indigenous people and tribes are either indifferent or apathetic to it, but that's not the same as being for it. . . . And even those people who are for it wouldn't allow anybody to come up to them or their children and address them by that name. They'd be liars if they said so." On both sides of the struggle over the team name one finds selectiveness, with individuals and organizations highlighting people who agree with them. The use of opinion, moreover, often has tended to be overly simplistic, avoiding nuance, history, and context while flattening the experiential elements that shape how and why people take or abdicate positions, whether that be to defend or oppose the use of Indianness by the franchise or to remain apathetic on the subject.[5] Such opinions do not fit into the neat boxes or narrow agendas of dominant society.

Three examples from Pine Ridge Reservation speak to the complexities and contradictions of opinion on the subject. Elaine Yellow Horse, when asked about the name, remarked, "I don't really worry about it. . . . There are just so many other things that I need to worry about before that." Similarly, her fellow student and tribal member John Reddy said when asked whether the team was offensive, "Ehh, whatever." The journalist Joe Flood pressed Reddy to consider a less abstract, "real-world situation . . . what he would think if a stranger showed up to his house and called his little brothers and sisters 'cute little redskins.' His answer: 'Well, I'd fuck him up.'"[6]

In contrast with Yellow Horse and Reddy, who have spent most of their lives on the reservation, Sara Jumping Eagle spent years away from her tribal community training to be a doctor. She has a decidedly different take on the subject.

I graduated from the University of North Dakota in 1993 and was president of the UND Indian Association for two years. . . . Their mascot is the Fighting Sioux. When I went to college I didn't know much about the issue at all, I was just 17 years old. But then I went to a hockey game and there were people there, drunk and dressed up in feathers, their faces painted up, acting ridiculous. During the homecoming parade, [the UND Indian Association] had a float and students dressed in Native regalia. During the parade, the float behind us started doing the Tomahawk Chop and playing that *duhm-duhm-duhm-duhm* war drum, [people] yelling, "Go back to the rez"

Jumping Eagle added that "she'd like to see the end of 'Redskins'—and Indians, and Braves, and all other Native-themed mascots."[7] Flood suggests that exposure to anti-Indian racism plays a crucial difference in the opinions formed by Yellow Horse, Reddy, and Jumping Eagle.

Drawing on her own experience, Adrienne Keene (Cherokee) reaches a similar, if more nuanced, conclusion:

The reason some folks on the rez don't care as much (which is also a dangerous stereotype, cause many of the lead activists in this, Amanda Blackhorse included, live on or near reservations) is because they aren't faced with all these examples I showed above on a daily basis. We in the city have to walk down the street and encounter this racism everyday, and we're separated from the counter-narratives and counter-representations that would surround us if we lived in our communities. Many of us don't have easy access to our ceremonies, our aunties, our grandmas, our land—the things that show us we aren't the harmful stereotypes we see at the sports arena. Folks on the rez do have those counter-examples, surrounding them at all times. Additionally, if you only interact with other Native people everyday, no one is going to call you a redsk*n as a slur.[8]

The relentless presence of anti-Indian racism, paired with more limited access to cultural resources and role models, fosters the development of a deeper awareness of its forms and impacts. While I think Keene and Flood are right that the ubiquity of anti-Indianism plays an important role in the emergence and articulation of critical attitudes for some, if this were the only factor, one would expect a larger number of American Indians to be more vocal in opposition to the team and its traditions. In other words, as I think they both would agree, it's complicated.

By the Numbers

Too often, in spite of these complexities, media coverage and public discourse reduce the controversy surrounding the Washington professional football team to measures of opinion. In the face of a charged ethical and political issue, polling offers an apparently objective, seemingly scientific, highly manageable index of how people feel, seemingly illuminating a clear course of action for policy makers, gatekeepers, and institutions. Counting and calculation largely replace discussions of history and racism. Consequently, critical thinking and moral reflection get lost in formulaic questions—do you believe the team should change its name?—which oversimplify complex issues and reinforce commonsense understanding of them. Oddly, the importance of polling to media and politics has risen precisely as the public has shifted away from landlines and their willingness to participate has continued to plummet. Nevertheless, surveys offer the promise of snapshots of public opinion, seemingly simple and straightforward statements of the facts.

To date, most polling has demonstrated wide public endorsement for the name of the Washington professional football team. In many respects, this is not surprising, particularly in light of my examination of history, racism, and sentiment. In a previous study, my colleagues and I found three patterns in our review of early surveys: "(a) EuroAmericans are more likely than Native Americans to support Native American mascots; (b) Native Americans do not agree about mascots, and some endorse them; and (c) population, techniques, questions asked, and so on have a profound effect on the findings. While survey results have varied, these patterns remain constant."[9] The majority of the public continues to support the team name, but over the past two decades that support has declined noticeably. A survey taken during the lead-up to the 1992 Super Bowl showed 89 percent of the public favored the team name; in 2014 it had dropped to 71 percent.[10] At the same time, although a majority of the public do not believe the team should change its name, the numbers have declined over the past fifteen years: while 88 percent objected to change in 1998, by 2014 only 60 percent held the same opinion.[11] The opinions of active NFL players virtually match those of the public as well.[12] Add to this noticeable changes in attitudes toward the word R*dskins: 59 percent of Americans understand why the term is offensive and 80 percent of Americans would not say it to an American Indian's face.[13]

While a shift appears to have happened, it is unclear at this writing whether the trend will intensify as more people sour on the team name or if it is sustainable and of lasting significance. It does seem that public opinion may be reaching a tipping point of sorts. In discussing his study of attitudes toward the team name in 1998, which suggested that 80.6 percent of DC-area residents and 88 percent of Americans supported the name and did not think it should be changed, Lee Seligman concluded,

> Simply put, the general public "just doesn't get it" with respect to these team names. Especially since actual Indians are a virtually invisible minority for most Americans, stereotypical images of Native Americans have long been widespread in American popular culture. As a consequence, a name like "Redskins" seems unlikely to become a source of widespread public outrage—far less likely than would be the case if a team had an unflattering name (or any name at all) signifying, say, blacks, Asians, or Jews. Many white Americans who understand that terms like "nigger" and "spic" are derogatory and who even know something about the history of such terms, may not recognize "redskin" as a derogatory term.[14]

Shifting attitudes toward the term and an increasing recognition of its derogatory content may be at the heart of the ongoing shift in public opinion and may prove central to the fate of the team name in the future.

Counting on American Indian Opinion

American Indian opinion has an especially important place in the ongoing struggles over the use of Indianness by the Washington professional football team. This derives in part from efforts to limit the terms of the struggle to personal, affective, and individual dimensions—is the team name offensive?—and to ways in which opinion on that question has been manipulated by the franchise, fans, the league, and the media. And while there have been numerous surveys of Native Americans, one poll has proven particularly instrumental in shaping perceptions of the issues and framing the debate. The 2004 National Annenberg Election Survey has come to dominate public discourse and to anchor the defense of the team and its traditions.[15] The franchise routinely invokes it, as Dan Snyder did in his letter to fans in October 2013, and the league has also relied on it to buttress its position.[16]

The telephone survey, conducted over the course of twelve months (October 2003 through September 2004), sought to gauge public opinion on a range of issues. It included one question on the team name and posed it to 768 self-identified American Indians. It trumpeted the findings in a sensational press release headlined "Most Indians Say Name of Washington 'Redskins' Is Acceptable While 9 Percent Call It Offensive, Annenberg Data Show."[17] Not surprisingly, those who support the team love this survey. Its findings would seem to render the controversy a nonissue; however, the survey has been subjected to much criticism since its release. It was problematic at the time and its continued use is even more problematic today.

The design and execution of the survey were flawed. Natasha Dhillon and her colleagues have summarize some of its key weaknesses, calling into question its validity and utility: "The reported results of this survey consist of (1) a single confusing question, (2) asked without context or reflection, (3) of people who self-identify as 'Native American or Indian,' (4) via a mode of communication less than half of Native Americans on reservations at the time were using." And it based its findings on a small sample size: less than 0.5 percent of the Native American population in the United States at the time.[18]

The question was confusing at best. It read, "The professional football team in Washington calls itself the Washington Redskins. As a Native American, do you find that name offensive or doesn't it bother you?" Wait, what? It is actually asking two things at once. "Do you find that name offensive OR doesn't it bother you. The two aren't mutually exclusive. You can find it offensive and 'not be bothered by it,' which . . . many people would go for, because they don't want to be seen as 'weak' or being bothered by an image."[19] At the very least, the competing answers would seem to render the finding unusable and meaningless.

Even if one can find merit in the flawed survey, one wonders about its continued relevance. One cannot make good policy now based on old data; one cannot understand how people feel today with polling results that are over a decade old. Indeed, one wonders whether there is any other issue of public importance in which it would be deemed good leadership or sound management to rely on data that is so dated; furthermore, in what other domain would journalists repeat without question the circulation of evidence of this nature? Is the suggestion that Native American attitudes are fixed and unchanging? Such a sentiment might be in keeping with the timelessness wrongly ascribed to indigenous cultures. "Like other surveys, that one reflected a moment in time," Annenberg director of communications Michael Rozansky has said. "If people are interested in knowing what Native Americans think of the issue today, it'd be best for someone to conduct a new survey to find out."[20] Perhaps such an endeavor would prove too costly or challenging, for after all, collecting sound data would take work and dedication. Maybe most Americans do not care what American Indians actually think. Or is the issue more self-serving? The poll results satisfy supporters and effectively quash debate. In fact, the finding not only endorses the legitimacy of the team name and suggests there in no need for further discussion, it also enable supporters to speak for American Indians, effectively silencing and marginalizing critics. "While Snyder speaks for himself, the 'scientific fact' of the Annenberg finding replaces the 'voice' of American Indians."[21]

Demanding a Recount

Of course, surveys of American Indian opinion on this subject neither started nor stopped in 2004. And while mainstream polls have shown support for the team name among Native Americans, these numbers are always smaller than the support shown by other racial and ethnic groups and never approach the figures in the 2004 Annenberg survey.[22] Two recent efforts to gauge American Indian opinion merit brief mention here. The sociologist James Fenelon (Lakota/Dakota) has undertaken a project in which he verifies the ethnic or racial claims of participants, often collecting data at powwows. Although his numbers are still small, they show that 67 percent of American Indians find the team name to be racist and 68 percent find it to be disrespectful.[23] Setting aside survey methodology, Adrienne Keene has used her blog to capture opinion in Indian Country. Specifically, she has asked Native Americans opposed to the name to sign a Google Doc online. As of March 31, 2015, nearly fifty-seven hundred American Indians had signed it.[24] Although her project was designed to counter the 2004 poll, she was more interested in representativeness and inclusiveness than randomness and objectivity. As she said in an interview, "It's a collective voice, thousands of indigenous peoples saying, 'We're here, and we care about the ways we are represented.'"[25]

Limits of Polling

A survey, no matter how reliable it may be, cannot settle the key questions. Relying on the logic of polling may prompt us to look to counting for the appropriate resolution. In a recent essay, the football analyst Ross Tucker fell into this line of thinking: "How many people need to be offended for a change to be made? Maybe more to the point, what percentage of the group in question, in this case Native Americans, needs to be offended before action should be taken? Is it more than 50 percent? Is it at least a solid 25 percent? Is just 1-to-5 percent enough for a change to be made?"[26] Such queries misunderstand the actual problem. "Neither the Washington team nor its owner appears to understand that there is no poll or financial transaction that can solve a moral problem."[27] Or, as my colleagues and I have phrased it,

> Of course, the greatest error of all may be the idea that polling people on these issues is appropriate from the outset. It suggests that popular opinion can settle troubling questions about prejudice, power, and privilege. Hence, if the majority support mascots (or racial segregation or sexual harassment), then such symbols and practices are acceptable. And worse . . . if members of marginalized and oppressed groups consent to their marginalization and oppression, then everything is OK. If most Blacks supported racial segregation, would it be a justifiable

system? If most women saw nothing wrong with sexual harassment, would we not still want to suggest such actions were reprehensible and problematic?[28]

Social justice, human rights, and individual dignity cannot be addressed through a survey question or conveyed by the results of a poll. They demand an acknowledgement of difference, a willingness to come to terms with the past, and a recognition of shared humanity.

Invoking American Indian High Schools

A recent study has found sixty-two high schools in twenty-two states that refer to their sport teams as the R*dskins; of these, three have majority Native American student bodies.[29] The franchise itself has pointed to high schools to defend its own continued use of the name. In fact, it posted an article on its website at roughly the same moment Cooperstown (NY) High School debated and ultimately decided to end its use of its R*dskin mascot. The articles points to several dozen schools with such a moniker, noting the deep connection between athletes and mascot at these high schools and in the NFL. It encapsulates the shared sentiments by quoting George Hemming, athletic director at Coshocton (OH) High School, "We are very proud of our athletic teams and very proud to be called Redskins!"[30]

American Indian high schools that share a team name with the Washington professional football franchise have provided supporters with a particularly powerful and problematic way to inject indigenous opinion into the ongoing controversy over the team and its traditions. The seeming contradiction posed by schools that at once serve primarily American Indian students and have a mascot identified as a slur by American Indian activists and organizations has proven too tantalizing for fans, journalists, and even the franchise to ignore. As such, it is worth considering what to make of such institutions and the ways that they get used in the larger struggle.

American Indian high schools in Kingston, Oklahoma; Red Mesa, Arizona; and Wellpinit, Washington, all use *R*dskins* to refer to their sport teams. Each of these schools has a special regard for the team.

In Kingston, which serves primarily Chickasaw and Choctaw students, according to the English teacher Brett Hayes (Choctaw), "It's a name that honors the people"; or, in the words of Assistant School Superintendent Ron Whipkey, "It is a prideful thing."[31] In Wellpinit, student Brodie Ford notes, "We don't see it as a derogatory name."[32] And in Red Mesa, echoing these sentiments, Superintendent Tommie Yazzie declares, "I don't find it derogatory. It's a source of pride."[33] These small, rural communities exhibit complications as well. Chet Bluff in Wellpinit traces the origin of the team name to the taking of bloody scalps, while government teacher Wesley Cobb in Red Mesa finds it to be "a profoundly racist name."[34] Finally, none of these schools has courted the national spotlight and all would prefer not to be drawn into the controversy. "One thing that annoys me," says John Teters, registrar for the school district, "is that we're used as an excuse for this asinine process. You name it, Cleveland Indians, Washington Redskins, whenever those names come up, the school gets called. 'If you guys can do it, why can't we?' We're somehow used as a justification."[35] They find themselves put to use once more. Like so many elements of the team, supporters take and remake Indianness—imagery, culture, practice, identity—for their own ends, regardless of cost or context.

And Teters is exactly right about how they are being used: these three high schools are made to excuse or endorse the DC NFL franchise. They provide a false equivalence that says, if American Indians use this word and it is okay, then we can use it. Like them, we too take pride in our team, honor indigenous people, and seek to convey respect; so our use, like theirs, cannot be a slur, read as racist. This is a false equivalence, however. It is different for the R*dskins to be used as a brand worth billions of dollars and for it to be used by a small high school on a reservation. It is different for American Indians to name themselves and imagine themselves and for Euro-Americans to name them, imagine them, and speak for them. Just as all uses of *n*gger* are not the same, so too not all uses of *r*dskin* are the same. Context matters, who speaks to whom about what matters. Joe Flood nicely captures some of these differences: "The Washington Redskins aren't a reservation high school re-appropriating a slur. . . . They're a white-owned team in the seat of the government that waged war against Native Americans for decades, a franchise with a long history of racism and no discernible connection to any particular tribe or Native American cause."[36] Adrienne Keene gets deeper, reminding her readers that what is at stake is not simply the word but a broader constellation of relations and representations: "The name being a racial slur is only one part of why the mascot needs to change. The disrespect, racism, and dishonor come from not just the name, but when you have non-Natives representing 'Native' cultures through the mascots, and opponents of the teams vilifying and mocking Native cultures in the name of sports rivalry." Moreover, speaking about Red Mesa specifically, she continues, explaining that one will not find dehumanizing stereotyping and anti-Indian racism there because "the audience, team, and school is nearly 100% Native. . . . They would be dishonoring and disrespecting their communities and relatives. The name doesn't have the same weight and urgency, or any weight and urgency, because, to them, it's self-referential. They have control over the name and image, they have the right and power to do with it what they want. If they want to change it, they can. Clearly, not the case outside of the Navajo Nation." This last point is crucial, highlighting a fundamental difference. Not only are the Navajos at Red Mesa High School creating images of themselves for themselves, but they have the power to define and determine themselves. Sovereignty and self-determination must inform how we interpret these schools. Significantly, American Indians cannot exercise autonomy or authority in relation to the Washington professional football team. In fact, the owner ignores those Native Americans who do not agree with him, speaks for them, and reminds them of their impotence in the face of anti-Indian racism, while fans routinely appropriate and invent Indianness for their amusement at games. Appreciating these power dynamics, Keene explains, "I don't think that any school should have the Redsk*ns as a mascot. But I respect the decision of the Red Mesa school officials, given the context of their school."[37]

Get Real

In announcing the establishment of OAF, Daniel Snyder suggested that the new philanthropic organization would address real concerns and pressing problems identified by American Indians, stating in part, "They have genuine issues they truly are worried about, and our team's name is not one of them."[38] In doing so, he sought to tell the general public which issues mattered, delimiting which topics Native Americans could speak about and mobilize against. Yet he excluded the team name. In a similar fashion, supporters will often tell critics of the franchise essentially to "get real," redirecting their opinions and energies to what supporters will often describe as bigger issues in Indian Country. In the process, they seek to trivialize the connection between representation, racism, and the real world, and thus they let the team off the hook while marginalizing oppositional opinion by claiming opponents' efforts are misguided, insensitive, and insincere. This strategy is yet another variation of speaking for indigenous people, a form that goes one step further by telling them what to care about.

Not surprisingly, many American Indians hear in this argument an arrogant and unreflective reiteration of the key principles of U.S. settler colonialism. Adrienne Keene, for instance, notes,

Yes, unequivocally, we have big things to tackle in Indian Country. We have pressing and dire issues that are taking the lives of our men and women everyday, and I am in absolutely no way minimizing this reality. But we also live in a state of active colonialism. In order to justify the genocide against Native peoples in this country, we must be painted as inferior—that's the colonial game. These images continue that process. The dominant culture therefore continues to marginalize our peoples, to ignore and erase our existence. We are taught everyday, explicitly in classrooms, and implicitly through messages from the media, that our cultures are something of the past, something that exists in negative contrast to "western" values, and something that can be commodified and enjoyed by anyone with $20 to buy a cheap plastic headdress. These stereotypical images like mascots feed into this ongoing cycle, and until we demand more, our contemporary existence (and therefore the "real" problems in Indian Country) simply doesn't exist in the minds of the dominant culture.[39]

Keene forcefully resists the denial of anti-Indianism as an anchor of efforts to distract and distort. She embeds the team name, along with other pressing problems, in a larger context of exploitation and exclusion, misrepresentation and miseducation, and appropriation and eradication. To deal with the other issues facing indigenous peoples in the United States, then, she argues, one must confront and change anti-Indian racism, as embodied by the Washington professional football team.

Dallas Goldtooth (Mdewakanton Dakota and Diné), a member of the 1491s and an activist engaged with several ongoing political struggles, concurs with Keene, offering a fuller appraisal of why so many in Indian Country fight the team name and simultaneously work to address other issues to better the lives of people in their tribes and communities:

> Many of us who are against the Red*kins name, also happen to be tribal leaders, ceremonial leaders, youth advocates, substance abuse counselors, professors, language revitalization teachers, community organizers against domestic violence, drugs, and environmental injustice—we are lawyers, tribal judges, tribal college presidents, doctors, athletes, writers, business owners, freelance journalists, work in the White House, artists, musicians, filmmakers, parents, and overall just badass native leaders who work day by day to make our communities healthier, stronger environments.
>
> And we still make derogatory mascots and imagery a priority because simply, its just another part of the work towards a better world.[40]

While supporters want to decontextualize the team and its traditions, disconnect interwoven issues and their origins, and dismiss uncomfortable opinions, opponents emphasize the importance of history and context, insist on intersectional approaches on multiple fronts, and refuse to be silenced.

Silence

While supporters of the teams and its tradition regularly highlight American Indian attitudes that they find pleasing, especially as measured by polls and demonstrated by their adoption of the embattled name, they also silence more critical perspectives. While they do not operate as a cabal actively censoring thought, their control of media and politics works to marginalize oppositional opinions.

In Virginia, for instance, American Indians do not feel it safe to speak their minds. At a powwow in 2014, reporters found opinions ranging from complacency—"I'm so used to Washington being called the Redskins, it doesn't offend me"—to critique—"The facts are it's a derogatory term." These attitudes register readings of the ubiquity of anti-Indianism, a structure of feeling that informs state politics as well, placing Native Americans in a precarious spot. "Who does most of Virginia root for?" Reggie Tupponce (Upper Mattaponi) asked rhetorically. "You can make a lot of enemies very quickly. If you look at our legislature, they have come out and done a caucus to support [the name] and a lot of native issues need support from the government." In other words, speaking out against the team and anti-Indian racism would put American Indians at odds with many in the state and their elected officials. A desire to maintain good relations and worries over punitive action undoubtedly quiet dissent in the state.[41]

Similarly, despite the active presence of news outlets like the *Washington Post* and the *City Paper*, the DC media market might be described as chilling. Snyder himself, through Red Zebra Broadcasting, owns six radio stations, including WTEM, which has a sports-talk format.[42] And other media providers have an interest in appearing neutral, that is, in not angering the franchise. It is not shocking to learn that two radio stations refused to run ads by an organization critical of the team name.[43] Silencing dissent is, of course, in these stations' best interest. To do otherwise threatens to alienate the team and the NFL more generally as well as their audience. The stations have glossed this as an effort to promote balanced discourse, guided by principles of fairness meant to protect their audience and open discussion of the issue. For its part, the NFL has opted to muzzle critics as well. It refused to run a commercial about the team name produced by the National Congress of American Indians during the 2014 Super Bowl.[44] It justified this decision by pointing to a long-standing prohibition of activist ads. Subsequent new coverage of the rejection ensured many Americans watched the spot; nevertheless, by silencing dissent, the league not only maintained control of its message and brand, but it also underscored its continued endorsement of anti-Indian racism. Another interesting measure of silencing can be found in a recent poll of NFL players' attitudes on a broad range of issues, including whether the DC franchise should change its name. While the players' views corresponded with those of the general public, of the fifty-one Washington players surveyed, twenty-four opted not to answer and twenty-six supported keeping the name.[45] A near majority felt they could not answer, and all but one of those who did reply endorsed the team, a striking deviation from the 58 percent average support for the question. In the end, much like Reilly and Snyder, who silence indigenous people by speaking for them, the radio stations and the league silence them, albeit in a more overt and direct fashion, by refusing to let the public hear their perspectives.

Ending the Misuse of Opinion

Too often, Native American opinion matters only because of how whites might use it. It cannot be heard in its original voice, terms, or context. For the franchise and its fans, the attitudes and perspectives of indigenous people have value to the extent they enhance the defense of the team. From surveys to schools, this often has meant simplifying, misrepresenting, and speaking for American Indians. Such efforts repeat a long-standing pattern of taking and remaking Indians for white ends, a process that typically has involved accentuation and erasure.

American Indian opinions about the Washington professional football team and its traditions are complicated, at times counterintuitive, and even contradictory. They do not nicely fit external agendas or neatly fit into simple binaries. A full understanding of the ongoing controversy comes into view only when we recognize the diverse perspectives in Indian Country, the conditions that rise to them, and the selective use and misuse of them. For many fans and pundits, the more complex the issue gets, the more they push to simplify it.

This may be what Rick Reilly was up to in his column. A charitable reading might suggest he was trying to resolve contradictions, manage complexity, and otherwise find a comfortable way to make sense of competing narratives. If I were his editor, I would have asked him to return to a piece he wrote nearly a quarter century ago. In it, Reilly troubled the increasingly intense debate over the DC NFL franchise; he wrote a column condemning American Indian mascots, wondering aloud, "Why are we still stuck with antiques of that old racism—the Washington Redskins and the Cleveland Indian?" In this piece, Reilly expressed a keen understanding of anti-Indianism: "Early white settlers regarded Indians as savages and animals, not a race of people. Subsequent generations of children have been permitted to reduce Indians to playground characters." He knows most fans today do not "mean any harm by their actions, Nobody does. But that doesn't mean harm isn't done."[46] Perhaps with his own sage insights from the past he would have recognized the dangers of misusing American Indian opinion and the possibility of combating anti-Indian racism while fostering respect for the diverse perspectives alive in Indian Country.

Change

10

In December 2014 the National Congress of American Indians launched a Kickstarter campaign designed to raise money to fund a commercial spot to coincide with the upcoming Super Bowl. While the organization hoped to place the ad on television during the game, it also hoped the ad, like a previous video, would go viral even if not aired, educating the broader public, prompting further dialogue in the media, and energizing activists. The campaign, in keeping with conventions of crowdsourcing, offered a stepped incentive program, in which donations were tied to specific rewards. For instance, gifts of thirty dollars would receive "a t-shirt in Washington colors stating either 'REPLACE,' 'RENAME,' or 'RETHINK,' and your name called out on our website." In the space of a month, the initiative had exceeded its goal, raising more than $22,000.[1]

When measured against the profits of the franchise or the league, this sum appears minuscule. It thus nicely illustrates the asymmetrical struggle to foster change. At the same time, it underscores the vitality, creativity, and diversity of opposition to the team and its traditions, which has emerged as a multifaceted movement, knitting together activists and fans to form a broad multiethnic coalition, rooted in indigenous communities and organizations, that has drawn on an array of strategies, including litigation, game day protests, social media, and grassroots networking. Moreover, the thematic pillars of the campaign, as represented in the t-shirts distributed to donors, point to the key objectives of the movement and core features of broader public conversations about change: rethink, rename, and replace. The push for change, in the NCAI initiative, in the larger movement, and as reflected in everyday engagements, cannot be understood as merely employing forms of negation. Instead, the various strands unite around efforts to rebuild community, reclaim dignity, and renovate accepted understandings, opening spaces to reimagine the self and the other, the past and the future, and recognition and belonging.

In this chapter I explore various facets of ongoing efforts to change the Washington professional football team and its traditions. I begin with a brief discussion of indigenous activism before turning to fans who have been moved to resist and even remake the face of the franchise. Next, I consider the array of alternative names proposed in recent years, probing their deeper significance for understanding of the core issues. Finally, I examine the fiscal costs and rewards for the franchise associated with any alteration to its name and logo. Throughout, I think critically about how and why individuals and organizations call on the team, the league, and the public to rethink, rename, and replace.

Rethink

The impetus for change has come from Indian Country and dates back more than four decades. Indeed, the efforts of countless Native Americans constitute the inspiration and foundation of the movement against the Washington professional football franchise. My account of the team and its traditions owes a deep debt to these individuals and organizations and my interpretation thus far has given voice to their interpretations, the context giving life to them, and their larger significance. Thus in this section I will not and cannot offer a full history of activism, which frankly deserves a dedicated monograph of its own. Instead, here I will provide a brief review of the recent intensification of opposition.

The struggle against the moniker today might be best understood as the fourth phase of activism. The first, described in the chapter on origin stories, had its roots in the broader indigenous renaissance of the 1960s, the emergence of Red Power, and diverse freedom struggles, particularly the civil rights movement. It was given its clearest expression in the demands for change in 1972, and it prompted the organization to make minor alterations, including changes in the lyrics of the fight song. Next, after a lull, efforts quickened again in the late 1980s and early 1990s in conjunction with a resurgent push across the country to retire mascots. Protests and rallies at RFK Stadium during this period, according to Charlene Teters (Spokane), who helped organize them, were usually small, ranging from twenty to fifty demonstrators, and arguably climaxed in demonstrations at Super Bowl XXVI in Minneapolis (see figure 9).[2] In the third phase, initiated in *Harjo et al. v. Pro-Football, Inc.*, the movement shifted tactics to the court room, pushing to the end the anti-Indianism associated with the name by stripping the team of its trademarks. The most recent incarnation of activism begins with the filing of *Blackhorse et al. v Pro-Football, Inc.*, which shared arguments and objectives with the previous case and which has in turn opened new forms of opposition while invigorating a new generation of activists.

The current moment of activism is arguably the most visible and influential to date, distinguished by novel uses of media, strategies, and networks. Resistance now manifests itself on multiple fronts: in demonstrations outside of games at FedEx Field and across the country; in the courtroom; in legislative action at the state, local, and federal levels; at academic conferences and political symposia; within traditional media outlets; and across social media. It is a national movement; it is pan-Indian, intertribal, and multiethnic. It has firm institutional footing across Indian Country, including in its longtime opponents the National Congress of American Indians, the National Museum of the American Indian, and the Oneida Indian Nation. They, in turn, have encouraged and even spawned new oppositional groups, including Change the Mascot and Not Your Mascots. Together they have anchored a more sustainable movement that can more persistently, systematically, and effectively intervene and incite, matching the franchise organizationally in placing its message in conventional media outlets. Arguably more importantly, the current iteration of the movement has masterfully used social media to advance the cause. It has made this virtual and viral space indigenous: it has organized online, recruiting new members, linking like-minded individuals, and diffusing its message widely; it has pushed back with websites and Twitterstorms targeting the franchise; it has raised money and consciousness; and it has created and disseminated videos, many of which have gone viral. And thanks in large part to research associated with litigation and a rising tide of scholarship, especially into the psychological, historical, and cultural dimensions, it has leveraged a powerful empirical case against the moniker that complements and extends its forceful moral argument against it. Throughout, the present phase of the movement remains committed to the ideals that gave life to opposition more than forty years ago, challenging anti-Indianism embodied by the team and its traditions, pushing for change to alleviate it, and showing determination to reclaim and revalue indigeneity.

For the past quarter century, the driving force and unwavering anchor of opposition to the team and its traditions has been Suzan Shown Harjo (Cheyenne and Hodulgee Muscogee), a recipient of the Presidential Medal of Freedom in 2014. Described by *Business Insider* as the "Native American grandmother who beat the Redskins," she has played a leading role in efforts to change the name, first through her leadership of NCAI and later as president of the Morning Star Institute. She had a decisive hand in the shift to the courtroom, a strategy that has proven key to unsettling the organization and calling into question racial entitlement more generally. Her regular columns in *Indian Country Today*, moreover, have nurtured community and given hope while encouraging scholars—like myself and Linda Waggoner, to name only two—to ask questions about the history and significance of the moniker. Finally, she was the guiding force behind the symposium on "Racist Stereotypes and Cultural Appropriation in American Sports" held at the National Museum of the American Indian in February 2013. This gathering of activists, journalists, policy makers, and academics focused a spotlight on the team and sparked intense public interest. In fact, to my mind, it is the catalyst of much of the recent push for change.[3]

Refashion

Preston Wells (Choctaw) gives voice to many of the fundamental insights and central arguments of indigenous activism in his poem "If the Indian Mascot Could Speak." Claiming the voice of the silenced icon and commodified totem, he speaks against the force of stereotypes and the enduring power of anti-Indianism. His reflections linger on branding and consumption, stressing their deep connections to the history of settler colonialism and its manifestation today in white privilege.

> You'll take off that shirt at day's end, but when will it be my turn?
> It's hard to breathe on cotton. Just another form of relocation.
> Throw me in with your dirty clothes, do your laundry.
> Wash me good enough to wipe my bravery weak.

Focusing on the familiar t-shirt as trophy case, he testifies to the manner in which such images distort, dislocate, disempower, and dehumanize. Significantly, the NCAI Kickstarter campaign seized upon the t-shirt as well, using the familiar color scheme of the Washington professional football team to question its legitimacy and call for change.[4]

Increasingly, poems and protests like these speak to fans of the franchise, prompting them to rethink the name, logo, and rituals associated with them. In December 2014 the former *Washington Post* columnist Mike Wise reported receiving emails from six hundred team boosters who had come to support changing the name. This number points to growing discontent among the die-hard fans. The messages Wise received included ones from people who described themselves as "old-school" and "lifelong" fans, who learned the fight song at the age of two, who watch every week, even after they moved away from DC, and who named a pet after running back John Riggins. Tried and true supporters, who have concluded that "the name needs to change," who cannot in "good conscience keep" using it, and who will be "distraught and upset" to see it change but admit that, "on a human level, it would make sense to me."[5] Such fans, too, often turn to branded garments to express their discomfort with the team and its traditions. For instance, longtime fan Jenn Rubenstein cancelled her season tickets after the 2013 season and "has since boycotted team gear." Similarly, Ben Becker has gone for more than a decade without purchasing team apparel and "he won't dress his sports-loving 3-year-old son in anything that prominently displays the name or logo," because, he explains, "I feel very uncomfortable putting my little boy, who doesn't have a say in the matter, in a shirt with a big

Indian face on it." Likewise, Brent Sower, a third-generation fan who, like Dan Snyder, fondly recalls attending games as a youth, has not permitted his three children to wear clothes carrying the team name or logo, noting that as a fan, "It really leaves you in a conflicted space when you love a team but hate their name."[6]

It may be because of this ambivalence, if not open antipathy, which has become pervasive among the public, that sales of team gear have dropped. In late summer 2004, for example, when sales of NFL apparel rose by 3 percent, sales for the DC franchise fell by 35 percent. One might attribute this in part to poor play undercutting revenues, but the gap is so significant that something more complex must be at play. Likely factors include fans finding the mascot racist, not wanting to be labeled as racist, or wanting to avoid the controversy altogether.[7]

A smaller set of fans have not only refused to buy or wear team gear, they have actively sought to refashion it, in essence renouncing the name while declaring their affiliation with the team. Ian Washburn provides the most visible example of such reclamations in DC. A lifelong fan, he decided not simply to refuse to wear team merchandise but to remake it, retaining what he found most meaningful. "After his epiphany, Washburn found a manufacturer that makes custom patches in China. Over eight months, he spent about 100 hours working with the company to perfect the font and colors of cloth strips that said, simply, 'WASHINGTON.' He ordered 30 extra in case, some day, other fans wanted to use them. Total cost: more than $300."[8] The time and expense personally invested here underscore how much Washburn loves his team and hates its name. His actions and his repositioning of his fandom have put him odds with other fans, who take affront, and with members of his family, who continue to support the team. This practice mirrors the move to de-chief the Cleveland baseball team by removing Chief Wahoo from hats and shirts.[9] Refashioning one's allegiance, whether by renunciation or active redesign, is an individual act, which can be hidden. Even when such acts are publicly known, they do not constitute a collective movement. Consequently, the kind and quality of pressure they can bring to bear on the organization is limited as to their effectiveness in bringing about structural change.

Rebrand

Ian Washburn has declared, "All the Native themes are going to go. They need to go. . . . I want this cancer to go away. And it is a cancer."[10] Arguably, fans hold the key to recognizing the problem and pushing for initiatives designed to foster healing. To date, many of their efforts have been isolated, even invisible, but sustained indigenous activism has proven unsettling, and as a result, it has prompted renewed examinations of race and representation; forced some to interrogate history, identity, and community; and encouraged others together to create fan-based oppositional organizations.

Fans for a New Tradition brings together dedicated and die-hard supporters of the team who have reached the conclusion that it is time for a change. Its website hails others in a similar position: "We've rooted for the Washington football team our entire lives. . . . We bleed that *burgundy and gold*." Ye, they know there is a problem because they have "read the stories and followed the debate" and have developed an appreciation of "the challenges facing Native Americans." They have concluded, despite their allegiance to the team, that its moniker "is an offensive racial slur." Importantly, "once we were able to acknowledge this fact, we made personal changes: we stopped claiming to be able to see both sides of the issue, we stopped wearing our team gear, didn't renew our season tickets, stopped referring to the team by its name." They share much with the fans discussed above, and they may have made the same choices, but "Dan Snyder said '*NEVER*.'" His recalcitrance incited action, prompting them to seek out others and to establish the website, which they hope will "be a forum and center of gravity for [like-minded fans]." The website offers helpful summaries of key issues, responds to frequently asked questions and common misconceptions, highlights individuals and organizations who have taken a stand, and provides links to resources. In many ways, it works to counter how the team has framed the debate and defended the team name while also educating its visitors. Believing "it's time for a new tradition in Washington, D.C. It's time for Washington and NFL fans across the country to have their voices heard," they placed a petition on the website calling for the franchise to change the name. To their minds, this will "allow all Washington fans to root for their team proudly" and "show the world that NFL fans, and Americans in general, will take a stand against prejudice and racial bigotry," without jeopardizing the more important aspects of the team's history and tradition, including the team colors, the Super Bowl victories, or the fans' memories.[11]

Another set of fans has established Rebrand Washington Football: Fans for a New Name (RBF), a self-described "grassroots advocacy group" dedicated to changing the name through advocacy and engagement. Josh Silver, Shelia Miles, and Ian Washburn came together to create the group. Each had independently come to the conclusion that the logo and name pose fundamental problems and had devised means to cope with, or even challenge, them. According to Silver, "All three of us became increasingly uncomfortable with the racist legacy of the name. I remember hiding the logo and name in 1990 when I was a graduate student. Ian 'rebranded' all of his team gear." Silver also took the initiative to promote political change. "I decided to do something about this in 2013. In the fall of 2013, I first contacted my county council of Montgomery County MD. The County Executive decided that the county would not use the name of the team in official county communications. The District of Columbia Council passed a resolution urging Dan Snyder, the owner of the team, to change the name. We have asked other public and private sector organizations to adopt similar positions." Silver and Washburn subsequently collaborated on a robocall campaign, facilitated by Change the Mascot, that reached some ten thousand residents in the Washington DC area. After this, the two created RBF with Miles. The trio regularly collect signatures in the metro area and have plans for continued activism to put pressure on the organization.[12]

Replace

As the movement for change has gained increasing traction and momentum, it has prompted many fans and activists, including some graphic designers and comedians, to imagine a time and a team after the slur. In light of the growing disease, it is not a surprise to learn that a recent solicitation for new names and logo designs received more than eighteen hundred pitches from nearly 350 designers. Kevin Meringolo, managing editor of Hogs Haven, which cosponsored the contest with the *Washington Post*, saw in the level of interest and quality of contributions a desire among many to be "part of a new chapter."[13] The opportunity to reimagine the team, to condense that new chapter into a word or image, has inspired playful, critical, and serious proposals to replace the existing moniker. These often take a position on current events as they push the team and the public to move in novel directions. Not surprisingly, because of the charged tone of the ongoing controversy, many of the suggestion deliver biting commentary on the team, race, and cultural politics today. Many other ideas, however, offer more serious alternatives. Here I will not endeavor to catalog all of the new concepts or monikers devised. Instead, I will briefly examine four types of proposals, which might be described as parody, minimalism, new honors, and departures.

Parody

The ongoing controversy has afforded critics and comedians ample opportunity to poke fun at the team and its owner and to comment on broader social issues. Renaming the team, in particular, has encouraged playful and humorous interventions, ranging from the silly—the Washington Fredskins (with the face of the animated character Fred Flintstone replacing the Indian head in the logo)—to insider humor—the Washington Redshirts, referencing *Star Trek* and including a version of the Star Fleet Insignia—to political jabs, like the Washington Drones, a clear comment on the ongoing war on terror.[14] And some commentators have found in the name change an opportune means of amplifying the culture wars through humor, lampooning what they see as "political correctness" by suggesting names like the LGBT Muslim Communists or the Thinskins, or critiquing the agenda of President Obama by proposing the name the Washington Welfare, with the image of Obama, a bong, and food stamps for the logo.[15]

It also affords an occasion for biting satire directed at the franchise. For example, in response to a call from the franchise for indigenous art, members of the comedy troupe the 1491s redesignated the team the Foreskins and redesigned the team logo accordingly. Their work effectively questions the team and its appeal for art, while underscoring how offensive, denigrating, and inappropriate its current name and logo are.[16] An equally unsettling renaming can be found in the many iterations of Deadskins as a replacement for the current moniker. Typically such renderings deface the current logo, transforming it into a bloody victim of assault, and worse.[17] Such stark renderings remind us of the violence and death animating the term, which, in Danielle Miller's words, cast "genocide as entertainment." "As many football fans know 'Deadskins' is used as an insult to mock the Redsk*ns team after a loss, or it's even [used] just as an insult from rival team fans. Its one of the many reasons that Natives find the name to be offensive. Corporations such as the NFL are part of the reason such stereotypes and caricatures are normalized to the point that people categorize them as mere entertainment."[18] Reclaiming the name *Deadskins* and redeploying it in this form makes visible practices and power held under erasure, questioning the legitimacy of the team and its traditions.

At the same time, parody allows commentators to call out the whiteness of the team. The comedian Hari Kondabolu underscores the power of such satirical interventions. Using social media, he began a campaign to replace the current logo with a more representative figure: "If the NFL's Washington Football team won't change their name, then perhaps they could change their logo to a severely sunburned white person." He has asked people to tweet images and has posted a selection on a dedicated Tumblr page.[19] Through humor, Kondabolu and his contributors highlight the absurdity of white racism and direct attention to the core of the controversy, what I described earlier as the white problem. Clearly, his satire raises consciousness as it extract a good laugh, but it does not promulgate transformation.

Minimalism

Arguably, the easiest solution and the one that makes many most comfortable would be to keep a familiar reference for the team and redefine it. Such a maneuver would obviously allow change but restrict its importance.

For more than a quarter century, people have proposed that the team remain the Redskins, substituting a foodstuff, most often a variety of potato, but also a peanut or even an onion, for an American Indian. A letter to the editor in 1987 suggested, "Don't change the name—just change the symbol. Why not have a peanut, a potato or an onion—all with red skins—as their symbol? With the help of a good graphic artist and a top-flight advertising firm . . . the possibilities are endless: a cuddly peanut, a hunky potato, a sexy onion." More recently, People for the Ethical Treatment of Animals has advocated a similar idea, marking a rare moment of agreement between it and the conservative talk-show host Rush Limbaugh, who has remarked, "Just change the icon to a potato, a red-skinned potato. You know, dress it up, have a flashy looking potato, maybe put a football helmet on the potato or something, and you can keep calling them the Washington Redskins. There are red-skinned potatoes out there. Aren't there?" Of course, this sleight of hand neither engages with the anti-Indianism central to the history of the team and its traditions nor addresses the deeper concerns about the hostile environment fostered on game day. Such a move, moreover, clings to the status quo, seeking to offer the illusion of change and sympathy through a superficial and hollow gesture. In a sense, one might read less sincere iterations of this idea as a form of satire in which the joke is not on the team but on its critics.[20]

The *Washington City Paper*, an independent weekly, took a stand against the current moniker in 2012.[21] In association with this move, the editors announced a plan to empower readers to give the team a new nickname. After gathering suggestions, it allowed readers to vote to rename the team, offering five choices: Pigskins, aka the Hogs, a tribute to the storied offensive line; Monuments, a reference to the well-known obelisk; Washingtons, the namesake of DC and the first president; Half-Smokes, a local sausage; and Bammas, a local put-down for a person without taste.[22] Ultimately, Pigskins, aka Hogs, won. The editors, for their part, were pleased with the name because of its obvious historical allusion and "one added benefit to the name: The 'Skins abbreviation still works. And even the team's fight song can fit our new style, with only slight modification: 'Hail to the Pigskins, hail victory, Hogs on the warpath, fight for old D.C.!'"[23] The *Washington City Paper* at once articulated a bold position by refusing to the use the current name in the DC media market and acquiesced to the comforts of familiarity that allow tradition to continue with only minimal reflection and superficial cleansing, as if to say, we don't have to be troubled by the uncomfortable realities of racism or come to terms with historic transgressions anchoring the team and its traditions.

New Honors

Whereas minimalism seeks to find a new name that changes the uneasiness caused by the moniker without addressing its foundations, others have proposed more striking changes that root the redesign in a rhetoric of honor, a rhetoric that has also supported the retention of the slur. While this effort is well intended to be sure, one may wonder if trademarks, commodities, and brands can actually honor individuals or groups. In fact, critics of the Washington professional football team have pushed back against this logic. This has not prevented proposals that the new name be conceived as a way of honoring others. While Michael Taube has pitched the idea of using the name change to enshrine the memory of Ronald Regan, most initiatives in this vein pivot around race, having a pronounced tendency to resuscitate the team's native fixation.[24]

The central place of Indianness in the history and identity of the team has led some to make this the foundation for a new name to honor Native Americans. For instance, in an otherwise sharp economic analysis of the team, Michael Lewis and Manish Tripathi "suggest that Mr. Snyder reach out to American Indian community leaders to propose a new team name and set of symbols that honor Indians. This would provide a continuity that would enable the team to retain much of its former brand equity while creating a new name capable of attracting previously offended consumers."[25] Although such a move would satisfy the sentiments of many in the public, it is not altogether clear how such a replacement would avoid the dangers and damaging impacts of stereotyping and prevent spectacles of dehumanization on the field and in the stands.

Concurring with this general suggestion, others have proposed that the team should take the name of a local tribe, such as the Potomac, as way to ground its legitimacy and convey a positive, respectful vision of indigeneity.[26] The Florida State University Seminoles, endorsed by the Seminole Tribe of Florida but not the Seminole Nation of Oklahoma, provide a clear argument against such arrangements, because, far from altering anti-Indianism, they in fact give it an approved space to fester, as evidenced by the dehumanizing caricature of Chief Osceola, the cartoonish anthem played by the band, the demeaning marketing campaigns, and the antics of fans, most notably in the form of the tomahawk chop.

Finally, another proposal playing off of Indianness encourages the team to rename itself in honor of the great Lakota leader Red Cloud. Bob Drury and Thomas Clavin, who authored a book on Red Cloud, argue that "such a move would not only ease tension between American Indians and the NFL, but naming the team after Red Cloud would also signify strength, intelligence and perseverance—qualities any NFL team would be proud to project." If this sounds like a more specific reiteration of the franchise's general defense of the current name through notions of honor and intention, it is. And, in common with minimalist renamings, such a change would not involve anything painful or probing, like, say, confronting anti-Indian racism: "It would involve minor alterations to the team's logo and even its famous fight song, which could be sung, without missing a beat, as 'Hail to the Red Clouds.'" Indeed, Drury and Clavin's proposal seems destined to encourage the disparaging representations of American Indians generally and Red Cloud specifically, as their argument itself recycles the demeaning allusions common in anti-Indian headlines since the team's inception: "The Washington Red Clouds would be a lock to emulate their namesake and rout 49ers, defeat Raiders, humiliate Cowboys, pluck Eagles, turn back Texans, break Broncos and generally leave quivering the remaining would-be Giants and Titans of the National Football League."[27] Where the honor is in all of this for the great Lakota leader or indigenous people is beyond me.

While a fixation with honoring Indians lingers in many proposals, some commentators have suggested that the team should use the opportunity to honor to African Americans. In particular, they assert the franchise should pay tribute to a set of African American airmen popularly known as the Red Tails, who flew in the Second World War. It would also provide a means for the team to acknowledge its connection to the city's black community and perhaps even make amends for its long commitment to segregation. DC Council member David Grosso, who originally proposed the idea, echoed many other advocates of change when he noted how easily the name could be adapted to the fight song: "Hail to the Red Tails."[28] Again, one wonders how the franchise, its fans, and its rivals would convey the proper respect and preserve the memory of the airmen and their sacrifice in halftime shows, marketing campaigns, and fight songs. More pressing, perhaps, even if it is good concept, is the concern that it is unclear whether it is a name that fans will embrace or find meaningful. And, finally, the minimalism that shapes this proposal poses problems as well. In the words of the sportswriter Vinnie Iyer, "Then there are those suggestions that keep 'Red' in the name, such as the Miami of Ohio–like Red Hawks or the Tuskegee Airmen–honoring Red Tails. The 'Red' is the part of 'Redskins' that emphasizes the slur. There's no reason to keep that element, and it's lazy to do so."[29]

Departures

To effect a meaningful transformation, the new name for the Washington professional football team must make a real break with the nomenclature, iconography, and rituals of the past. Some of the more popular names in the design competition do just this. Renegades and Griffins have surfaced as two especially fecund alternatives that refuse a minimalist path, cast aside the native fixation, and do not court comfort by connecting to the color red or encouraging an easy fight song revision. While these may or may not be the best fit with the community, the region, or the history of the team (I will leave this to fans and supporters to sort out), they do mark powerful departures, opening a new chapter. Other names have the potential to do this as well but present complications worthy of reflection.

Warriors, for instance, has a special appeal for many participants in the recent redesign competition and in broader public conversations. It surely speaks to the place of patriotism and militarism in the region and, depending on how it were framed, might pay tribute to veterans. It does, however, carry an association with American Indians and the history of playing Indians. Arguably, this can be expunged, and an emphasis on national symbols, patriotism, and veterans may temper that, while allow-ing the many past and present indigenous people who have served the United States to be represented alongside others as cultural citizens and national heroes equal in every way. This is essentially what the sports-writer Mike Wise encouraged Dan Snyder to do in 2013: "I name them the Washington Warriors. I do away with the spears, the logo and all native peoples' imagery. I honorably retire the old name in a ceremony to include tribal chiefs and I dedicate the new name to the Wounded Warriors and every soldier who has served our country—including the scores of tribal elders who honorably served the U.S. military over the years. If I were Snyder, I would actually give a percentage of all paraphernalia on new items purchased to a fund for wounded veterans."[30] If this is how it were executed, it would go a long way toward transforming the team. "The most important thing you can do to promote Native human and civil rights in the mascotting arena," according to Suzan Shown Harjo, "is to advocate for a name and image that offends no one, and not to advocate for a name and image that are only a 'little racist.'"[31]

Revenue

When Edward Bennett Williams met with American Indians critical of the Washington professional football team in 1972, he suggested that change would be prohibitively expensive. Laura Wittstock (Seneca) replied, "You've made money off this Indian stereotype for years . . . and we refuse to accept this kind of argument now."[32] More than forty years later, the franchise, the league, the media, and many others continue to profit off of racism, so not surprisingly, financial impact remains an important concern. The organization, of course, has not engaged the issue, for its still holds that the moniker honors American Indians, and that will not change. Like Wittstock, I do not believe that revenue provides a foundation to defend the team. It cannot be a barrier to ethical engagement. More importantly, the fiscal costs associated with change appear to be more imagined than real, and they do not constitute a practical barrier either.

While the name, logo, and associated traditions have great sentimental value for Dan Snyder and many fans, they do not have much bankable worth. When the Cooke family put the franchise up for sale in 1998, Morgan Stanley Dean Witter, in outlining the "benefits of owning the club," did not reference the team name as an asset for potential buyers.[33] Moreover, according to Peter Keating, only 6.5 percent of the value of the DC team comes from brand equity, "the value teams get from fans being able to identify with individual franchises." "The bottom line," he continues, is that "a team's value comes from its monopoly rights, TV deals, market size and, lastly, brand identity, which in turn largely depends on what fans experience—how it plays and treats its customers. Not its mascot."[34] Worse, the organization is one of two in the NFL with negative brand equity—the other also having an American Indian motif, the Kansas City Chiefs.[35] And it has failed to adequately build its fan equity. By some estimates, for instance, it should have roughly sixty thousand more Twitter followers.[36]

Although the value of the name itself may not be especially great or constitute a substantial portion of the total equity of the team, the selection of a new name and logo sounds like a costly expense. After all, one must conduct research; secure trademarks; create new uniforms; redo signage, letterhead, and other essentials of doing business; pay lawyers; and so on. When the Charlotte professional basketball franchise opted to change its moniker from Bobcats back to Hornets, the total cost came to almost $4 million.[37] To create a new name would likely be even costlier. At a minimum, the DC NFL franchise, according to Allen Adamson of Landor Associates, would have to spend between $10 and $15 million to create a new name and logo.[38] This is no small sum, but for a franchise worth over $2 billion, with revenues approaching $400 million, this seems like a relatively small cost. To put it in perspective, heading into the 2015 season, more than a dozen players had contracts in excess of $15 million.[39]

Even if the moniker does not have the value some assume and the costs of change are not prohibitive, one might worry how the change will affect the sales of merchandise or attendance at games. No parallels exist in professional sports, but changes over the past few decades in intercollegiate athletics do reveal a noteworthy pattern. The economists Michael Lewis and Manish Tripathi, in a review of colleges and universities that have replaced an Indian themed mascot, found "an insignificant effect on revenue in the year immediately following a name change, and a positive revenue trend in the subsequent years." Far from hurting the bottom line, such changes appear to be beneficial over time.

To Lewis and Tripathi, "This suggests that the segment of the fan base opposed to such a change, however vocal, tends to be small, that threats of boycotts are empty and that there are eventual financial benefits to dropping an American Indian mascot."[40] Business analysts agree that the organization might enjoy something of a marketing "bonanza" but emphasize that proactive and smart implantation would be necessary to get maximum fan buy-in and to maximize fan buying power.[41]

A greater cost to the team may be intransigence or falling out of favor with fans. "When people who might buy team merchandise start worrying about whether it'll get them sent home from school—or simply be regarded as tawdry or racist by passers-by—there's a direct financial impact." Indeed, although we have not reached such a space yet, "What happens when you own a team whose merchandise is seen, even by five percent of potential consumers, as too distasteful to wear outside?"[42]

Lewis and Manish conclude that the only prudent thing for a well-run business to do under the circumstances would be to change the name, logo, and associated traditions. "Our research, the marketing logic and the survey data all point to the same conclusion: Retaining the Redskins name borders on managerial malpractice. . . . In this case, doing the morally right thing is also the correct business decision."[43]

This Is the End?

While the sportswriter Peter King may have been overly optimistic when he suggested that the Washington professional football team would have a new name in 2016, his intimate knowledge of the league may indicate that the franchise, the NFL, or society more generally have neared a tipping point on this issue.[44] His pronouncement may portend that it is only a matter of time. A former *Washington Post* columnist echoed such a sentiment when he declared, "The name is the past. . . . That's all Dan can effectively sell to keep the windfall coming in: the past. . . . Sometimes I don't think he owns a football team as much as he owns a museum."[45] Although one may balk at this reduction of the team and its traditions to a collection of dead relics enshrined to inspire, enlighten, or entertain, their contested presence ensures that many profit from the persistence of racism and settler colonialism, which invigorates anti-Indianism and extends the unsustainable privileges of whiteness. Snyder and his supporters have effectively turned their backs on the present, preferring the nostalgic comforts of saccharine stories and simulated Indianness to the more challenging opportunities and obligations to reaffirm sport and society as inclusive, affirming, and empowering for all.

In contrast, indigenous leaders, activists, fans, and myriad others have demanded that the team, the NFL, and the public rethink history and reconceive the present by renaming the franchise. Their endeavors to end one highly visible, damaging, and divisive iteration of anti-Indianism have called forth transformative possibilities. For Paul Kendrick, a long-time fan, this has meant coming to the realization that "loving our team no longer means defending the Redskin name; now it means loving our team enough to say that I'm in for the future. I'm in for changing our name for the better."[46] In the pursuit of something better, such fans have laid claim to Indianness, demanded dignity, and imagined community anew, envisioning an alternative future. They have set in motion the end: "There's gonna come a time—I don't know when it is, 20 years, 40 years, whenever—there's gonna come a time when people are gonna look back and say *can you believe those idiots thought Redskins was appropriate?* ... That day is coming, because the Redskins will be so far removed from the NFL you're gonna need a microscope to find it. It's here for now, but it won't be for long."[47] Until then, rethink, rename, replace.

Ends

11

On November 2, 2014, Native Americans and their allies demonstrated against the Washington professional football team on the occasion of its game against the Minnesota Vikings in Minneapolis (see figs. 10 and 11). Olympic gold medalist Billy Mills (Lakota) marched with thousands of others, calling on the franchise to do the right thing and make a change while reminding it and the general public that American Indians are "not your mascot." Mills felt compelled to participate, finding the team name to be "among the most vulgar" references to indigenous people, which cannot convey the respect and honor many supporters read into it. As he noted in an interview at the time, "I think my reason is because it's time to change. It's time for America to move on. It's time for those individuals and those teams who think they're honoring us to recognize that we bring honor to ourselves and our tribal nations. In honoring our tribal nations, we bring honor to America. I think it's time for the owner of the Washington Redskins, for example, to bring honor to himself—by changing the name of the Washington Redskins." Mills not only reclaimed the notion of honor and the locus of power in his comments, but elsewhere in his discussion he resituated the slur in the broader history of violence against Native America, drawing explicit comparisons to the Holocaust.[1]

Echoing Mills's assertion, the "Proud to Be" campaign, spearheaded by the National Congress of American Indians and released to coincide with Super Bowl XLVIII, reframed the issue, reclaiming the right to name indigeneity while pushing back against the franchise. The public service announcement, released on social media and later aired during the NBA Championship in late spring 2014, features a series of images of American Indians paired with keywords. It opens with a "Proud," pivots to "Forgotten," and closes the stanza with "Indian." Throughout, it follows a similar syncopated pattern. It references specific tribes and historic figures, capturing scenes of the everyday and the extraordinary. It includes images of poverty and underdevelopment as well as of powwows, laughter, and beauty. "Proud to Be" employs

> a strategy of copia, going on and on and cycling back on themes to stress the vast diversity of Native American peoples before climbing to an assertive final note: "Unyielding, Strong, Indomitable. Native Americans call themselves many things. The one thing they don't..." and the increasingly rapid music and image montage cut to black. The pregnant pause gives way to a slow fade on the Redskins helmet logo and a football that stay on the screen in silence. The argument here is simple: despite all of the terms that the commercial has shared, it will not stoop to saying the derogatory word. The NFL and viewers nationwide should do the same.[2]

The short video has immense power, evoking an array of emotions. It is not perfect, but it does render indigenous people as fully human, presenting images that likely defy many viewers' expectations and in turn challenging their stereotypes.[3] It makes an important intervention in the debate and, more importantly perhaps, imprints an alternative visual and rhetorical repertoire on the public imagination, defined not by sport franchises, the entertainment industries, or academics, but on and in indigenous terms. In addition to visibility and voice, "Proud to Be" might be best read as a reclamation project intent on rehabilitating understandings and identities as it repossesses Indianness. In the words of Simon Moya-Smith, (Lakota), "And as Native Americans are seen beyond the stereotypes, and as we use our voices to speak out, we give visibility to who we are, as well as the issues we are working to solve. This visibility allows for a rehumanization. That is important, and not just for the sake of a brand name of a professional football team."[4]

The demonstration and the commercial are but two of the emergent ways American Indians and their allies have devised to raise consciousness, shift the debate, and ultimately force the Washington professional football franchise to change its name, logo, and brand. They give evidence of a re-energized opposition to the team and its traditions and a deeper resurgence across Indian Country. At once hopeful, inspiring, and empowering, they seem to point to an inevitable end. The short-lived satisfaction of earlier victories, most notably the initial ruling in *Harjo et al. v. Pro-Football, Inc.*, and the capacity of the organization to deflect such criticism for more than four decades should temper expectations. Indeed, the end may not be what so many want it to be; it may be an impasse; it may be marked a refusal to engage the real issues. More likely than not, the end will be multiple, unfinished, and undetermined. As such, it will not be simple, but complex and contradictory, something to celebrate, to be sure, as well as a signal to get back to it, as it will initiate another phase in a much larger process or struggle.

Of course, the end is not here yet. I cannot say when the end will come and cannot describe precisely how it will play out, but I do believe that the movement against the team and its traditions has begun to near a critical mass and that it may soon reach a tipping point. At some point in the near future, the franchise, perhaps under pressure from the NFL, perhaps as a result of *Blackhorse et al. v. Pro-Football, Inc.* stripping the team of a number of its trademarks, or perhaps because of changes within its calculations or sensibilities (business, political, and/or moral), will make a change to its brand. An often unexplored question will occupy my thoughts in this concluding chapter: what kind of change is really necessary to make a substantive difference in the lives of indigenous peoples, in the popular uses and understandings of Indianness, and in the shape and significance of anti-Indian racism? In part, my reply, like my analysis to this point, will foreground the importance of bringing anti-racist interventions and decolonial projects into the dialogue. It emphasizes that just as the struggle is about more than the name, so too positive resolution and productive reconciliation depend on something more than the franchise selecting a new name and logo. Moreover, for a change to be truly meaningful, in the end, whites must actively engage and address history, power, and race as manifested in U.S. settler colonialism.

It may be too early to worry, but as I think toward the end, I do worry. I worry that when change comes it will be superficial or stop with the slur.

The franchise might replace the name but retain the logo. In keeping the core of the brand but repackaging it around, say, the Warriors, the team could project an air of sensitivity and progressivism while shielding its anti-Indian traditions. Although partial and problematic, as discussed in the previous chapter, such a move would let the team off the hook, making it far less contentious for most Americans because it would fall within the boundaries of good taste. The rebranded team would be akin to the Chicago Blackhawks. Such a possibility has prompted the sportswriter Mike Florio to ask, "If the profile of a Native American represents an acceptable logo for the Chicago Blackhawks, why isn't the profile of a Native American an acceptable logo for the Washington NFL franchise?"[5] A minor change to nomenclature need not address underlying issues or historical structures. In fact, it would give the franchise and fans permission to use Indianness as they see fit and abuse American Indians in the process. An NHL game featuring Chicago routinely includes fans playing Indian, dressing in feathers, and otherwise dehumanizing indigenous peoples to express team loyalty and to intensify their amusement.

Even if legal challenges, persistent media attention, continued protests, declining merchandising revenue, and changing public attitudes prompt the franchise to change its name and its logo, I worry that the success may not be transferable precisely because for many the problem is the slur. For instance, Bob Costas, in his highly visible commentary calling for change, actually said as much, asserting that the DC NFL franchise was indefensible because of its use of a slur, while other mascots, like Warriors or Braves, convey honor and positivity. I have argued against such narrow, ahistorical readings throughout this book. Yet it is this logic that makes the Blackhawks and the Chiefs seem acceptable to most in the public: the r-word is a slur; it is bad; it must go; however, American Indian mascots can be okay, positive, and defensible. This contradictory thinking, which has its roots in white entitlement, the appropriations of settler colonialism, and erasures and inventions of anti-Indianism, remains undisturbed by the focus on the slur and may make it difficult to harness the momentum of an as-yet-hypothetical victory.

For alterations to the team and its traditions to be truly meaningful, I believe they have to be situated within larger processes of reflection and revision, included as a part of ongoing efforts to rethink and refashion sport and society. Rather than describe the end, here I identify a number of paths forward that take us closer to it. While American Indians have played a leading role as advocates for change, those who produced, profited from, took pleasure in, and otherwise participated in the creation, circulation, and consumption of the brand and its pseudo-Indian play must seize the opportunity and take up the obligation to forge these paths. Finally, in outlining these proposals I do not mean to create an exhaustive list or to overdetermine action but instead to highlight an assemblage of antiracist and decolonial interventions: specifically, stop stereotyping, divest, recognize humanity, educate, come to terms, honor, and create new images.

Stop Stereotyping. Perhaps it goes without saying, but the identification and eradication of stereotypes constitutes the first step. I have worried over this above as the final step. This is not the end, but the beginning of the end. We have entered this phase in recent years as more and more fans, journalists, policy makers, and religious leaders not only have recognized the problems with but also have spoken out against the name, logo, and associated rituals. These practices, I have argued, reduce American Indians to a flat, fixed image, one of a noble savage frozen in time like a museum piece or hunting trophy; encapsulate them through a racial slur with deep roots in genocidal violence; deny them cultural citizenship and a capacity to be recognized as embodied equals in everyday life; and transform them into props and playthings, customs to be worn for fantasy and escape during the game and caricatures to be bought and sold. Above all else, each of these practices relies on and recycles stereotypes that dehumanize and denigrate Native Americans. Only by stopping the creation and consumption of such imagery can we begin to conceive an ending that restores, respects, and renews indigenous and settler alike.

Divest. Because so much of the team and its traditions hinges on entitlement, in the sense that Euro-Americans both have a right to Indianness and have title to it or own it, divestment has to be a primary objective moving forward. This demands at once unlearning the racial and settler privileges of not knowing, not remembering, and not thinking; it prompts a realization that one can neither possess Indianness nor take and remake it at will; it necessitates a renunciation of a long tradition, not the least that one cultivated by the organization and its partners, of profiting off of anti-Indianism; and it encourages a recognition of one's social and historical position. Reflecting on the team name, Zach Mitcham gave voice to some of the issues to be faced: "There were thousands of years of human life here before the immigration of Europeans. I think of where we live now and how those who lived here before us were driven off the land, how so many were killed and how I'm a descendant beneficiary. I think it's important to recognize how my own good fortune is tied by time's rope to harm that came before."[6] Such reflections may prove painful and may only be partial for some, but they are a crucial step in the larger process.

Recognize Humanity. Since much of the history of the franchise hinges on misrecognition and misrepresentation of American Indians, working through and against it necessitates efforts and interventions directed at rehumanization, the recognition of indigenous people as fully human and representational practices that fully and accurately convey their humanity to a society that for so long was (and is) devoted to denying, destroying, or distorting it. Whereas mascots, logos, and practices like those animating the DC NFL brand, which confine American Indians to the past, to a limited range of human possibility most often associated with violence, nature, savagery, and masculinity, and almost invariably for the delight of and at the direction and discretion of white authors and audiences, rehumanization, as the "Proud to Be" public service announcement demonstrates, instead embraces diversity (cultural, geographic, tribal, lifestyle, class, gender, and so on), locates Native Americans in the present, and appreciates the complex mix of similarities and differences at play in Indian Country. Moreover, recognizing humanity means listening to indigenous people and acknowledging, incorporating, and empowering their perspectives. This is not to say American Indians are always right or should dictate the course of events and social arrangements. Rather, it suggests arrangements in which one works to understand in context what is being said and why and to engage sincerely with indigenous interlocutors as coequals, integrating them where conventionally they have been silenced, ignored, and rendered invisible. Finally, rehumanizing means regarding Native Americans on their own terms, hearing them in their own voices, and working to develop the tools to do so, always mindful of their diverse cultures, histories, and experiences.

Educate. Native American mascots and other stereotypes persist because most Americans remain thoughtless, lacking the resources, knowledge, and skills to think critically about them. Most Americans have not received adequate historical instruction nor had exposure to indigenous peoples and perspectives as living, vital, and valuable; they have not, moreover, cultivated toolkits to enable them to unpack the construction and circulation of images and texts. In many ways, while most Americans can read, they remain illiterate: they cannot read media, history, or society in a critical fashion because they learn about these subjects, particularly as they relate to indigenous peoples, from movies and television shows, stump speeches and national monuments, football games and fashion trends. To reverse the ingrained illiteracy that makes it possible to have a football team and its traditions built around a racial slur, and makes it possible for thousands to not only endorse but also defend such practices, demands better education. On the one hand, more and better-quality instruction about indigenous cultures and histories is crucial; it should integrate native and scholarly findings and interpretations. A good first step might be for state legislatures and school boards to mandate increased mainstreaming of American Indian history. On the other hand, increased emphasis on media literacy and critical thinking will enable students and citizens to make sense of what is being said in a given moment and why it matters, allowing them to assess images, unpack rhetoric, and decipher significance in a more sophisticated and systematic fashion. Education, then, has the potential to replace illiteracy and thoughtlessness with more informed and engaged understandings of context and content.

Come to terms. Most Americans live in denial. Comforted by national narratives (Pocahontas, the first Thanksgiving, the winning of the West, and heroic pioneers) and cherished concepts (nation of immigrants, Manifest Destiny, the frontier, and so), they do not have to face the past or consider its afterlives. For fans and supporters, origin stories and simulated support in Indian Country serve the same purpose, reconciling and explaining away contradictions, as they legitimate existing practices. Education and divestment challenged these patterns of strategic ignorance and settled thoughtlessness. They initiate an essential if long-avoided and eternally deferred obligation, coming to terms with a history of displacement, dispossession, and death, the associated enabling structures of racism and anti-Indianism, and their legacies in contemporary ways of seeing and being in the world.

Erma J. Vizenor offers eloquent testimony about the significance of the past in the present struggle against the team and its traditions. For her, whatever the intention, the brand always invokes a slur: "In my experience the term has never been used in a respectful way that honors our people, but rather used in a derogatory manner to separate us out as savages or to signify in some way that we are less than human beings." And more, it does not simply misrepresent or dehumanize, it has been used to "justify the genocide that remains a part of our shared history." Vizenor purposely emphasizes a collective past, which unites those who defend and those who oppose the team. "As Americans, we must not only celebrate our proud heritage, but also come to terms with the historic violence and racism that this country was founded upon and, to some degree, remains with us today. We must begin to heal, not by sweeping the past under the proverbial rug and denying involvement, denying intent and denying relevance. To heal, we must instead be allowed to speak our truths and begin to reconcile past hurts and injustices." And this may be the most important part of facing the past and its afterlives: the encounter opens the possibility of speaking and hearing truth, fostering reconciliation, and facilitating rehabilitation. As Vizenor says, again with reference to the Washington professional football team, "So let's start healing today by admitting this truth; the use of racist and derogatory 'Indian' sports mascots, logo or symbols is harmful and perpetuates negative stereotypes of America's first peoples, my people. . . . I believe with all my heart that my daughters and grandchildren deserve a legacy built upon our values, traditions and perseverance as a people. I also believe all children deserve something better than a legacy constructed on hate and misunderstanding."[7] Ultimately, then, coming to terms facilitates healing, laying the foundation for a more just, inclusive future.

Honor. Respect and honor have a place moving forward; however, we have to reconceive and redirect them. In a recent editorial cartoon, Marty Two Bulls highlights the dimensions and distinctions I have in mind in his rendering of the current charade of honor preferred by the team and its supporters (see figure 12). While the current defense essentially says, "We are honoring you with this name and logo," what I have in mind here, following the ideas of a number of indigenous people, is a reformulation whereby "we have an obligation to honor past treaties." In this frame, respect is not about intention but action, not about projection but practice: it simultaneously acknowledges indigenous sovereignty, recognizing American Indians as tribal groups with political autonomy; embraces concrete covenants between nations; and conveys the value and vitality of indigenous people. Brian Cladoosby (Swinomish), president of the National Congress of American Indians, captures much of this when he notes, "We have many non-Native friends—businesses, organizations and foundations—that partner with us. Our greatest successes have come when our allies respect our sovereignty, listen to us and do what they can to support our self-determination."[8] Engaging native nations on these terms has the advantage of regarding them as equals, as fully human, and demanding that those in mainstream society cast aside notions of entitlement and superiority, challenging the anti-Indianism grounding the settled state of everyday life in the United States. Moreover, the remembrance, reflection, and responsibility central to honoring the treaties also contributes to broader processes of individual empowerment, community development, and tribal growth in Indian Country.

Create New Images. We need more images of American Indians in American society to overwhelm and overwrite existing inventions and misrepresentations. In part, as the National Congress of American Indians puts it, a corrective is order: "Creating positive images and role models is essential in helping Native youth more fully and fairly establish themselves in today's society."[9] More than just representations that we can feel good about, though, we need the voices and imaginings in Indian Country to receive broader circulation and more serious consideration, and we need more of them. In a sense, we need a new semiotic economy. In an ideal world, part of the end of the current representation regime around professional football in Washington DC would entail investing substantial capital in such an economy, funding authors, artists, and educators, building infrastructure, and attracting audiences. I am not certain that Dan Snyder, who knows a thing or two about running media infrastructure, would willingly invest in such an enterprise; I would, however, strongly argue that the organization, the league, and its media partners should pay reparations for decades of knowingly profiting off of racism. These reparations might be leveraged for this new economy. In identifying the importance of increased cultivation and circulation, I have in mind what Scott Richard Lyons has termed "rhetorical sovereignty," which "aim[s] [to] recover the losses from the ravages of colonization," pursuing "the inherent right and ability of peoples to determine their own communicative needs and desires . . . to decide for themselves the goals, modes, styles, and languages of public discourse."[10] Ultimately, a new semiotic economy holds the promise of altering creation, consumption, and control of Indianness, which could be the greatest end to come from the end of a racial slur posing as a sports brand.

NOTES

1. INTRODUCTION

1. Kogod, "Bob Costas on Redskins Name."
2. Anderson, "How Media Organizations Are Handling the Redskins Name"; Beaujon, "Here's a List"; Keene, "Who Has Spoken Out?"
3. Burke, "'Redskins' Mentions Down 27%"; Bene, "Broadcasters Really Are Saying 'Redskins' a Lot Less."
4. Anderson, "How Media Organizations Are Handling the Redskins Name"; Beaujon, "Here's a List"; Keene, "Who Has Spoken Out?" On the ethics of using the name in news coverage, see Jensen, "Banning 'Redskins'"; Lindsay, "Representing Redskins."
5. Wulf, "Why Use of Native American Nicknames."
6. On the team, see Coombe, "Sports Trademarks and Somatic Politics"; Goddard, "I Am a Red-Skin"; Harjo, "Fighting Name-Calling"; Sigelman, "Hail to the Redskins?"; Strong, "Trademarking Racism"; Waggoner, "On Trial." Good introductions to the subject of American Indian mascots include Davis, "Protest against the Use of Native American Mascots"; Guiliano, *Indian Spectacle*; C. R. King, "Re/Claiming Indianness"; C. R. King, *Native American Mascot Controversy*; C. R. King, *Unsettling America*; C. R. King and Springwood, *Team Spirits*; Pewewardy, "Native American Mascots and Imagery"; Spindel, *Dancing at Halftime*; Springwood, "I'm Indian Too!"; Staurowsky, "Act of Honor or Exploitation?"; Staurowsky, "Cleveland Indians"; Strong, "Mascot Slot"; Taylor, *Contesting Constructed Indian-ness*. Importantly, only Staurowsky deals exclusively with professional athletics, in her studies of the Cleveland Indians.
7. "11 Trending Words of 2014."

8. Brady, "Poll."
9. Steinberg, "Pizza Chain Apologizes."
10. Krauthammer, "Redskins and Reason."
11. "Washington Redskins Valuation."
12. Odle, "What's in a Name?"
13. Fruehling, "We Won't Use Redskins Anymore."
14. Ley, "Washington Merchandise Sales Are Down."
15. "Washington Redskins Valuation."
16. Guiliano, *Indian Spectacle*.
17. Blackhorse, "This Is What Dehumanization Looks Like."
18. Blackhorse, "This Is What Dehumanization Looks Like."

2. ORIGINS

1. Hayley Munguia, "2,128 Native American Mascots."
2. On these challenges, see Reid, "Why the 'Redskins' Is a Racist Name."
3. Wise, "Questionable Naming Rights."
4. B. Allen, "Letter to Harry Reid."
5. "The Facts"; see also Kessler, "Fact Checking the New Web Site."
6. Goddard, "I Am a Red-Skin." Goddard's website offers excerpts and copies of original source material, http://anthropology.si.edu/goddard/redskin -examples.htm.
7. Vaughan, "From White Man to Redskin"; Shoemaker, *Strange Likeness*.
8. Shoemaker, *Strange Likeness*, 129.
9. Shoemaker, *Strange Likeness*, 130; Vaughan, "From White Man to Redskin," 921.
10. Shoemaker, *Strange Likeness*, 130; see also Vaughan, "From White Man to Redskin," 921.
11. Shoemaker, *Strange Likeness*, 130–31.
12. Vaughan, "From White Man to Redskin," 949.
13. Reid, "Why the 'Redskins' Is a Racist Name."
14. Shoemaker quoted in Sanders, "Pundit Claims."
15. Holmes, "'Redskin' Is the Scalped Head"; see also Holmes, "Update"; Harjo, "The R-Word Is Even Worse"; Harjo, "Washington 'Redskins' Is a Racist Name."
16. Odle, "What's in a Name?"
17. *Merriam-Webster Dictionary*; *The American Heritage Dictionary of the English Language*, 5th ed.; Dictionary.com; *Webster's College Dictionary*; *Collins English Dictionary*.
18. Harding, "Simple Case."
19. Nunberg, "When Slang Becomes a Slur."
20. Kogod, "Sonic Apologizes."

21. U.S. Patent and Trademark Office, Trademark Trial and Appeal Board, Petitioners' Trial Brief.

22. Stapleton, *Redskins*, 101.

23. Baum, Editorial.

24. Stapleton, *Redskins*, 101.

25. Stapleton, *Redskins*, 101.

26. See Waggoner, "On Trial," for a broader history of this context and a detailed accounting of this change.

27. D. Snyder, "Letter from Washington Redskins Owner."

28. Barr, "Was Redskins' First Coach a Fraud?"

29. "Boston Braves Grid Men Become 'Redskins'"; see also Waldron, "81-Year-Old Newspaper Article"; McCartney, "1933 News Article."

30. "Braves Pro Gridmen to Be Called Redskins."

31. Leiby, "Legend of Lone Star Dietz."

32. Hylton, "Before the Redskins Were the Redskins."

33. Waggoner, "On Trial"; Waggoner, "Reclaiming James One Star." See also Benjey, *Keep A-Goin'*.

34. B. Allen, "Letter to Harry Reid."

35. Mansch, "Don Wetzel"; Engberg, "Who Made the Redskins Logo?"; "Washington's Nickname Controversy."

36. Engberg, "Who Made the Redskins Logo?"

37. Scolari, "Indian Warriors and Pioneer Mothers," 52–88.

38. Tomassen, "Redskins Name Change"; Dunetz, "Liberal Media Attacks"; Lowry, "Liberals Fabricate Outrage."

39. Zirin, "Assassinating of Native American Voices."

40. Page, "Indian Raid."

41. Gross quoted in U.S. Patent and Trademark Office, Trademark Trial and Appeal Board, Petitioners' Trial Brief.

42. TsalagiMahariel, "Alcatraz Is Not an Island"; Boyer, "Reflections on Alcatraz."

43. Steinberg, "Edward Bennett Williams's 1972 Letter."

44. Steinberg, "Great Redskins Name Debate."

45. Strong, "Trademarking Racism."

46. Edward Lazarus, letter to *Washington Post*, January 4, 1992, quoted in Powell, "Recycling the Redskins," 10.

47. Waggoner, interview.

3. USES

1. McKenna, "This Dated Video."

2. *Exploiting Indians*.

3. See Guiliano, *Indian Spectacle*.

4. C. R. King, "Uneasy Indians."
5. C. R. King and Springwood, "Best Offense."
6. T. G. Smith, *Showdown.*
7. Quoted in Zirin and Zill, "History Lesson."
8. Waggoner, "On Trial."
9. Peterseim, "Not Just Whistling Dixie in DC"; Griffith, *My Life with the Redskins.*
10. Griffith, *My Life with the Redskins.*
11. Griffith, *My Life with the Redskins*, 42; Holley, "Slingin' Sammy Baugh."
12. Considine story in Griffith, *My Life with the Redskins*, 37–39.
13. Considine quoted in Griffith, *My Life with the Redskins*, 94.
14. "Washington Is Capital of Football World."
15. Waldron, "NFL Commissioner."
16. Berkhofer, *White Man's Indian.*
17. Griffith, *My Life with the Redskins*, 228.
18. U.S. Patent and Trademark Office, Trademark Trial and Appeal Board, Petitioners' Trial Brief, 35.

4. ERASURE

1. "Official Extremeskins Tailgate."
2. Cox, "Redskins Protesters Gearing Up"; Cox, "At FedEx Field."
3. Cox, "Redskins Protesters Gearing Up."
4. Cook-Lynn, *Anti-Indianism in Modern America*, xx.
5. Steinberg, "Notah Begay."
6. Cox, "At FedEx Field"; Houska, "Dehumanization, Racism, and Disrespect." See also Klemko, "Redskins."
7. Powell, "Recycling the Redskins."
8. Blackhawk, *Violence over the Land*, 4.
9. Odle, "What's in a Name?"
10. Wolfe, "Settler Colonialism."
11. National Congress of American Indians, *Ending the Legacy of Racism*, 5.
12. W. Smith, "Fighting for His People."
13. Starr, "We Need to Stop."
14. Jae, "Is the R*dskins Name Really Offensive?"
15. Buchanan, "Hail to the Redskins."
16. "Report: Redskins' Name Only Offensive."
17. See Pewewardy, "Native American Mascots and Imagery"; Staurowsky, "American Indian Imagery."
18. Gover, "Unraveling the 'Redskins' Lie."
19. Faleomavaega, "Ignorance Is Bliss."
20. Garcia-Vargas, "Redskins Say."
21. Cook, "Stupid Americans."

22. Shakely, "Problem with the 'R' Word?"
23. Faleomavaega, "Ignorance Is Bliss."
24. Bryant, "Battle over Nickname Continues."
25. Zirin, "You Can't Unsee It."
26. Moya-Smith, "Mea Culpa."
27. Saunt, "This Land Is Their Land."

5. SENTIMENT

1. "ESPN's Mike Ditka on Redskins' Name Debate." After this initial statement, Ditka clarified his position slightly. See Cahill, "Mike Ditka."
2. Lovely, "Redskins."
3. Steinberg, "Dan Snyder Bought."
4. Steinberg, "Matthew McConaughey and the Redskins." See also Steinberg, "Matthew McConaughey Tells Larry Michael."
5. D. Snyder, "Letter from Washington Redskins Owner."
6. Geoghegan, "Washington Redskins."
7. Tomasky, "Dan Snyder's Trail."
8. Quoted in "NFL Commissioner Tells Congress."
9. "Daniel Snyder Defends the 'Redskins.'"
10. L. Smith, "Redskins' Nickname Honors Indian Warriors."
11. "Theismann: 'Skins Name Is Meaningful."
12. Cox, "Redskins Protesters Gearing Up."
13. Steinberg, "Redskins Lawyer Says."
14. Vargas and Shin, "President Obama Says."
15. Steinberg, "Cowboys Owner Jerry Jones Says."
16. Kogod, "Bob Costas on Redskins Name."
17. Strong, "Trademarking Racism."
18. Walker, "Meet the Native American Grandmother."
19. Brady, "New Generation of American Indians"; Pensoneau, "I'll Fucking Cut You."
20. Gambini, "Research Shows Native American Imagery Hurts."
21. Fryberg, Markus, Oyserman, and Stone, "Of Warrior Chiefs and Indian Princesses."
22. LaRocque, McDonald, Weatherly, and Ferraro, "Indian Sports Nicknames/Logos."
23. Freng and Willis-Esqueda, "Question of Honor"; Chaney, Burke, and Burkley, "Do American Indian Mascots = American Indian People?"; Kim-Prieto, Goldstein, Okazaki, and Kirschner, "Effect of Exposure."
24. Hoskins, "Washington Redskins."
25. Friedman, "Harmful Psychological Effects."
26. Wulf, "Why Use of Native American Nicknames."

27. Steinfeldt et al., "Racism in the Electronic Age."

28. Stokes, "5 Studies."

29. Hoskins, "Washington Redskins."

30. National Congress of American Indians, *Ending the Legacy of Racism*, 5.

31. Friedman, "Harmful Psychological Effects."

32. Wise, "To Seattle Native Americans."

33. Cladoosby, "A Good Project for Synder's Foundation?"

34. Vargas, "Granddaughter of Former Redskins Owner" (emphasis in original).

6. BLACK/WHITE

1. Ironwing, "Remarks on Wichita North Redskins."

2. Steinberg, "John Kent Cooke."

3. Ansell, *New Right, New Racism*; Collins, *Black Sexual Politics*; Bonilla-Silva, *Racism without Racists*.

4. Collins, *Black Sexual Politics*, 54.

5. Ansell, *New Right, New Racism*, 59.

6. Bonilla-Silva, *Racism without Racists*.

7. Bonilla-Silva, *Racism without Racists*, 28.

8. Picca and Feagin, *Two-Face Racism*.

9. Steinberg, "From Riley Cooper to 'Redskins.'"

10. Shelburne, "Sad Last Chapter."

11. Ramsey, "Seahawks Richard Sherman."

12. Friedman, "NBA Schools the NFL."

13. Page, "Now It's Time."

14. Lone Hill, "Refusal to Rename the Redskins."

15. Steinberg, "Drake Takes a Shot."

16. "Chris Rock."

17. Ralbovsky, "Indian Affair."

18. Carley, "Is Chief Noc-a-Homa Racist?"

19. Giago, "R-word Just as Insulting."

20. "Shoni Schimmel Calls for End."

21. "NFL Official."

22. Wise, "Questionable Naming Rights."

23. Hendricks, "Champ Bailey."

24. Tribou, "Bobby Mitchell." See also Steinberg, "Former Redskins Receiver Charlie Brown."

25. Swayney, "Redskins Just a Name?"

7. OWNERSHIP

1. Shin, "Redskins Name Change Demanded." See also C. R. King, "Looking Back to a Future End."

2. Brady, "Daniel Snyder Says."

3. Freeman, "Why Dan Snyder Won't Relent."

4. Wood, "If You Are Offended"; "Top 10 Strongest Takes."

5. C. R. King and Springwood, *Beyond the Cheers*, 160.

6. Strong, "Mascot Slot."

7. Harris, "Whiteness as Property"; Lipsitz, "Possessive Investment in Whiteness."

8. Povich, "George Preston Marshall," 16.

9. Povich, "George Preston Marshall," 17.

10. Povich, "George Preston Marshall," 18.

11. See T. G. Smith, *Showdown*.

12. McKenna, "Fight for New Dixie."

13. T. G. Smith, *Showdown*; Basen, "Fifty Years Ago."

14. See T. G. Smith, *Showdown*; Basen, "Fifty Years Ago."

15. T. G. Smith, *Showdown*, 159.

16. Steinberg and Jenkins, "Black Fans."

17. Wulf, "Why Use of Native American Nicknames."

18. "Redskins Prepare for Return."

19. Milloy, "Battle Over the Redskins' Name."

20. Hinkle, "Washington Redskins Are About to Fleece."

21. "Financing New Stadiums."

22. See Steinberg, "Daniel Snyder"; Snider, "Dan Snyder's Path Past 'Never.'"

23. Steinberg, "Vinny Cerrato Says."

24. On privilege, see McIntosh, "White Privilege"; Kendall, *Understanding White Privilege*; Kimmel and Ferber, *Privilege*.

25. Johnson, "What Is a 'System of Privilege'?"

26. Kwiatek, "Another Voice."

27. Kwiatek, "Another Voice."

28. "Daniel Snyder Defends the 'Redskins.'"

29. Brady, "Redskins' Trademark Attorney."

30. "Dan Snyder to 'Redskins' Critics."

31. Deloria, *Playing Indian*.

32. Salaita, "Nothing Scarier."

33. Vargas, "U.S. Patent Office Cancels"; U.S. Patent and Trademark Office, Trademark Trial and Appeal Board, Opinion, *Blackhorse et al. v. Pro-Football Inc.*

34. Shapira, "Federal Judge Orders Cancellation."

35. Handy, "Complex and Hidden Story."

36. Vargas, "From Pork Rinds to Cheerleaders."

37. "Trademark Decision against the Redskins"; "Patent Office Comanches."

38. Treadway, "Twitter Has Plenty of Suggestions."

39. Washington Redskins "Statement by Bob Raskopf," (emphasis in original).
40. But see Boren, "Who Is Amanda Blackhorse?"
41. Walker, "Meet the Native American Grandmother."
42. See U.S. Patent and Trademark Office, Trademark Trial and Appeal Board, Opinion, *Harjo et al. v. Pro-Football Inc.*
43. Salaita, "Nothing Scarier."
44. Boraas, "Aniak Halfbreeds?"
45. Salaita, "Nothing Scarier."
46. White Eyes, "Indian Mascots, a Privileged Fight."

8. SIMULATION

1. Deal, "I Have Been Indian My Whole Life."
2. Deal, "Redskin."
3. Regan, "Gregg Deal's Performance."
4. Deal, "Redskin: Indigenous Art and Identity."
5. Deal, "I've Been Indigenous My Whole Life."
6. Deal, "I've Been Indigenous My Whole Life."
7. Milloy, "Battle Over the Redskins' Name."
8. Harjo, "Washington Chief-Making." Many thanks to Linda Waggoner for drawing this article to my attention.
9. "Navajo Code Talkers Leader Defends."
10. Zirin, "Redskins Owner Dan Snyder Says."
11. Brady, "Woman Suing Redskins Says."
12. Petchesky, "Disgraced, Soon-to-Be-Former Navajo Nation President"; Toensing, "Navajo Medicine Men Pass Anti-Redskins Resolution"; Shapira, "Dan Snyder and the Navajo Nation"; Hendley, "Navajo Representative Wants."
13. Shapiro, "Princess Pale Moon."
14. Sager, "Princess Pale Moon."
15. "Pale Moon Bounced from Expo."
16. Franklin, "Give It Back for Tax Breaks."
17. Sager, "Princess Pale Moon."
18. Savilla, "Interview with Floyd Red Crow Westerman."
19. McKenna, "Is the Redskins' 'VIP' Indian Defender a Fake Indian?"; Capozza, "Charity Scams."
20. "Native American Chief Talks about Redskins."
21. McKenna, "Redskins' Indian-Chief Defender."
22. McKenna, "Redskins' Indian-Chief Defender."
23. McKenna, "Is the Redskins' 'VIP' Indian Defender a Fake Indian?"
24. D. Snyder, "Letter to Everyone." See also the Washington Redskins Original Americans Foundation website.

25. Vargas and Jackman, "CEO of New Washington Redskins Foundation."
26. "Native Americans Tell Redskins Owner."
27. Brady, "Notah Begay."
28. Levin, "Here, Take This Coat."
29. J. King, "Native American Groups Are Not Impressed."
30. Enote, "We Are Not Redskins."
31. D. Snyder, "Letter to Everyone."
32. Steinberg, "Redskins Launch New 'Redskins Facts' Campaign."
33. Brady, "Montana Indian Tribe."
34. Jodie, "Washington Redskins Donate $30,000."
35. Wharton, "NFL's Washington Team Offers Donation."
36. "Las Vegas Paiute Tribe Rejected 'Gift.'"
37. "Quechan Skate Park Project."
38. Keene, "Kwatsan Tribe Refuses."
39. Cohen, "Dan Snyder Seeks."
40. Wise, "Latest Redskins Nickname Outreach."
41. "Snyder's Blood Money."
42. Van Bibber, "Dan Snyder's Latest Cigar Store Indian."
43. D'Errico, "NFL Franchise Channels Puritan Colonists."
44. Cladoosby, "A Good Project for Synder's Foundation?"
45. Treuer, "Price of a Slur."
46. Guy, "Washington Redskins."
47. Deal, "I Have Been Indian My Whole Life"; "Indigenous Artist Gregg Deal."
48. Cox, "Tribe's Infighting."

9. OPINION

1. Reilly, "Have the People Spoken?"
2. Zirin, "Rick Reilly."
3. Burns, "Blackfeet Elder Says Rick Reilly Misquoted Him."
4. Vargas, "One Native American Family."
5. Vargas, "One Native American Family."
6. Flood, "How the 'Redskins' Debate Goes Over."
7. Flood, "How the 'Redskins' Debate Goes Over."
8. Keene, "Missing the Point."
9. C. R. King et al., "Of Polls and Race Prejudice," 390.
10. Nucklos, "US Poll Finds Widespread Support"; "3rd Annual NFL Poll."
11. Sigelman, "Hail to the Redskins?"; "60% Don't Think Washington Redskins Should Change."
12. Babin, "NFL Player Poll."
13. Brady, "Poll"; Waldron, "83 Percent."
14. Sigelman, "Hail to the Redskins?," 323.

15. Annenberg Public Policy Center, "Most Indians Say."
16. D. Snyder, "Letter from Washington Redskins Owner."
17. Annenberg Public Policy Center, "Most Indians Say."
18. Dhillon, Hemmings, Scales, and Stanley, "11 Reasons to Ignore."
19. Keene, "Missing the Point."
20. McCartney, "We Need a Fresh, Reliable Opinion Poll."
21. Staurowsky, "Exploring the 'Science.'"
22. Laveay, Callison, and Rodriguez, "Offensiveness of Native Americans Mascots." See also C. R. King et al., "Of Polls and Race Prejudice."
23. Fenelon, "Survey on Redskins Team Name."
24. Keene, "Native against Redsk*ns."
25. Moya-Smith, "Scholar Launches Google Doc 'Collective Voice' Campaign."
26. Tucker, "Redskins Nickname Issue Too Divisive."
27. Waldron, "Why a Poll Showing Americans Support."
28. C. R. King et al., "Of Polls and Race Prejudice," 390–91.
29. Song, "Other Redskins."
30. "We Are Very Proud."
31. Reilly, "Have the People Spoken?"
32. Lacitis, "For Wellpinit Students."
33. Shapira, "In Arizona."
34. Lacitis, "For Wellpinit Students"; Shapira, "In Arizona."
35. Lacitis, "For Wellpinit Students."
36. Flood, "How the 'Redskins' Debate Goes Over."
37. Keene, "Missing the Point."
38. D. Snyder, "Letter to Everyone."
39. Keene, "Missing the Point."
40. Goldtooth, "To All the Red*kins Supporters or Deniers."
41. St. George, "Why Va. Tribes Have Stayed Out." An interesting counterpoint here would be the alliance between the Seminole Tribe of Florida and Florida State University. Adrienne Keene has a nice piece here on the subject, "Interest Convergence, FSU, and the Seminole Tribe of Florida."
42. Fahri, "Dan Snyder Expands Radio Empire."
43. "Breaking News."
44. Irwin, "Most Important Super Bowl Ad."
45. Babin, ""NFL Player Poll."
46. Reilly, "Let's Bust Those Chops."

10. CHANGE

1. "Funding the Next #ChangetheMascot SuperBowl Ad"; Moya-Smith, "NCAI Seeks to Fund New Super Bowl Ad."
2. Cox, "Redskins Protesters Gearing Up."

3. Walker, "Meet the Native American Grandmother;" Harjo, "Fighting Name-Calling"; C. R. King, "Looking Back." Video streams from the symposium "Racist Stereotypes and Cultural Appropriation in American Sports" are available on the National Museum of the American Indian's website at http://nmai.si.edu/connect/symposia/archive/#stereotype.

4. Stretten, "If the Indian Mascot Could Speak"; White Eyes, "Indian Mascots, a Privileged Fight."

5. Wise, "Rooting for Washington's NFL Team."

6. Cox, "Redskins Name."

7. "Redskins Gear Stiff-Armed by Fans."

8. Cox, "Fierce, Lifelong Redskins Fan."

9. Lukas, "Hail to De-chiefing"; Cheney-Rice, "#DeChiefing Is the Anti-Racist Protest."

10. Cox, "Fierce, Lifelong Redskins Fan."

11. Fans for a New Tradition (emphasis in original).

12. Josh Silver, personal communication (email), April 20, 2015. See also Rebrand Washington Football.

13. Vrentas, "Battle of Washington."

14. "10 New Mascots"; DeadBatDesigns, "Washington Redshirts 'Uniform Look' Shirts"; Powers, "Satire."

15. "6 Suggestions for New Redskins Mascots."

16. Newell, "For Sale."

17. Keene, "10 Examples."

18. Miller, "Genocide as Entertainment."

19. "New Logo for the Washington Redskins"; see also "Creative New Way to Help People."

20. S. Allen, "People Have Been Making."

21. Madden, "Hail to the _____!"

22. Madden, "Vote to Rename the Team."

23. Madden, "Hail to the Pigskins!"

24. Taube, "Why Not the Washington Reagans."

25. Lewis and Tripathi, "Redskins Is Bad Business."

26. Sullivan, "Patawomeck Tribe."

27. Drury and Calvin, "Washington Red Clouds."

28. Craig, "D.C. Council May Push."

29. Iyer, "There's Only One Redskins Name Change."

30. Wise, "There's Really No Debate."

31. Suzan Shown Harjo's Facebook page, posted July 1, 2014.

32. Steinberg, "Great Redskins Name Debate."

33. Keating, "Washington Has Everything to Lose."

34. Keating, "What's In a Name?"

35. Lewis and Tripathi, "Redskins Is Bad Business."
36. Keating, "Washington Has Everything to Lose."
37. Seiffert, "Inside Slant."
38. McCarthy, "Redskins Rebrand Would Cost $15 Million."
39. "Washington Redskins Contracts."
40. Lewis and Tripathi, "Redskins Is Bad Business."
41. Seiffert, "Inside Slant."
42. Schaffer, "Here's How the Washington Football Team's Name Controversy Will End."
43. Lewis and Tripathi, "Redskins Is Bad Business."
44. Steinberg, "Peter King Explains."
45. Freeman, "Why Dan Snyder Won't Relent."
46. Kendrick, "How I Realized."
47. Steinberg, "From Riley Cooper to 'Redskins'" (emphasis in original).

11. ENDS

1. Dafron, "Billy Mills."
2. Schmitt, "Struggling, Resilient."
3. For a critical reading that nicely highlights the tropes and blind spots of the PSA, see Keene, "Proud to Be."
4. Moya-Smith, "Reclaiming the Native Voice."
5. Florio, "If Name Changes."
6. Mitcham, "Why 'Redskins' Must Go."
7. Vizenor, "Nickname Is Highly Offensive."
8. Cladoosby, "A Good Project for Synder's Foundation?"
9. National Congress of American Indians, *Ending the Legacy of Racism*, 5.
10. Lyons, "Rhetorical Sovereignty," 449–50.

BIBLIOGRAPHY

Allen, Bruce. "Letter to Harry Reid." May 23, 2014. http://files.redskins.com/pdf/letter
-from-bruce-allen.pdf.

Allen, Scott. "People Have Been Making the Same Redskins Potato Suggestion for
(at Least) 27 Years." *Washington Post*, June 19, 2014. http://www.washingtonpost
.com/blogs/dc-sports-bog/wp/2014/06/19/people-have-been-making-the-same
-redskins-potato-suggestion-for-at-least-27-years/.

Anderson, Monica. "How Media Organizations Are Handling the Redskins Name." Pew
Research Center, October 30, 2013. http://www.pewresearch.org/2013/10/30/how
-media- organizations-are-handling-the-redskins-name/.

Annenberg Public Policy Center. "Most Indians Say Name of Washington 'Redskins'
Is Acceptable While 9 Percent Call It Offensive, Annenberg Data Show." News
release, September 24, 2004. http://www.annenbergpublicpolicycenter.org/wp
-content/uploads/2004_03_redskins_09-24_pr2.pdf.

Ansell, Amy. *New Right, New Racism: Race and Reaction in the United States*. New York:
New York University Press, 1997.

Babin, Jason. "NFL Player Poll: Redskins Name ok." ESPN, September 3, 2014. http://
espn.go.com/nfl/story/_/id/11452022/nfl-nation-confidential-majority-players
-support-washington-redskins-nickname.

Barr, John. "Was Redskins' First Coach a Fraud?" ESPN, September 3, 2014. http://
espn.go.com/espn/otl/story/_/id/11455467/was-washington-redskins-first
-coach-fraud.

Basen, Ryan. "Fifty Years Ago, Last Outpost of Segregation in N.F.L. Fell." *New York
Times*, October 6, 2012. http://www.nytimes.com/2012/10/07/sports/football
/50-years-ago-redskins-were-last-nfl-team- to-integrate.html?_r=0.

Baum, Frank. Editorial. *Aberdeen (SD) Pioneer*, December 20, 1890. http://www2
.warwick.ac.uk/fac/arts/english/currentstudents/undergraduate/modules
/fulllist/second/en213/term1/l_frank_baum.pdf.

Beaujon, Andrew. "Here's a List of Outlets and Journalists That Won't Use the Name 'Redskins.'" Poynter Mediawire, June 19, 2014. http://www.poynter.org/news /mediawire/256258/heres-a-list-of-outlets- and-journalists-who-wont-use-the -name-redskins/.

Bene, Ross. "Broadcasters Really Are Saying 'Redskins' a Lot Less This Year." Deadspin, September 17, 2014. http://regressing.deadspin.com/broadcasters-really -are-saying-redskins-a-lot-less-th-1635806862.

Benjey, Tom. *Keep A-Goin': The Life of Lone Star Dietz*. Carlisle PA: Tuxedo Press, 2006.

Berkhofer, Robert F. *The White Man's Indian: Images of the American Indian from Columbus to Present*. New York: Vintage/Random House, 1978.

Blackhawk, Ned. *Violence over the Land: Indians and Empires in the Early American West*. Cambridge MA: Harvard University Press, 2006.

Blackhorse, Amanda. "This Is What Dehumanization Looks Like." *Indian Country Today*, March 20, 2015. http://indiancountrytodaymedianetwork.com/2015/03/20 /blackhorse-what-dehumanization-looks-159694.

Bonilla-Silva, Eduardo. *Racism without Racists: Color-Blind Racism and the Persistence of Racial Inequality in America*. Lanham MD: Rowan and Littlefield, 2003.

Boraas, Alan. "Aniak Halfbreeds? Proud Name; Washington Redskins? Racist Slur." *Alaska Dispatch News*, September 19, 2014. http://www.adn.com/article/20140919/aniak -halfbreeds-proud-name-washington-redskins-racist-slur.

Boren, Cindy. "Who Is Amanda Blackhorse in Redskins' Trademark Case?" *Washington Post*, June 18, 2014. http://www.washingtonpost.com/blogs/early-lead/wp/2014/06 /18/who-is-amanda-blackhorse-in-redskins-trademark-case/.

"Boston Braves Grid Men Become 'Redskins.'" *Hartford Courant*, July 6, 1933, 15.

Boyer, LaNada. "Reflections on Alcatraz." In *American Indian Activism: Alcatraz to the Longest Walk*, edited by Troy R. Johnson, Joane Nagel, and Duane Champagne, 88–103. Urbana: University of Illinois Press, 1997.

Brady, Erik. "Daniel Snyder Says Redskins Will Never Change Name." *USA Today*, May 10, 2013. http://www.usatoday.com/story/sports/nfl/redskins/2013/05/09 /washington-redskins-daniel-snyder/2148127/.

———. "Montana Indian Tribe Happy to Take Redskins' Money." *USA Today*, July 31, 2014. http://www.usatoday.com/story/sports/nfl/2014/07/31/washington-redskins -original-americans-foundation-indian-tribes/13422205/.

———. "New Generation of American Indians Challenges Redskins." *USA Today*, May 10, 2013. http://www.usatoday.com/story/sports/nfl/redskins/2013/05/09 /native-americans-washington-mascot-fight/2148877/.

———. "Notah Begay: Snyder's Redskins Foundation a 'Gimmick.'" *USA Today*, April 22, 2014. http://www.usatoday.com/story/sports/nfl/2014/04/22/daniel -snyder-team-name-controversy-foundation-notah-begay/8014797/.

————. "Poll: 83% Would Not Call Native American a 'Redskin.'" *USA Today*, November 20, 2014. http://www.usatoday.com/story/sports/nfl/redskins/2014/11/20 /washington-redskins-poll-name-controversy-daniel-snyder/19297429/.

————. "Poll: Majority See Why Redskins Name Offensive." *USA Today*, October 16, 2013. http://www.usatoday.com/story/sports/nfl/redskins/2013/10/15/redskins -oneida-indian-nation-name/2990743/.

————. "Redskins' Trademark Attorney Debates Meaning of 'Redskin.'" *USA Today*, June 19, 2014. http://ftw.usatoday.com/2014/06/redskins-trademark-attorney-debates -meaning-of-redskin.

————. "Woman Suing Redskins Says Code Talkers Honor 'Sugarcoats' Racism." *USA Today*, November 27, 2013. http://www.usatoday.com/story/sports/nfl /redskins/2013/11/27/amanda-blackhorse-redskins-navajo-code-talkers-honor /3767981/.

"Braves Pro Gridmen to Be Called Redskins." *Boston Herald*, July 6, 1933, 20.

"Breaking News: D.C. Radio Stations Won't Run Anti-mascot Ad." *Indian Country Today*, October 19, 2013. http://indiancountrytodaymedianetwork.com/2013/10/19 /breaking-news-dc-radio-stations-wont-run-anti-mascot-ad-151842.

Bryant, Howard. "Battle over Nickname Continues." *ESPN Magazine*, September 2, 2014. http://espn.go.com/nfl/story/_/id/11185859/washington-redskins-nickname -does-not-honor-native-americans-espn-magazine.

Buchanan, Patrick J. "Hail to the Redskins." *World Net Daily*, October 21, 2013. http:// www.wnd.com/2013/10/hail- to-the-redskins/#OMrtYwPsqj5fBZUQ.99.

Burke, Timothy. "'Redskins' Mentions Down 27% on NFL Game Broadcasts in 2014." *Deadspin*, December 30, 2014. http://regressing.deadspin.com/redskins-mentions -down-27-on-nfl-game-broadcasts-in-1676147358.

Burns, Bob. "Blackfeet Elder Says Rick Reilly Misquoted Him; Wants 'Redskins' Banned." *Indian Country Today*, October 10, 2013. http://indiancountrytodaymedianetwork .com/2013/10/10/blackfeet-elder-says-rick-reilly-misquoted-him-wants-redskins -banned-151696.

Cahill, Dan. "Mike Ditka: If 'Redskins' Is Offensive to American Indians, 'I'm All for Changing It.'" *Chicago Sun-Times*, August 22, 2014. http://voices.suntimes.com /sports/mike-ditka-if-redskins-is-offensive- to-american-indians-im-all -for-changing-it/.

Capozza, Koren. "Charity Scams: Making Big Business Out of Native American Poverty." *Colorlines*, December 15, 2000.

Carley, William M. "Is Chief Noc-a-Homa Racist? Many Indians Evidently Think He Is?" *Wall Street Journal*, January 27, 1972.

Chaney, John, Amanda Burke, and Edward Burkley. "Do American Indian Mascots = American Indian People? Examining Implicit Bias towards American Indian People and American Indian Mascots." *American Indian and Alaska Native Mental Health Research* 18 (2011): 42–62.

Cheney-Rice, Zak. "#DeChiefing Is the Anti-racist Protest That Pro Sports Badly Needs." Mic.com, April 5, 2014. http://mic.com/articles/86947/dechiefing-is -the-anti-racist-protest-that-pro-sports-badly-needs.

"Chris Rock: 'Redskins? That's Not Nice. That's a Racial Slur.'" *Indian Country Today*, July 30, 2014. http://indiancountrytodaymedianetwork.com/2014/07/30/chris -rock-redskins-thats-not-nice-thats-racial-slur-156126.

Cladoosby, Brian. "A Good Project for Synder's Foundation? Fighting the Use of the Word Redskins." *Washington Post*, April 4, 2014. http://www.washingtonpost.com/opinions /a-good-project-for-snyders-foundation-fighting-the-use-of-the-word-redskins /2014/04/04/7b736380-baab-11e3-9a05-c739f29ccb08_story.html.

Cohen, Rick. "Dan Snyder Seeks Original Native American Art to Redwash Foundation." *Nonprofit Quarterly*, August 8, 2014. https://nonprofitquarterly.org /policysocial-context/24644-dan-snyder-seeks-original-native-american-art-to -redwash-foundation.html.

Collins, Patricia Hill. *Black Sexual Politics: African Americans, Gender and the New Racism*. New York: Routledge, 2005.

Cook, Ray. "Stupid Americans Doing What Stupid Americans Have Always Done." *Indian Country Today*, October 27, 2014. http://indiancountrytodaymedianetwork.com /2013/10/27/stupid-americans-doing-what-stupid-americans-have-always -done.

Cook-Lynn, Elizabeth. *Anti-Indianism in Modern America: A Voice from Tatekeya's Earth*. Urbana: University of Illinois Press, 2001.

Coombe, Rosemary J. "Sports Trademarks and Somatic Politics: Locating the Law in Critical Cultural Studies." In *SportCult*, edited by R. Martin and T. Miller, 262–88. Minneapolis: University of Minnesota Press, 1999.

Cox, John Woodrow. "At FedEx Field, Redskins Name Protesters Exchange Sharp Words with Fans" *Washington Post*, December 28, 2014. http://www.washingtonpost .com/local/at-fedex-field-redskins-name-protesters-exchange-sharp-words -with-fans/2014/12/28/f3aa1acc-8ed3-11e4-a412-4b735edc7175_story.html.

———. "A Fierce, Lifelong Redskins Fan Takes a Stand against His Beloved Team's Name." *Washington Post*, November 21, 2014. http://www.washingtonpost.com /local/a-rabid-lifelong-redskins-fan-takes-a-stand-against-his-beloved-teams -name/2014/11/21/34848708-6fb7-11e4-8808-afaa1e3a33ef_story.html.

———. "Redskins Name: 'A pr Dumpster Fire.'" *Washington Post*, November 21, 2014. http://www.washingtonpost.com/blogs/local/wp/2014/11/21/redskins-name-a -pr-dumpster-fire/.

———. "Redskins Protesters Gearing Up for FedEx Field Rally Offended by Nearby Event's Title." *Washington Post*, December 26, 2014. http://www.washingtonpost .com/local/redskins-protesters-gearing-up-for-fedex-field-rally-offended-by -nearby-events-title/2014/12/26/e72ee1ce-8d2f-11e4-a085-34e9b9f09a58_story .html.

———. "Tribe's Infighting Offers Glimpse into Redskins Foundation's Tactics." *Washington Post*, April 2, 2015. http://www.washingtonpost.com/local/tribes-infighting-offers -glimpse-into-redskins-foundations-tactics/2015/04/02/be7c9a22-d8c1-11e4 -8103-fa84725dbf9d_story.html.

Craig, Tim. "D.C. Council May Push Washington Redskins into 'Washington Redtails.'" *Washington Post*, April 30, 2013. http://www.washingtonpost.com/local /dc-politics/dc-council-may-push-washington-redskins-into-washington-redtails /2013/04/30/456cb72c-b1a7-11e2-bbf2-a6f9e9d79e19_story.html.

"A Creative New Way to Help People Understand How Racism Works." Upworthy, October 16, 2014. http://www.upworthy.com/a-creative-new-way-to-help-people -understand-how-racism-works-dont-panic-white-folks-its-funny.

Dafron, Bryan. "Billy Mills: Name Calls to Mind 'Our Own Holocaust.'" *Indian Country Today*, September 11, 2013. http://indiancountrytodaymedianetwork .com/2013/11/09/billy-mills-redskins-name-calls-mind-our-own-holocaust -152165.

"Daniel Snyder Defends the 'Redskins.'" ESPN, August 6, 2014. http://espn.go.com /nfl/story/_/id/11313245/daniel-snyder-redskins-term-honor-respect.

"Dan Snyder to 'Redskins' Critics: 'We're Not an Issue.'" *USA Today*, April 22, 2014. http:// www.usatoday.com/story/sports/nfl/redskins/2014/04/22/redskins-snyder-says -team-name-is-not-an-issue/8011455/.

Davis, Laurel R. "Protest against the Use of Native American Mascots: A Challenge to Traditional, American Identity." *Journal of Sport and Social Issues* 17 (1993): 9–22.

DeadBatDesigns. "Washington Redshirts 'Uniform Look' Men's and Ladies Shirts." Etsy. com, listed April 23, 2015. https://www.etsy.com/listing/183161779/washington -redshirts-uniform-look-mens?ref=related-2.

Deal, Gregg. "I Have Been Indian My Whole Life." Creative Mornings lecture, Washington DC, August 12, 2014. https://www.youtube.com/watch?v=d1dilz 5ph9u.

———. "I've Been Indigenous My Whole Life: Images of Indigenous Art and Activism." Lecture delivered at the National Museum of the American Indian, December 9, 2014. https://www.youtube.com/watch?v=1faaaaSHt2e.

———. "Redskin." [Undated, Fall 2014.] http://greggdeal.com/redskin.

———. "Redskin: Indigenous Art and Identity." Indiegogo crowdfunding page. 2014. https://www.indiegogo.com/projects/redskin-indigenous-art- and-identity.

Deloria, Philip L. *Playing Indian*. New Haven CT: Yale University Press, 1998.

D'Errico, Peter. "NFL Franchise Channels Puritan Colonists." *Indian Country Today*, April 18, 2014. http://indiancountrytodaymedianetwork.com/2014/04/18/nfl -franchise-channels-puritan-colonists.

Dhillon, Natasha, Justin Hemmings, Maggie Scales, and William Stanley. "11 Reasons to Ignore the 10-Year-Old Annenberg Survey about the Washington Football Team's Offensive Name." Glushko-Samuelson Intellectual Law Clinic,

Washington College of Law, American University, February 11, 2014. http://
ipclinic.org/2014/02/11/11-reasons-to-ignore-the-10-year-old-annenberg-survey
-about-the-washington-football-teams-offensive-name/.

Drury, Bob, and Thomas Calvin. "The Washington Red Clouds: A Team Name to
Honor a Great Warrior and Leader." *Washington Post*, November 1, 2013. http://
www.washingtonpost.com/opinions/the-washington-red-clouds-a-team-name-to
-honor-a-great-warrior- and-leader/2013/11/01/292f20c4-40e3-11e3-a624
-41d661b0bb78_story.html.

Dunetz, Jeff. "Liberal Media Attacks the Washington Redskins Thanksgiving Message."
Truth Revolt, November 28, 2014. http://www.truthrevolt.org/news/liberal
-media-attacks-washington-redskins-thanksgiving-message.

"11 Trending Words of 2014." Dictionary.com, December 18, 2014. http://blog.dictionary
.com/trending-words-2014/.

Engberg, Daniel. "Who Made the Redskins Logo?" *New York Times*, November 15, 2013.
http://www.nytimes.com/2013/11/17/magazine/who-made-that-redskins-logo
.html?_r=0.

Enote, Jim. "We Are Not Redskins." *Indian Country Today*, August 11, 2014. http://indian
countrytodaymedianetwork.com/2014/08/11/we-are-not-redskins.

"ESPN's Mike Ditka on Redskins' Name Debate." Redskinshistorian.com, [undated,
August 2014]. http://www.redskinshistorian.com/content/mike-ditka-redskins
-nickname-controversy.

Exploiting Indians (blog). http://exploitingtheindians.blogspot.com.

"The Facts." Redskinsfacts.com. http://www.redskinsfacts.com/facts.

Fahri, Paul. "Dan Snyder Expands Radio Empire." *Washington Post*, June 5, 2008.
http://www.washingtonpost.com/wp-dyn/content/article/2008/06/04/ar20080
60404080.html.

Faleomavaega, Eni. "Ignorance Is Bliss . . . for Supporters of the Washington Redskins."
Hill, June 9, 2014. http://thehill.com/opinion/op-ed/208725-ignorance-is-bliss
-for-supporters-of-the-washington-redskins.

Fans for a New Tradition. http://fansforanewtradition.com.

Fenelon, James V. "Survey on Redskins Team Name Found Most American Indians
Believe It to Be Offensive and Racist." Press release, California State University,
San Bernardo, undated. http://cips.csusb.edu/docs/PressRelease.pdf.

"Financing New Stadiums." *New York Times*, May 7, 1998. http://www.nytimes.com
/1998/05/07/opinion/financing-new-stadiums.html.

Flood, Joe. "How the 'Redskins' Debate Goes Over on an Actual Indian Reservation."
Buzzfeed, October 3, 2013. http://www.buzzfeed.com/joeflood/how-the-redskins
-debate-goes-over-on-an-actual-indian-reserv#.vaMzomVWw.

Florio, Mike. "If Name Changes, Would Washington Logo Be Acceptable?" *Pro
Football Talk*, June 1, 2014. http://profootballtalk.nbcsports.com/2014/06/01/if
-name-changes-would-washington-logo-be-acceptable/.

Franklin, Mary Beth. "Give It Back for Tax Breaks." *Los Angeles Times*, February 10, 1985.

Freeman, Mike. "Why Dan Snyder Won't Relent on 'Redskins,' and Why I Did." *Bleacher Report*, June 10, 2014. http://bleacherreport.com/articles/2088756-why-dan-snyder -wont-relent-on-redskins-and-why-i-did.

Freng, Scott, and Willis-Esqueda, Cynthia. "A Question of Honor: Chief Wahoo and American Indian Stereotype Activation among a University-Based Sample." *Journal of Social Psychology* 151 (2011): 577–91.

Friedman, Michael A. "The Harmful Psychological Effects of Washington's Redskins Mascot." *Indian Country Today*, September 27, 2013. http:// indiancountrytodaymedianetwork.com/2013/09/27/harmful-psychological -effects-washingtons-redskins-mascot.

———. "The NBA Schools the NFL on How to Handle Racism." *Psychology Today*, May 6, 2014. https://www.psychologytoday.com/blog/brick-brick/201405/the-nba-schools -the-nfl-how-handle-racism-0.

Fruehling, Douglas. "We Won't Use Redskins Anymore." *Washington Business Journal*, August 1, 2014. http://www.bizjournals.com/washington/print-edition/2014/08/01 /we-won-t-use-redskins-anymore.html.

Fryberg, Stephanie A., Hazel Rose Markus, Daphna Oyserman, and Joseph M. Stone. "Of Warrior Chiefs and Indian Princesses: The Psychological Consequences of American Indian Mascots." *Basic and Applied Social Psychology* 30 (2008): 208–18.

"Funding the Next #ChangetheMascot SuperBowl Ad." Crowdsourcing campaign. https://www.kickstarter.com/projects/1036961755/change-the-mascot/updates.

Gambini, Bert. "Research Shows Native American Imagery Hurts All Ethnic Groups, Says ub Psychologist." News release, University of Buffalo, March 11, 2015. http:// www.buffalo.edu/news/releases/2015/03/021.html.

Garcia-Vargas, Andrea. "The Redskins Say Their Name Is 'Respectful'—Here's the Truth They Need to See," Mic.com, May 20, 2014. http://www.mic.com/articles/87629/the -redskins-say-their-name-is-respectful-here-s-the-truth-they-need-to-see.

Geoghegan, Tom. "Washington Redskins: Time to Change the Name?" *BBC Magazine*, September 14, 2013. http://www.bbc.com/news/magazine-24027457.

Giago, Tim. "R-word Just as Insulting as the N-word." Indianz.com, December 4, 2006. http://www.indianz.com//news/2006/017185.asp.

Goddard, Yves. "'I Am a Red-Skin': The Adoption of a Native-American Expression (1769–1826)." *European Review of Native American Studies* 19, no. 2 (2005). http:// anthropology.si.edu/goddard/redskin.pdf.

Goldtooth, Dallas. "To All the Red*kins Supporters or Deniers." Facebook post, October 2014. https://www.facebook.com/dallasgoldtooth/posts/10103575063421053.

Gover, Kevin. "Unraveling the 'Redskins' Lie: Americans Don't Know Native History." *Indian Country Today*, October 29, 2014. http://indiancountrytodaymedianetwork .com/2014/10/29/unraveling-redskins-lie-americans-dont-know-native-history.

Griffith, Corrine. *My Life with the Redskins*. New York: as Barnes, 1947.

Guiliano, Jennifer. *Indian Spectacle: College Mascots and the Anxiety of Modern America.* New Brunswick NJ: Rutgers University Press, 2015.

Guy, Ronald. "Washington Redskins: The Original Americans Foundation Falls Silent." Football.com, March 28, 2015. https://www.football.com/en-us/washington -redskins-the-original-americans-foundation-falls-silent/.

Handy, Bruce. "The Complex and Hidden Story behind the Washington Redskins Trademark Decision." *Vanity Fair*, June 25, 2014. http://www.vanityfair.com/news /2014/06/story-behind-washington-redskins-name.

Harding, Robert. "A Simple Case for the NFL's Washington Redskins to Change their Racist Name." *Auburn (NY) Citizen*, March 26, 2014. http://auburnpub.com /blogs/in_the_pros/a-simple-case-for-the-nfl-s-washington-redskins-to/article _4c7ff33c-b546-11e3-959c-001a4bcf887a.html.

Harjo, Suzan Shown. "Fighting Name-Calling: Challenging 'Redskins' in Court." In *Team Spirits: Essays on the History and Significance of Native American Mascots*, edited by C. Richard King and Charles Fruehling Springwood, 189–207. Lincoln: University of Nebraska Press, 2001.

——. "Washington Chief-Making and the R-Word." *Indian Country Today*, February 4, 2002. http://indiancountrytodaymedianetwork.com/2002/02/04/washington -chief-making-and-r-word-87474.

——. "The R-Word Is Even Worse Than You Think." Politico, June 23, 2014. http:// www.politico.com/magazine/story/2014/06/washington-football-team-108213 .html.

——. "Washington 'Redskins' Is a Racist Name: U.S. Pro Football Must Disavow It." *Guardian*, January 17, 2013. http://www.theguardian.com/commentisfree/2013/jan /17/washington-redskins-racism-pro-football.

Harris, Cheryl I. "Whiteness as Property." *Harvard Law Review* 106 (1993): 1710–91.

Hendley, Matthew. "Navajo Representative Wants Washington Redskins' Name Changed." *Phoenix New Times*, October 28, 2014. http://blogs.phoenixnewtimes.com /valleyfever/2014/10/washington_redskins_name_change_navajo_jamescita _peshlakai.php.

Hendricks, Maggie. "Champ Bailey: Controversial 'Redskins' Name Like N-Word." *USA Today*, June 11, 2014. http://q.usatoday.com/2014/06/11/champ-bailey -controversial-redskins-name-like-n-word/.

Hinkle, A. Barton "The Washington Redskins Are About to Fleece Virginia Taxpayers." *Reason*, June 18, 2012. http://reason.com/archives/2012/06/18/the-washington -redskins-are-about-to-fle.

Holley, Joe. "Slingin' Sammy Baugh Passed His Way into Gridiron History." *Washington Post*, February 4, 2006. http://www.washingtonpost.com/wp-dyn/content /article/2006/02/03/ar2006020302966_pf.html.

Holmes, Baxter. "A 'Redskin' Is the Scalped Head of a Native American, Sold, Like a Pelt, for Cash." *Esquire*, June 17, 2014. http://www.esquire.com/news-politics/news /a29445/true-redskins-meaning.

———. "Update: Yes, a 'Redskin' Does, in Fact, Mean the Scalped Head of a Native American, Sold, Like a Pelt, for Cash." *Esquire*, June 18, 2014. http://www.esquire.com /news-politics/news/a29318/redskin-name-update/.

Hoskins, Tansy. "Washington Redskins: Do Offensive Team Names Endanger Public Health?" *Guardian*, October 25, 2013. http://www.theguardian.com/sustainable -business/washington-redskins-native-american-stereotypes-bullying.

Houska, Tara. "Dehumanization, Racism, and Disrespect: A Walk through a Tailgate at FedEx Field." Notyourmascot.org, January 3, 2015. http://www.notyourmascots.org /2015/01/03/dehumanization-racism-and-disrespect/.

Hylton, J. Gordon. "Before the Redskins Were the Redskins: The Use of Native American Team Names in the Formative Era of American Sports, 1857–1933." *North Dakota Law Review* 86 (2010): 879–904.

"Indigenous Artist Gregg Deal on 'Redskins' Name Controversy." Creative Resistance, [undated]. http://www.creativeresistance.org/indigenous-artist-gregg-deal-on -redskins-name-controversy/.

Ironwing, Clem. "Remarks on Wichita North Redskins, Mascot/Identity Committee Hearing." November 11, 1996. Copy in author's files.

Irwin, Ben. "The Most Important Super Bowl Ad You Didn't See." *Huffington Post*, April 5, 2014. http://www.huffingtonpost.com/ben-irwin/the-most-important-super -_b_4717316.html.

Iyer, Vinie. "There's Only One Redskins Name Change That Works." *Sporting News*, June 18, 2014. http://www.sportingnews.com/nfl/story/2014-05-22/washington-redskins -name-change-nfl-daniel-snyder-americans-redtails-cowboys.

Jae, Johnnie. "Is the R*dskins Name Really Offensive? Why Yes, Yes It Is." Good Men Project, June 2, 2014. http://goodmenproject.com/featured-content/redskns-name -really-offensive-yes-yes-hesaid/.

Jensen, Robert. "Banning 'Redskins' from the Sports Page: The Ethics and Politics of Native American Nicknames." *Journal of Mass Media Ethics* 9 (1994): 16–25.

Jodie, Quentin. "Washington Redskins Donate $30,000 to Local School." *Navajo Times*, August 26, 2014. http://navajotimes.com/rezsports/washington-redskins-donate -30000-local-school/#.VKo1r1rsdUQ.

Johnson, Allan G. "What Is a 'System of Privilege'?" 2013. http://www.agjohnson.us/glad /what-is-a-system-of-privilege/.

Jones, Mike. "Bruce Allen: No Plans to Change Redskins' Name." *Washington Post*, February 14, 2013. http://www.washingtonpost.com/blogs/football-insider/wp/2013/02/14 /bruce-allen-no-plans-to-change-redskins-name/.

Keating, Peter. "What's in a Name?" *ESPN Magazine*, June 27, 2014. http://espn.go .com/nfl/story/_/id/9540075/dan-snyder-refuses-change-washington-redskins -mascot-espn-magazine.

——. "Washington Has Everything to Lose." ESPN, September 3, 2014. http://espn
.go.com/nfl/story/_/id/11419303/washington-redskins-losing-money-keeping
-name.

Keene, Adrienne. "Interest Convergence, fsu, and the Seminole Tribe of Florida."
Native Appropriations (blog), January 22, 2013. http://nativeappropriations
.com/2013/01/interest-convergence-fsu-and-the-seminole-tribe-of-florida
.html.

——. "Kwatsan Tribe Refuses Dan Snyder's 'Blood Money.'" *Native Appropriations* (blog),
July 17, 2014. http://nativeappropriations.com/2014/07/kwatsan-tribe-refuses
-dan-snyders-blood-money.html.

——. "Missing the Point on the Red Mesa Redsk*ns." *Native Appropriations* (blog),
October 28, 2014. http://nativeappropriations.com/2014/10/missing-the-point-on
-the-red-mesa-redskns.html.

——. "Native against Redsk*ns." *Native Appropriations* (blog), [undated, Summer
2014]. http://nativeappropriations.com/nativesagainstredskins.

——. "'Proud to Be': NCAI's Answer to the R-word Mascot Debate." *Native
Appropriations* (blog), February 1, 2014. http://nativeappropriations.com/2014/02
/proud-to-be-ncais-answer- to-the-r-word-mascot-debate.html.

——. "10 Examples of Indian Mascots 'Honoring' Native Peoples." *Native Appropriations*
(blog), December 8, 2013. http://nativeappropriations.com/2013/12/10-examples
-of-indian-mascots-honoring-native-peoples.html/deadskin.

——. "Who Has Spoken Out against the Redskins?" *Native Appropriations* (blog), June
23, 2014. http://nativeappropriations.com/2014/06/who-has-spoken-out-against
-the-redskns.html.

Kendall, Frances E. *Understanding White Privilege*. 2nd ed. New York: Routledge, 2013.

Kendrick, Paul. "How I Realized Loving the Washington Redskins Means Demanding a
Name Change." *Huffington Post*, October 6, 2014. http://www.huffingtonpost.com
/paul-kendrick/how-i-realized-loving-the_b_5940300.html.

Kessler, Glenn. "Fact Checking the New Web Site, 'RedskinsFacts.com.'" *Washington
Post*, July 31, 2014. http://www.washingtonpost.com/blogs/fact-checker/wp
/2014/07/31/fact-checking-the-new-web-site-redskinsfacts-com/.

Kimmel, Michael S., and Abby Ferber, eds. *Privilege: A Reader*. Boulder CO: Westview
Press, 2003.

Kim-Prieto, Chu, Lizabeth A. Goldstein, Sumie Okazaki, and Blake Kirschner. "Effect
of Exposure to an American Indian Mascot on the Tendency to Stereotype a
Different Minority Group." *Journal of Applied Social Psychology* 40 (2010): 534–53.

King, C. Richard. "Looking Back to a Future End: Reflections on the Symposium on
Racist Stereotypes in American Sport at the National Museum of the American
Indian." *American Indian Quarterly* 38 (2014): 135–42.

——, ed. *The Native American Mascot Controversy: A Handbook*. Lanham md: Scarecrow
Press, 2011.

——. "On Being a Warrior: Race, Gender, and American Indian Imagery in Sport." *International Journal of the History of Sport* 23 (2006): 313-29.

——, ed. "Re/Claiming Indianness: Critical Perspectives on Native American Mascots." Special Issue, *Journal of Sport and Social Issues* 28, no. 1 (2004).

——. "Uneasy Indians: Creating and Contesting Native American Mascots at Marquette University." In *Team Spirits: The Native American Mascot Controversy*, edited by C. Richard King and Charles Fruehling Springwood, 281-303. Lincoln: University of Nebraska Press, 2001.

——. *Unsettling America: Indianness in the Contemporary World*. Lanham md: Rowman and Littlefield, 2013.

King, C. Richard, and Charles Fruehling Springwood. "The Best Offense . . . Dissociation, Desire, and the Defense of the Florida State University Seminoles." In *Team Spirits: The Native American Mascot Controversy*, edited by C. Richard King and Charles Fruehling Springwood, 129-56. Lincoln: University of Nebraska Press, 2001.

——. *Beyond the Cheers: Race as Spectacle in College Sports*. Albany: State University of New York Press. 2001.

——, eds. *Team Spirits: Essays on the History and Significance of Native American Mascots*. Lincoln: University of Nebraska Press, 2001.

King, C. Richard, Ellen J. Staurowsky, Lawrence Baca, Laurel R. Davis, and Cornel Pewewardy. "Of Polls and Race Prejudice: *Sports Illustrated*'s Errant 'Indian Wars.'" *Journal of Sport & Social Issues* 26 (2002): 381-402.

King, Jamillah. "Native American Groups Are Not Impressed by Dan Snyder's Latest Move." *Colorlines*, March 25, 2014. http://colorlines.com/archives/2014/03/native_american_groups_are_not_impressed_by_dan_snyders_latest_move.html.

Klemko, Robert. "Redskins: Right or Wrong?" *Sports Illustrated*, December 31, 2014. http://mmqb.si.com/2014/12/31/washington-redskins-nickname-protest-nfl/.

Kogod, Sarah. "Bob Costas on Redskins Name: 'It's an Insult, a Slur.'" *Washington Post*, October 13, 2013. http://www.washingtonpost.com/blogs/dc-sports-bog/wp/2013/10/13/bob-costas-on-redskins-name-its-an-insult-a-slur/.

——. "Redskins Respond to Team Name Controversy, Kind Of." *Washington Post*, February 12, 2013. http://www.washingtonpost.com/blogs/dc-sports-bog/wp/2013/02/12/redskins-respond-to-team-name-controversy-kind-of/.

——. "Sonic Apologizes for Offensive Chiefs-Redskins Sign." *Washington Post*, December 9, 2013. http://www.washingtonpost.com/blogs/dc-sports-bog/wp/2013/12/09/sonic-apologizes-for-offensive-chiefs-redskins-sign/.

Krauthammer, Charles. "Redskins and Reason." *Washington Post*, October 17, 2013. http://www.washingtonpost.com/opinions/charles-krauthammer-redskins-and-reason/2013/10/17/cbb11eee-374f-11e3-ae46-e4248e75c8ea_story.html.

Kwiatek, Beth. "Another Voice: Redskins Debate Misses the Larger Point of White Privilege." *Buffalo News*, April 1, 2015. http://www.buffalonews.com/opinion/another

-voice/another-voice-redskins-debate-misses-the-larger-point-of-white-privilege
-20150401.

Lacitis, Erik. "For Wellpinit Students, 'Redskins' a Source of Pride, Tradition." *Spokane (WA) Spokesman Review*, July 2, 2014. http://www.spokesman.com/stories/2014/jul/02/for-wellpinit-students-redskins-a-source-of-pride/.

LaRocque, Angela R., Douglas J. McDonald, Jeff N. Weatherly, and Richard F. Ferraro. "Indian Sports Nicknames/Logos: Affective Differences between American Indian and Non-Indian College Students." *American Indian and Alaska Native Mental Health Research* 18 (2011): 1–16.

"Las Vegas Paiute Tribe Rejected 'Gift' from NFL Team's Foundation." Indiaz.com, August 29, 2014. http://www.indianz.com/News/2014/014912.asp.

Laveay, Fraser, Coy Callison, and Ann Rodriguez. "Offensiveness of Native Americans Mascots and Logos in Sports: A Survey of Tribal Leaders and the General Population." *International Journal of Sport Communication* 2 (2010): 81–99.

Leiby, Richard. "The Legend of Lone Star Dietz: Redskins Namesake, Coach—and Possible Impostor?" *Washington Post*, November 6, 2013. www.washingtonpost.com/lifestyle/style/the-legend-of-lone-star-dietz-redskins-namesake-coach—and-possible-imposter/2013/11/06/a1358a76-466b-11e3-bf0c-cebf37c6f484_story.html.

Levin, Josh. "Here, Take This Coat." *Slate*, March 25, 2014. http://www.slate.com/articles/sports/sports_nut/2014/03/dan_snyder_washington_nfl_team_the_owner_s_cynical_new_effort_to_squelch.html.

Lewis, Michael, and Manish Tripathi. "Redskins Is Bad Business." *New York Times*, June 24, 2014. http://www.nytimes.com/2014/06/25/opinion/redskins-is-bad-business.html.

Ley, Tom. "Washington Merchandise Sales Are Down 35 Percent," *Deadspin*, September 5, 2014. http://deadspin.com/washingtons-merchandise-sales-are-down-35-percent-1631023843.

Lindsay, Peter. "Representing Redskins: The Ethics of Native American Team Names." *Journal of the Philosophy of Sport* 35 (2008): 208–24.

Lipsitz, George. "The Possessive Investment in Whiteness: Racialized Social Democracy and the 'White' Problem in American Studies." *American Quarterly* 47 (1995): 369–87.

Lone Hill, Dana. "The Refusal to Rename the Redskins Is Far Worse Than Sterling's Racist Remarks." *Guardian*, April 30, 2014. http://www.theguardian.com/commentisfree/2014/apr/30/rename-the-washington-redskins-racism.

Lovely, Lori. "Redskins: What's in a Name? Native Americans Protest the Racial Slur That Is a Mascot" *Nuvo*, December 3, 2014. http://www.nuvo.net/indianapolis/redskins-whats-in-a-name/Content?oid=2982102.

Lowry, Rich. "Liberals Fabricate Outrage Over 'Redskins'," *National Review*, October 8, 2013. http://www.nationalreview.com/article/360614/liberals-fabricate-outrage-over-redskins-rich-lowry.

Lukas, Paul. "Hail To De-chiefing." ESPN, April 24, 2014. http://espn.go.com/mlb/story/_/id/10715887/uni-watch-some-fans-removing-chief-wahoo-logos-protest.

———. "Native Americans Speak on Sports Imagery." espn, February 13, 2013. http://espn.go.com/blog/playbook/fandom/post/_/id/18144/native-americans-speak-on-sports-imagery.

———. "Tribe Supports Native American Mascots." espn, February 20, 2013. http://espn.go.com/blog/playbook/fandom/post/_/id/18484/tribe-supports-native-american-mascots.

Lyons, Scott Richard. "Rhetorical Sovereignty: What Do American Indians Want from Writing?" *College Composition and Communication* 51 (2000): 447–68.

Madden, Mike. "Hail to the _____!" *Washington City Paper*, October 1, 2012. http://www.washingtoncitypaper.com/blogs/citydesk/2012/10/01/hail-to-the--_____/.

———. "Hail to the Pigskins!" *Washington City Paper*, October 18, 2012. http://www.washingtoncitypaper.com/blogs/citydesk/2012/10/18/hail-to-the-pigskins/.

———. "Vote to Rename the Team." *Washington City Paper*, October 9, 2012. http://www.washingtoncitypaper.com/blogs/citydesk/2012/10/09/vote-rename-the-team/.

Mansch, Scott. "Don Wetzel: Don't Call Redskins Logo Offensive." *Great Falls (MT) Tribune*, February 19, 2014. http://www.greatfallstribune.com/story/news/2014/02/16/don-wetzel-dont-call-redskins-logo-offensive/5528647/.

Maske, Mike. "Redskins Name Change Would Have to Pass Muster with NFL, Sponsors." *Washington Post*, February 24, 2013. http://www.washingtonpost.com/sports/redskins/redskins-name-change-would-have-to-pass-muster-with-nfl-sponsors/2013/02/24/c4fa763c-7b0b-11e2-9c27-fdd594ea6286_story.html.

McCarthy, Michael. "Redskins Rebrand Would Cost $15 Million." *AdAge*, September 24, 2013. http://adage.com/article/news/redskins-rebrand-cost-15-million/244295/.

McCartney, Robert. "1933 News Article Refutes Cherished Tale That Redskins Were Named to Honor Indian Coach." *Washington Post*, May 28, 2014. http://www.washingtonpost.com/local/1933-news-article-refutes-cherished-tale-that-redskins-were-named-to-honor-indian-coach/2014/05/28/19ad32e8-e698-11e3-afc6-a1dd9407abcf_story.html.

———. "We Need a Fresh, Reliable Opinion Poll to Show What Indians Today Think of 'Redskins' Name." *Washington Post*, February 19, 2014. http://www.washingtonpost.com/local/we-need-a-fresh-reliable-opinion-poll-to-show-what-indians-today-think-of-redskins-name/2014/02/19/6afdb02c-99a0-11e3-b88d-f36c07223d88_story.html.

McIntosh, Peggy. "White Privilege: Unpacking the Invisible Backpack." 1989. https://www.isr.umich.edu/home/diversity/resources/white-privilege.pdf.

McKenna, Dave. "Fight for New Dixie." *Washington City Paper*, September 2, 2011. http://www.washingtoncitypaper.com/articles/41422/why-a-washington-baltimore-game-sparked-redskins-segregation-policy-protests.

———. "Is the Redskins' 'vip' Indian Defender a Fake Indian?" Deadspin, October 7, 2014. http://deadspin.com/is-the-redskins-vip-indian-defender-a-fake-indian-1642991295.

———. "Redskins' Indian-Chief Defender: Not a Chief, Probably Not Indian." *Deadspin*, June 27, 2013. http://deadspin.com/redskins-indian-chief-defender-not-a-chief-probably-590973565.

———. "This Dated Video Helped Make the Case against the Redskins Trademarks." Deadspin, June 19, 2014. http://deadspin.com/this-dated-video-helped-make-the-case-against-the-redsk-1592685513.

Miller, Danielle. "Genocide as Entertainment." Last Real Indians, July 3, 2014. http://lastrealindians.com/deadskins-genocide-as-entertainment-by-danielle-miller/.

Milloy, Courtland. "The Battle over the Redskins' Name Is about the Exploitation of a Stereotype for Profit." *Washington Post*, June 1, 2014. http://www.washingtonpost.com/local/the-battle-over-the-redskins-name-is-about-the-exploitation-of-a-stereotype-for-profit/2014/06/01/694b7084-e99b-11e3-93d2-edd4be1f5d9e_story.html.

Mitcham, Zach. "Why 'Redskins' Must Go," *Madison (GA) Journal Today*, July 7, 2014. http://www.madisonjournaltoday.com/archives/7022-opinion-Why-Redskins-must-go.html.

Moya-Smith, Simon. "Mea Culpa: Washington Football Team Fan Apologizes for Flipping Off Protesters." *Indian Country Today*, January 13, 2015. http://indiancountrytodaymedianetwork.com/2015/01/13/mea-culpa-washington-football-team-fan-apologizes-flipping-off-protesters-158682.

———. "ncai Seeks to Fund New Super Bowl Ad; Goal Set at $20,000." *Indian Country Today*, December 11, 2014. http://indiancountrytodaymedianetwork.com/2014/12/11/ncai-seeks-fund-new-super-bowl-ad-goal-set-20000-158240.

———. "Reclaiming the Native Voice." cnn, June 18, 2014. http://www.cnn.com/2014/06/18/living/obama-redskins-native-american-visibility/.

———. "Scholar Launches Google Doc 'Collective Voice' Campaign to Opposes 'Redskins' Name." *Indian Country Today*, July 7, 2014. http://indiancountrytodaymedianetwork.com/2014/07/07/scholar-launches-google-doc-collective-voice-campaign-opposes-redskins-name-155684M.

Munguia, Hayley. "The 2,128 Native American Mascots People Aren't Talking About." FiveThirtyEight, September 5, 2014. http://fivethirtyeight.com/features/the-2128-native-american-mascots-people-arent-talking-about/.

National Congress of American Indians. *Ending the Legacy of Racism in Sports & the Era of Harmful "Indian" Sports Mascots.* Washington dc, 2013. http://www.ncai.org /resources/ncai-publications/Ending_the_Legacy_of_Racism.pdf.

"Native American Chief Talks about Redskins." Redskins.com, May 3, 2013. http:// www.redskins.com/news-and-events/article-1/Native-American-Chief-Talks -About-Redskins/cdb3c94e-f5c6-4d98-9acd-18d7fb768bb7.

"Native Americans Tell Redskins Owner: I'm #Not4Sale." Aljazeera America, March 25, 2013. http://america.aljazeera.com/watch/shows/the-stream/the-stream -officialblog/2014/3/25/native-americanstellredskinsownerimnot4sale.html.

"Navajo Code Talkers Leader Defends Redskins Name." nfl.com, November 28, 2013. http:// www.nfl.com/news/story/0ap2000000289096/article/navajo-code-talkers -leader-defends-redskins-name.

Newell, Sean. "For Sale: Native-Made Washington 'Foreskins' Logo." Deadspin, August 11, 2014. http://deadspin.com/wanted-native-art-with-redskins-logo-and-colors -drunk-1618686583/1619788490.

"A New Logo for the Washington Redskins." http://newredskinslogo.tumblr.com.

"NFL Commissioner Tells Congress 'Redskins' Is a Positive Name." *Indian Country Today*, June 11, 2013. http://indiancountrytodaymedianetwork.com/2013/06/11/nfl -commissioner-tells-congress-redskins-positive-name-149843.

"NFL Official: Redskins 'Not a Slur.'" ESPN, June 1, 2014. http://espn.go.com/nfl/story/_ /id/11007769/nfl-official-says-washington-redskins-name-not-slur.

Nucklos, Ben. "US Poll Finds Widespread Support for Redskins Name." Associated Press, May 2, 2013. http://bigstory.ap.org/article/us-poll-finds-widespread-support -redskins-name.

Nunberg, Geoffrey. "When Slang Becomes a Slur." *Atlantic*, June 23, 2014. http://www .theatlantic.com/entertainment/archive/2014/06/a-linguist-on-why-redskin-is -racist-patent-overturned/373198/.

Odle, Mairin. "What's in a Name? On Sports Teams and Scalp Bounties." *Junto* (blog), December 22, 2014. http://earlyamericanists.com/2014/12/22/guest-post-whats-in -a-name-on-sports-teams- and-scalp-bounties/.

"Official Extremeskins Tailgate 12/28 vs Dallas—Shave Out Cancer." Discussion board, extremeskins.com, started December 23, 2014. http://es.redskins.com/topic /385980-official-extremeskins-tailgate-1228-vs-dallas-shave-out-cancer/.

Page, Clarence. "Indian Raid on Cooke's Wallet." *Baltimore Sun*, September 22, 1992. http://articles.baltimoresun.com/1992-09-22/news/1992266025_1_jack -kent-cooke-chicago-blackhawks-redskins.

———. "Now It's Time to Turn on Redskins Owner." *Green Bay (WI) Gazette*, May 4, 2014. http://www.greenbaypressgazette.com/article/20140504/gpg06/305040361 /Clarence-Page-column-Now-s-time-turn-Redskins-owner.

"Pale Moon Bounced from Expo." *Native Nevadan* (Reno), June 30, 1992, 21.

"Patent Office Comanches." *Wall Street Journal*, June 18, 2014. http://www.wsj.com/articles/patent-office-comanches-1403132099.

Pensoneau, Migizi. "'I'll Fucking Cut You': Behind the Scenes of the 1491s' Segment on 'The Daily Show.'" *Missoula (MT) Independent*, September 26, 2014. http://missoulanews.bigskypress.com/GreenRoom/archives/2014/09/26/ill-fucking-cut-you-behind-the-scenes-of-the-1491s-segment-on-the-daily-show.

Petchesky, Barry. "Disgraced, Soon-to-Be-Former Navajo Nation President Attends 'Skins Game." Deadspin, October 12, 2014. http://deadspin.com/disgraced-soon-to-be-former-navajo-nation-president-at-1645509844.

Peterseim, Locke. "Not Just Whistling Dixie in dc." ESPN, undated]. http://espn.go.com/page2/wash/s/closer/020315.html.

Pewewardy, Cornel D. "Native American Mascots and Imagery: The Struggle of Unlearning Indian Stereotypes." *Journal of Navaho Education* 9 (1991): 19–23.

Picca, Leslie Houts, and Joe Feagin. *Two-Face Racism: Whites in the Backstage and Frontstage*. New York: Routledge, 2007.

"Positive Reactions to Cooperstown Central Changing School Mascot." *Indian Country Today*, February 25, 2013. http://indiancountrytodaymedianetwork.com/2013/02/25/positive-reactions-cooperstown-central-changing-school-mascot-147875.

Povich, Shirley. "George Preston Marshall." In *The Redskin Book*, 16–36. Washington dc: Washington Post, 1998. http://www.washingtonpost.com/wp-srv/sports/redskins/longterm/book/.

Powell, Robin. "Recycling the Redskins." *Turtle Quarterly* 5, no. 1 (Winter 1993): 8–11.

Powers, Nicholas. "Satire: The Washington Drones Win the Superbowl." *Indypendent*, November 25, 2013. https://indypendent.org/2013/11/25/satire-washington-drones-win-superbowl.

"Quechan Skate Park Project Turns Down 'Bribe Money' from Redskins," *Indian Country Today*, July 17, 2014. http://indiancountrytodaymedianetwork.com/2014/07/17/quechan-skate-park-project-turns-down-bribe-money-redskins-155901.

Ralbovsky, Marty. "An Indian Affair: American Indian Students Concerned about Nicknames, Mascots in Sports." *New York Times*, November 14, 1971, 9.

Ramsey, David. "Seahawks Richard Sherman Sees Need to Change Redskins Racist Moniker." *Colorado Springs Gazette*, May 7, 2014. http://gazette.com/seahawks-richard-sherman-sees-need-to-change-redskins-racist-moniker/article/1525607.

Rebrand Washington Football. http://www.rebrandwf.org.

"Redskins Gear Stiff-Armed by Fans." CNN, September 4, 2014. http://money.cnn.com/2014/09/04/news/companies/redskins-merchandise/.

"Redskins Prepare for Return to Carlisle." *Washington Times*, July 25, 2001. http://www.washingtontimes.com/news/2001/jul/25/20010725-024425-8141r/.

Regan, Tim. "Gregg Deal's Performance Art Exposes the Real-Life Effects of the Washington Football Team's Name." *Washington City Paper*, September 23, 2014. http://www.washingtoncitypaper.com/blogs/artsdesk/performance- and -dance/2014/09/23/gregg-deals-performance-art-exposes-the-real-life-effects -of-the-washington-football-teams-name/.

Reid, Darren R. "Why the 'Redskins' Is a Racist Name." Podcast, [undated]. http://www. darrenreidhistory.co.uk/why-the-redskins-is-a-racist-name/#sthash.db5fdsb2 .dpuf.

Reilly, Rick. "Have the People Spoken?" ESPN, September 19, 2013. http://espn.go.com /nfl/story/_/id/9689220/redskins-name-change-not-easy-sounds.

———. "Let's Bust Those Chops." *Sports Illustrated*, October 28, 1991, 110.

"Report: Redskins' Name Only Offensive If You Think about What It Means." *Onion*, August 12, 2013. http://www.theonion.com/articles/report-redskins-name -only-offensive-if-you-think-a,33449/.

Sager, Mike. "Princess Pale Moon Rising with Her Message." *Spokane (WA) Spokesman-Review*, June 23, 1982, 25.

Salaita, Steven. "Nothing Scarier Than a Nervous White Man: The 'Redskins' Debate Is Really about White Privilege." Salon, September 29, 2013. http://www.salon.com /2013/09/29/nothing_scarier_than_a_nervous_white_man_the_redskins_debate _is_really_about_white_privilege/.

Sanders, Katie. "Pundit Claims Redskins Historically Used as 'Term of Respect.'" Politifact, June 4, 2014. http://www.politifact.com/punditfact/statements/2014/jun /04/pete-hegseth/pundit-claims-redskins-historically-used-term-resp/.

Saunt, Claudio. "This Land Is Their Land." *Slate*, July 6, 2014. http://www.slate.com /articles/sports/sports_nut/2014/07/washington_nfl_team_tribal_land_the_braves _chiefs_and_dan_snyder_s_franchise.html.

Savilla, Elmer M. "An Interview with Floyd Red Crow Westerman." *Seminole Tribune*, December 13, 1991, 9.

Schaffer, Michael. "Here's How the Washington Football Team's Name Controversy Will End." *New Republic*, October 14, 2013. http://www.newrepublic.com/article/115178 /redskins-name-will-change-because-merchandise-sales.

Schmitt, Casey. "Struggling, Resilient: The National Congress of American Indians Gives Washington Some Alternatives." *Rhetorically Speaking* (blog), February 13, 2014. http://rhetoric.commarts.wisc.edu/?p=102.

Scolari, Paul. "Indian Warriors and Pioneer Mothers: American Identity and the Closing of the Frontier in Public Monuments, 1890–1930." Dissertation, University of Pittsburgh, 2005.

Seiffert, Kevin. "Inside Slant: Presumed Redskins Bonanza." ESPN, June 30, 2014. http://espn.go.com/blog/nflnation/post/_/id/130696/inside-slant-presumed -redskins-bonanza.

Shakely, Jack. "The Problem with the 'R' Word? A Muskogee/Creek Indian Explains It All for You." *Los Angeles Times*, October 8, 2014. http://www.latimes.com/opinion /op-ed/la-oe-shakely-redskins-indians-sports-teams-mascot-20141009-story .html.

Shapira, Ian. "Dan Snyder and the Navajo Nation: It's Complicated." *Washington Post*, October 27, 2014. http://www.washingtonpost.com/blogs/local/wp/2014/10/27 /dan-snyder- and-the-navajo-nation-its-complicated/.

———. "Federal Judge Orders Cancellation of Redskins' Trademark Registrations." *Washington Post*, July 8, 2015. http://www.washingtonpost.com/local/judge -upholds-cancellation-of-redskins-trademarks-in-a-legal-and-symbolic -setback-for-team/2015/07/08/5a65424e-1e6e-11e5-aeb9-a411a84c9d55_story .html.

———. "In Arizona, a Navajo High School Emerges as a Defender of the Washington Redskins." *Washington Post*, October 26, 2014. http://www.washingtonpost.com /local/in-arizona-a-navajo-high-school-emerges-as-a-defender-of-the -washington-redskins/2014/10/26/dcfc773a-592b-11e4-8264-deed989ae9a2 _story.html.

Shapiro, Leonard. "Princess Pale Moon Draws Special Note; aim 'Totally Opposed' to Her Anthem Role." *Washington Post*, November 3, 1991, d9.

Shelburne, Ramona. "The Sad Last Chapter of Sterling's Life." ESPN, June 21, 2014. http:// espn.go.com/nba/story/_/id/11105717/sad-last-chapter-donald-sterling-life.

Shin, Annys. "Redskins Name Change Demanded at Smithsonian Forum." *Washington Post*, February 7, 2013. http://www.washingtonpost.com/local/redskins-name -change-demanded-at-smithsonian-forum/2013/02/07/40923a6c-714f-11e2 -ac36-3d8d9dcaa2e2_story.html.

Shoemaker, Nancy. *A Strange Likeness: Becoming Red and White in Eighteenth-Century North America*. Oxford: Oxford University Press, 2004.

"Shoni Schimmel Calls for End to Racist Sports Mascot." Indianz.com, November 8, 2013. http://indianz.com/news/2013/011712.asp.

Sigelman, Lee. "Hail to the Redskins? Public Reactions to a Racially Insensitive Team Name." *Sociology of Sport Journal* 15 (1998): 317–25.

"6 Suggestions for New Redskins Mascots." *Free Republic*, October 19, 2013. http:// www.freerepublic.com/focus/news/3081502/posts.

"60% Don't Think Washington Redskins Should Change Their Name." Rasmussen Reports, June 2014. http://www.rasmussenreports.com/public_content/lifestyle /sports/june_2014/60_don_t_think_washington_redskins_should_change_their _name.

Smith, Loren. "Redskins' Nickname Honors Indian Warriors." *Washington Examiner*, March 12, 2013. http://washingtonexaminer.com/op-ed-redskins-nickname-honors -indian-warriors/article/2524105.

Smith, Thomas G. *Showdown: JFK and the Integration of the Washington Redskins.* Boston: Beacon Press, 2013.

Smith, Wes. "Fighting for His People." *Chicago Tribune*, March 28, 1993. http://articles .chicagotribune.com/1993-03-28/features/9303280387_1_michael-haney-fight -for-indian-rights-museum-s-exhibit.

Snider, Rick. "Dan Snyder's Path Past 'Never' Changing the Redskins Name." *Washington Post*, June 18, 2014. http://www.washingtonpost.com/express/wp/2014/06 /18/dan-snyders-path-past-never-changing-the-redskins-name/.

Snyder, Dan. "Letter from Washington Redskins Owner Dan Snyder to Fans." *Washington Post*, October 9, 2013. http://www.washingtonpost.com/local/letter-from -washington-redskins-owner-dan-snyder- to-fans/2013/10/09/e7670ba0-30fe -11e3-8627-c5d7de0a046b_story.html.

———. "Letter to Everyone in Our Washington Redskins Nation." March 24, 2014. http://files.redskins.com/pdf/Letter-from-Dan-Snyder-032414.pdf.

"Snyder: We Will Never Drop Redskins Name." *Indian Country Today*, May 15, 2013. http://indiancountrytodaymedianetwork.com/2013/05/15/snyder-we-will-never -drop-redskins-name-149367.

"Snyder's Blood Money: The Zuni Need Our Love and Support." *Indian Country Today*, August 11, 2014. http://indiancountrytodaymedianetwork.com/2014/08/11 /snyders-blood-money-zuni-need-our-love- and-support-156332.

Song, Kelyn. "The Other Redskins." Capital News Service, April 2, 2013. http:// cnsmaryland.org/interactives/other-redskins/.

Spindel, Carol. *Dancing at Halftime: Sports and the Controversy over American Indian Mascots.* New York: New York University Press, 2002.

Springwood, Charles Fruehling. "'I'm Indian Too!' Claiming Native American Identity, Crafting Authority in Mascot Debates." *Journal of Sport & Social Issues* 28 (2004): 56–70.

Stapleton, Bruce. *Redskins: Racial Slur or Symbol of Success.* Lincoln ne: Writers Club Press, 2001.

Starr, Terrell Jermaine. "We Need to Stop 'Playing Cowboys and Indians' with Native Americans." *NewsOne*, October 21, 2013. http://newsone.com/2743075/redskins -name-change/.

Staurowsky, Ellen J. "An Act of Honor or Exploitation? The Cleveland Indians' Use of the Louis Francis Sockalexis Story." Sociology of Sport Journal 15, no. 4 (1998): 299–316.

———. "American Indian Imagery and the Miseducation of America." *Quest* 51 (1999): 382–92.

———. "The 'Cleveland Indians': A Case Study of American Indian Cultural Dispossession." Sociology of Sport Journal 17, no. 4 (2000): 307–30.

———. "Exploring the 'Science' behind the Poll Snyder Cites to Defend His Redsk*ns." *Indian Country Today*, December 16, 2013. http://indiancountrytodaymedianetwork

.com/2013/12/16/exploring-science-behind-poll-snyder-cites-defend-his
-redskns-152739.

Steinberg, Dan. "Cowboys Owner Jerry Jones Says Redskins Name 'Is One of Pride.'" *Washington Post*, October 21, 2014. http://www.washingtonpost.com/blogs/dc -sports-bog/wp/2014/10/21/cowboys-owner-jerry-jones-says-redskins-name-is -one-of-pride/.

——. "Daniel Snyder: Redskins Have Begun Planning for Their New Stadium." *Washington Post*, August 27, 2014. http://www.washingtonpost.com/blogs/dc-sports -bog/wp/2014/08/27/daniel-snyder-redskins-have-begun-planning-for-their -new-stadium.

——. "Dan Snyder Bought Some 'Keep the Name' T-Shirts in Richmond." *Washington Post*, August 3, 2014. http://www.washingtonpost.com/blogs/dc-sports-bog/wp /2014/08/03/dan-snyder-bought-some-keep-the-name-t-shirts-in-richmond/.

——. "Drake Takes a Shot at the Redskins Name in espys Monologue." *Washington Post*, July 17, 2014. http://www.washingtonpost.com/blogs/dc-sports-bog/wp/2014 /07/17/drake-takes-a-shot-at-the-redskins-name-in-espys-monologue/.

——. "Edward Bennett Williams's 1972 Letter to Pete Rozelle about the Redskins Name." *Washington Post*, June 18, 2014. http://www.washingtonpost.com/blogs/dc-sports -bog/wp/2014/06/18/edward-bennett-williamss-1972-letter- to-pete-rozelle -about-the-redskins-name/.

——. "Former Redskins Receiver Charlie Brown Says 'It's Nonsense' to Compare Team Name with Slurs against Blacks." *Washington Post*, January 27, 2015. http:// www.washingtonpost.com/blogs/dc-sports-bog/wp/2015/01/27/former-redskins -receiver-charlie-brown-says-its-nonsense- to-compare-team-name-with-slurs -against-blacks/.

——. "From Riley Cooper to 'Redskins.'" *Washington Post*, August 2, 2013. http:// www.washingtonpost.com/blogs/dc-sports-bog/wp/2013/08/02/from-riley -cooper- to-redskins/.

——. "The Great Redskins Name Debate of . . . 1972?" *Washington Post*, June 3, 2014. http://www.washingtonpost.com/blogs/dc-sports-bog/wp/2014/06/03/the -great-redskins-name-debate-of-1972/.

——. "John Kent Cooke Was Once Deposed about the Redskins Name, at Incredible Length." *Washington Post*, June 18, 2014. http://www.washingtonpost.com/blogs/dc -sports-bog/wp/2014/06/18/john-kent-cooke-was-once-deposed-about-the -redskins-name-at-incredible-length/.

——. "Matthew McConaughey and the Redskins." *Washington Post*, November 1, 2013. http://www.washingtonpost.com/blogs/dc-sports-bog/wp/2013/11/01/matthew -mcconaughey- and-the-redskins/.

——. "Matthew McConaughey Tells Larry Michael He Used to Wear a Head-ress to Redskins Games in Dallas." *Washington Post*, June 5, 2014. http:// www.washingtonpost.com/blogs/dc-sports-bog/wp/2014/06/05/matthew

-mcconaughey-tells-larry-michael-he-used-to-wear-a-headress-to-redskins
-games-in-dallas/.

———. "Notah Begay Calls Redskins Nickname Institutionalized Degradation." *Washington Post*, February 25, 2013. http://www.washingtonpost.com/blogs/dc-sports-bog
/wp/2013/02/25/notah-begay-calls-redskins-nickname-institutionalized
-degradation/.

———. "Peter King Explains His 2016 Redskins Name Change Prediction." *Washington Post*, July 28, 2014. http://www.washingtonpost.com/blogs/dc-sports-bog
/wp/2014/07/28/peter-king-explains-his-2016-redskins-name-change
-prediction/.

———. "Pizza Chain Apologizes for Using 'Wrong, Offensive, and Hurtful' Redskins Name."
Washington Post, September 19, 2014. http://www.washingtonpost.com/blogs/dc
-sports-bog/wp/2014/09/19/pizza-chain-apologizes-for-using-wrong-offensive
-and-hurtful-redskins-name/.

———. "Redskins Launch New 'Redskins Facts' Campaign as Former Players Travel to Reservation." *Washington Post*, July 29, 2014. http://www.washingtonpost.com
/blogs/dc-sports-bog/wp/2014/07/29/redskins-launch-new-redskins-facts
-campaign-as-former-players-travel- to-reservation/.

———. "Redskins Lawyer Says 'Put It in Caps' Language Will Change." *Washington Post*, October 9, 2013. http://www.washingtonpost.com/blogs/dc-sports-bog/wp
/2013/10/09/snyder-lawyer-says-put-it-in-caps-language-will-change/.

———. "Vinny Cerrato Says Daniel Snyder's defense of the Redskins Name Goes Back to His Father." *Washington Post*, July 2, 2014. http://www.washingtonpost.com
/blogs/dc-sports-bog/wp/2014/07/02/vinny-cerrato-says-daniel-snyders
-defense-of-the-redskins-name-goes-back- to-his-father/.

Steinberg, Dan, and Chris Jenkins. "Black Fans Have Grown to Love the Redskins."
Washington Post, October 26, 2011. http://www.washingtonpost.com/sports/redskins
/black-fans-have-grown- to-love-the-redskins/2011/10/26/giqa8q7eKM_story
.html.

Steinfeldt, Jesse A., Brad D. Foltz, Jennifer K. Kaladow, Tracy N. Carlson, Louis A. Pagano Jr., Emily Benton, and M. Clinton Steinfeldt. "Racism in the Electronic Age: Role of Online Forums in Expressing Racial Attitudes about American Indians." *Cultural Diversity and Ethnic Minority Psychology* 16 (2010): 362–71.

St. George, Joe. "Why Va. Tribes Have Stayed Out of Redskins Name Controversy." wtvr, November 17, 2014. http://wtvr.com/2014/11/17/virginia-tribes-on-redskins-name
-controversy.

Stokes, Dashanne. "5 Studies That Prove Dan Snyder Is Wrong about 'Redskins.'" *Indian Country Today*, April 21, 2014. http://indiancountrytodaymedianetwork.com
/2014/04/21/5-studies-prove-dan-snyder-wrong-about-redskins.

Stretten, Amy. "If the Indian Mascot Could Speak." *Fusion*, January 15, 2014. http://
fusion.net/story/4666/if-the-indian-mascot-could-speak-a-poem/.

Strong, Pauline Turner. "The Mascot Slot: Cultural Citizenship, Political Correctness, and Pseudo-Indian Sports Symbols." *Journal of Sport & Social Issues* 28 (2004): 79–87.

——. "Trademarking Racism: Pseudo-Indian Symbols and the Business of Professional Sports." *Anthropology Now*, September 2014. http://anthronow.com /print/trademarking-racism-pseudo-indian-symbols- and-the-business-of -professional-sports.

Strong, Pauline Turner, and Laurie Posner. "Selves in Play: Sports, Scouts, and American Cultural Citizenship." *International Review of the Sociology of Sport* 45 (2010): 390–409.

Sullivan, Mark. "Patawomeck Tribe: Snyder Could Rename Redskins After Us." *American Spectator*, July 3, 2014. http://spectator.org/articles/59851/patawomeck -tribe-snyder-could-rename-redskins-after-us.

Swayney, Kina. "Redskins Just a Name?" *Cherokee One Feather*, January 5, 2015. http:// theonefeather.com/2015/01/commentary-redskins-just-a-name/.

Taube, Michael. "Why Not the Washington Reagans?" *Washington Times*, June 24, 2014. http://www.washingtontimes.com/news/2014/jun/24/taube-why-not-the -washington-reagans/?page=1.

Taylor, Michael. *Contesting Constructed Indian-ness: The Intersection of the Frontier, Masculinity, and Whiteness in Native American Mascot Representations.* Lanham md: Rowman and Littlefield, 2014.

"10 New Mascots for Dan Snyder's 'Redskins.'" *Indian Country Today*, November 9, 2013. http://indiancountrytodaymedianetwork.com/2013/11/09/10-new-mascots-dan -snyders-redskins-152163.

"Theismann: 'Skins Name Is Meaningful." FoxSports, June 21, 2013. http://msn .foxsports.com/nfl/story/joe-theismann-i-represented-native-american-nations -with-washington-redskins-062113.

"3rd Annual NFL Poll." January 2, 2014. http://www.publicpolicypolling.com/main /2014/01/3rd-annual-nfl-poll.html.

Toensing, Gale Courey. "Navajo Medicine Men Pass Anti-Redskins Resolution." *Indian Country Today*, March 17, 2014. http://indiancountrytodaymedianetwork .com/2014/03/17/navajo-medicine-men-pass-anti-redskins-resolution-154032.

Tomasky, Michael. "Dan Snyder's Trail of Crocodile Tears." *Daily Beast*, March 28, 2014. http://www.thedailybeast.com/articles/2014/03/28/dan-snyder-s-trail-of -crocodile-tears.html.

Tomassen, Chris. "Redskins Name Change 'Festered by Liberals,' Former qb Billy Kilmer Says." *St. Paul Pioneer Press*, November 1, 2014. http://www.twincities.com/sports /ci_26836562/redskins-name-change-festered-by-liberals-billy-kilmer.

"Top 10 Strongest Takes about the Redskins Losing Their Trademark." UPROXX, June 18, 2014. http://kissingsuzykolber.uproxx.com/2014/06/top-10-strongest-takes -about-the-redskins-losing-their-trademark.html.

"Trademark Decision against the Redskins Is a Victory for Tolerance." *Washington Post*, June 18, 2014. http://www.washingtonpost.com/opinions/trademark-decision -against-the-redskins-is-a-victory-for- tolerance/2014/06/18/aaf666e2-f71f-11e3 -8aa9-dad2ec039789_story.html.

Treadway, Dan. "Twitter Has Plenty of Suggestions about What the #NewRedskinsName Should Be." *Sports Illustrated*, June 18, 2014. http://extramustard.si.com/2014/06/18 /twitter-has-plenty-of-suggestion-about-what-the-newredskinsname-should-be/.

Treuer, David. "The Price of a Slur." *New York Times*, April 3, 2014. http://www .nytimes.com/2014/04/03/opinion/the-price-of-a-slur.html.

Tribou, Doug. "Bobby Mitchell, Washington's First Black Player, Addresses Redskins Controversy." Only a Game, May 31, 2014. http://onlyagame.wbur.org /2014/05/31/bobby-mitchell-washington-redskins-team-name.

TsalagiMahariel. "Alcatraz Is Not an Island." Deviantart.com, [undated]. http:// tsalagimahariel.deviantart.com/art/Alcatraz-Is-Not-an-Island-505488477.

Tucker, Ross. "Redskins Nickname Issue Too Divisive for Sudden Change." *Sporting News*, April 2, 2014. http://www.sportingnews.com/nfl/story/2014-04-01/washington -redskins-name-change-native-americans-offended-percentage-pride-daniel -snyder-foundation-research.

U.S. Patent and Trademark Office, Trademark Trial and Appeal Board. Opinion. *Blackhorse et al. v. Pro-Football Inc.* June 18, 2014. http://ttabvue.uspto.gov/ttabvue /v?pno=92046185&pty=CAN&eno=199.

———. Opinion. *Harjo et al. v. Pro-Football Inc.* May 27, 1998. http://www.uspto.gov/web /offices/com/sol/foia/ttab/2aissues/1999/21069.pdf.

———. Petitioners' Trial Brief. *Blackhorse et al v. Pro-Football, Inc.* 2012. http://www .washingtonpost.com/wp-srv/business/trial-brief.pdf.

van Bibber, Ryan. "Dan Snyder's Latest Cigar Store Indian." SB Nation, March 28, 2014. http://www.sbnation.com/nfl/2014/3/28/5557304/dan-snyder -wasington-redskins-nickname-controversy-foundation-president.

Vargas, Theresa. "From Pork Rinds to Cheerleaders, the Trademark Office Rejects the Word 'Redskins.'" *Washington Post*, January 28, 2014. http://www.washingtonpost.com /blogs/local/wp/2014/01/28/from-pork-rinds- to-cheerleaders-the-trademark -office-rejects-the-word-redskins/.

———. "Granddaughter of Former Redskins Owner George P. Marshall Condemns Team's Name." *Washington Post*, July 23, 2014. http://www.washingtonpost.com/local /granddaughter-of-former-redskins-owner-george-p-marshall-condemns-teams -name/2014/07/22/eb9dd3b0-11cd-11e4-9285-4243a40ddc97_story.html.

———. "One Native American Family with Redskins Ties Disagrees on Whether Name Is Offensive." *Washington Post*, July 6, 2014. http://www.washingtonpost.com/local /one-native-american-family-with-redskins-ties-disagrees-on-whether-name -is-offensive/2014/07/06/ea8c5b46-fc8c-11e3-932c-0a55b81f48ce_story .html.

———. "U.S. Patent Office Cancels Redskins Trademark Registration, Says Name Is Disparaging." *Washington Post*, June 18, 2014. http://www.washingtonpost.com/local /us-patent-office-cancels-redskins-trademark-registration-says-name-is -disparaging/2014/06/18/e7737bb8-f6ee-11e3-8aa9-dad2ec039789_story.html.

Vargas, Theresa, and Tom Jackman. "ceo of New Washington Redskins Foundation Connected to 'Defective' Federal Contract." *Washington Post*, March 28, 2014. http:// www.washingtonpost.com/local/ceo-of-new-washington-redskins-foundation -connected-to-defective-federal-contract/2014/03/28/382142b4-b678-11e3-a7c6 -70cf2db17781_story.html.

Vargas, Theresa, and Annys Shin. "President Obama Says, 'I'd Think about Changing' Name of Washington Redskins." *Washington Post*, October 5, 2013. http://www .washingtonpost.com/local/president-obama-says-id-think-about-changing -name-of-washington-redskins/2013/10/05/e170b914-2b70-11e3-8ade-a1f23cda 135e_story.html.

Vaughan, Alden T. "From White Man to Redskin: Changing Anglo-American Perceptions of the American Indian." *American Historical Review* 87 (1982): 917–53.

Vizenor, Erma J. "Nickname Is Deeply Offensive in Any Context." *Bemidji (MN) Pioneer*, October 30, 2014. http://www.bemidjipioneer.com/content/erma-j-vizenor -nickname-deeply-offensive-any-context.

Vrentas, Jenny. "Battle of Washington." *Sports Illustrated*, April 3, 2014. http://mmqb.si .com/2014/04/03/washington-nfl-team-name-debate/7/.

Waggoner, Linda M. Interview by John Barr. *Outside the Lines* (ESPN), August 28, 2014. Copy in author's files.

———. "On Trial—The Washington R*dskins' Wily Mascot: Coach William Lone Star Dietz." *Montana: The Magazine of Western History* 63, no. 1 (Spring 2013): 24–47. http://nmai.si.edu/sites/1/files/pdf/seminars-symposia/WaggonerWEBSpr 2013.pdf.

———. "Reclaiming James One Star." *Indian Country Today*, August 4, 2004. http:// indiancountrytodaymedianetwork.com/2004/08/04/reclaiming-james -one-star-part-five-93839.

Waldron, Travis. "The 81-Year-Old Newspaper Article That Destroys the Redskins' Justification for Their Name." *Think Progress* (blog), May 30, 2014. http:// thinkprogress.org/sports/2014/05/30/3443168/redskins-founder-i-didnt-name -team- to-honor-native-americans/.

———. "83 Percent of Americans Wouldn't Say 'Redskin' to a Native American's Face." *Think Progress* (blog), November 24, 2014. http://thinkprogress.org/sports /2014/11/24/3596182/83-percent-of-americans-wouldnt-say-redskin-to-a -native-americans-face/.

———. "NFL Commissioner: Redskins Name an Honor for Native Americans." *Think Progress* (blog), January 31, 2014. http://thinkprogress.org/sports/2014/01/31 /3233961/goodell-redskins-honor-native-americans/.

———. "Why a Poll Showing Americans Support the 'Redskins' Name Matters." *Think Progress* (blog), January 3, 2014. http://thinkprogress.org/sports/2014/01/03/3116081/poll-showing-people-like-redskins-matters/.

Walker, Hunter. "Meet the Native American Grandmother Who Just Beat the Washington Redskins." *Business Insider*, June 18, 2014. http://www.businessinsider.com/meet-the-native-american-grandmother-who-just-beat-the-redskins-2014-6#ixzz3u6j7g1lU.

"Washington Is Capital of Football World as Redskins Swell 'Home' City's Pride." *New York Times*, December 7, 1937, 34.

Washington Redskins. "Statement by Bob Raskopf, Trademark Attorney for the Washington Redskins." Press release, June 18, 2014. http://files.redskins.com/pdf/Statement-by-Bob-Raskopf-Trademark-Attorney-for-the-Washington-Redskins.pdf.

"Washington Redskins Contracts." Spotrac.com. http://www.spotrac.com/nfl/washington-redskins/.

Washington Redskins Original Americans Foundation. http://www.washingtonredskinsoriginalamericansfoundation.org.

"Washington Redskins Valuation." *Forbes*, August 2014. http://www.forbes.com/teams/washington-redskins/.

"Washington's Nickname Controversy." ESPN, September 3, 2014. http://espn.go.com/espn/otl/story/_/id/11446278/questions-answers-debate.

"We Are Very Proud to Be Called Redskins." Redskins.com, February 11, 2013. http://www.redskins.com/news-and-events/article-1/We-Are-Very-Proud-to-Be-Called-Redskins/d4d7c05d-be39-4a27-9244-d06cfae46797.

Wharton, Tom. "NFL's Washington Team Offers Donation to Monument Valley." *Salt Lake City Tribune*, September 12, 2014. http://www.sltrib.com/sltrib/mobile/mobileopinion/58365453-82/team-schools-monument-nfl.html.csp.

White Eyes, Autumn. "Indian Mascots, a Privileged Fight." *Last Real Indians*, January 14, 2014. http://lastrealindians.com/indian-mascots-a-privileged-fight-by-autumn-white-eyes/.

Williams, Dana M. "Patriarchy and 'The Fighting Sioux': A Gendered Look at Racial College Sports Nicknames." *Race, Ethnicity and Education* 9 (2006): 325–40.

Wise, Mike. "Latest Redskins Nickname Outreach Is a Step, but Without a Direction." *Washington Post*, March 25, 2014. http://www.washingtonpost.com/sports/redskins/latest-redskins-nickname-outreach-is-a-step-but-without-a-direction/2014/03/25/3df18260-b46d-11e3-8020-b2d790b3c9e1_story.html.

———. "Only RG III Can Make the Redskins Change Their Name. Here's Why He Won't." *Washington Post*, January 11, 2013. http://articles.washingtonpost.com/2013-01-11/opinions/36312460_1_redskins-change-robert-griffin-iii-conscientious-objector.

———. "Questionable Naming Rights." *Washington Post*, September 17, 2005. http://www
.washingtonpost.com/wp-dyn/content/article/2005/09/16/AR2005091601640
.html.

———. "Rooting for Washington's NFL Team Has Become Tiresome; One Move Could
Make It Easier." *Washington Post*, December 10, 2014. http://www.washingtonpost
.com/sports/redskins/rooting-for-washingtons-nfl-team-has-become-tiresome
-one-move-could-make-it-easier/2014/12/10/925632ac-8086-11e4-8882-03cf
08410beb_story.html.

———. "There's Really No Debate—Redskins' Name Must Go." *West Lebanon (NH)
Valley News*, March 12, 2013. http://www.vnews.com/home/5058604-95/team
-harjo-redskins-american.

———. "To Seattle Native Americans, Redskins Are the Shame of the Game." *Washington Post*,
January 14, 2006. http://www.washingtonpost.com/wp-dyn/content/article/2006
/01/13/ar2006011301863.html.

Wolfe, Patrick. "Settler Colonialism and the Elimination of the Native." *Journal of
Genocide Research* 8, no. 4 (2006): 387–409.

Wood, Genevieve. "If You Are Offended, Get Over It: Redskins Should Get to Decide
Their Own Name." *Daily Signal*, August 26, 2014. http://dailysignal.com/2014
/08/26/youre-offended-get-redskins-get-decide-name/.

Wulf, Steve. "Why Use of Native American Nicknames Is an Obvious Affront." ESPN,
September 3, 2014. http://espn.go.com/espn/otl/story/_/id/11426021/why-native
-american-nicknames-stir-controversy-sports.

Zirin, Dave. "The Assassinating of Native American Voices by the Cowards Palin, Ditka
and Snyder." *Nation*, August 27, 2014. http://www.thenation.com/blog/181372
/assassinating-native-american-voices-cowards-palin-ditka- and-snyder.

———. "Redskins Owner Dan Snyder Says 'Some of My Best Friends Are Navajo Code
Talkers!'" *Nation*, November 26, 2013. http://www.thenation.com/blog/177368
/redskins-owner-dan-snyder-says-some-my-best-friends-are-navajo-code
-talkers#.

———. "Rick Reilly and the Most Irredeemably Stupid Defense of the Redskins Name
You Will Ever Read." *Nation*, September 18, 2013. http://www.thenation.com/blog
/176260/rick-reilly- and-most-irredeemably-stupid-defense-redskins-name
-you-will-ever-read#.

———. "You Can't Unsee It: Washington Football Name and Quiet Acts of Resistance."
Nation, September 5, 2014. http://www.thenation.com/blog/181502/you-cant
-unsee-it-redskins- and-quiet-acts-resistance.

Zirin, Dave, and Zach Zill. "A History Lesson for the Redskins Owner." *Nation*, February
9, 2011. http://www.thenation.com/article/158409/history-lesson-redskins-owner.

INDEX

OTHER WORKS BY C. RICHARD KING

MONOGRAPHS

Beyond Hate: White Power and Popular Culture, with David J. Leonard (2014)

Unsettling America: Indianness in the Contemporary World (2013)

Animating Difference: Race, Gender, and Sexuality in Contemporary Films for Children (2009)

Media Representations of Native Americans (2005)

Beyond the Cheers: Race as Spectacle in College Sports, with Charles Fruehling Springwood (2001)

Colonial Discourses, Collective Memories, and the Exhibition of Native American Cultures and Histories in the Contemporary United States (1998)

EDITED COLLECTIONS

Asian American Athletes in Sport and Society (2015)

Sport in the Pacific: Colonial and Post-Colonial Consequences (2014)

Commodified and Criminalized: African American Athletes and New Racism, coedited with David J. Leonard (2010)

The Native American Mascot Controversy: A Sourcebook (2010)

Native Americans and Sport in North America: Other People's Games (2008)

Visual Economies of/in Motion: Sport and Film, coedited with David J. Leonard (2006)

Native Athletes in Sport and Society (2005)

Team Spirits: The Native American Mascot Controversy (2001)

Postcolonial America (2000)